THE *Middle East*
THE ARAB STATES

in pictures

Coordinating Editor: E. W. Egan
Research Editors: Camille Mirepoix
Eugene Gordon
Jon Teta

The Holy Kaaba rises above a sea of the faithful. In the foreground, two pilgrims sit in an archway of the Great Mosque's tower.

STERLING PUBLISHING CO., INC. NEW YORK

Oak Tree Press Co., Ltd.   London & Sydney

Other Books of Interest

"China: The Dream of Man?"
Visual Geography Series

Much of the material in this book has been derived from
the following books of which Sterling Publishing Co., Inc.,
Two Park Avenue, New York, New York 10016, is the copyright
owner:
"Egypt—in Pictures," copyright 1979, 1978, 1975, 1974, 1973
"Iraq—in Pictures," copyright 1976, 1974, 1973, 1971, 1970
"Jordan—in Pictures," copyright 1978, 1976, 1974
"Kuwait—in Pictures," copyright 1977, 1974, 1972, 1970
"Lebanon—in Pictures," copyright 1978, 1974, 1972, 1971, 1969
"Saudi Arabia—in Pictures," copyright 1979, 1976, 1975, 1974, 1973

*An old engraving portrays a ceremony called "Stoning the Devil,"
which is part of the Mecca pilgrimage ritual.*

Contents

Color section begins opposite page 192

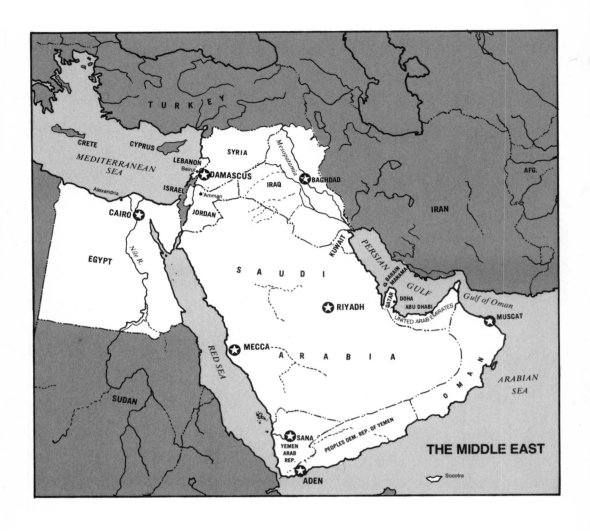

THE MIDDLE EAST

*A Neo-Babylonian seal found in Bahrain
dates from the 7th century B.C.*

Bahrain

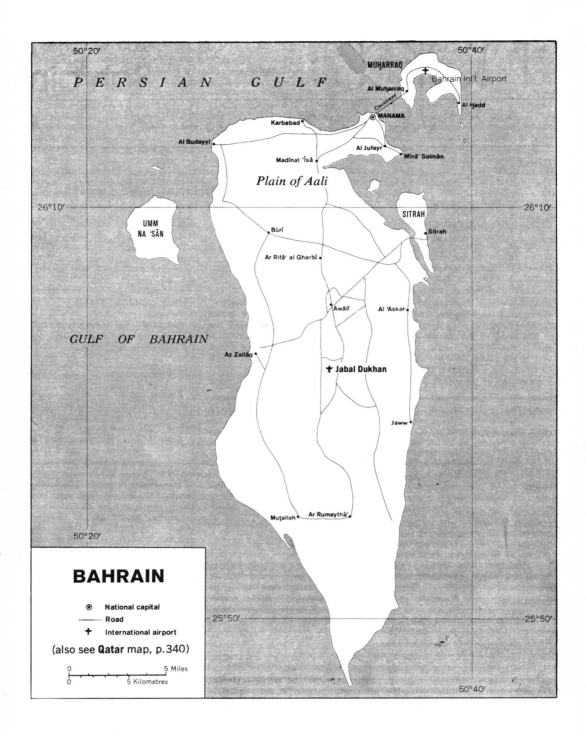

PERSIAN GULF

50°20'
50°40'

MUHARRAQ

Bahrain Int'l. Airport

Al Muharraq

Causeway

Al Hadd

MANAMA

Karbabad

Al Budayyi'

Al Jufayr

Madīnat 'Īsā

Mīnā' Salmān

Plain of Aali

26°10'
26°10'

UMM
NA 'SĀN

SITRAH

Būrī

Sitrah

Ar Rifā' al Gharbī

Awālī

Al 'Askar

GULF OF BAHRAIN

Az Zallāq

✝ **Jabal Dukhan**

Jaww

50°20'

Muṭallah
Ar Rumaythā'

50°20'

BAHRAIN

⊛ National capital

—— Road

✝ International airport

(also see **Qatar** map, p.340)

0 ————— 5 Miles
0 ————— 5 Kilometres

25°50'
25°50'

50°40'

6 ◇ BAHRAIN

Welders work in the shipyard of the Bahrain Ship Repairing and Engineering Company.

I. THE LAND

THE STATE OF BAHRAIN is a small island emirate in the Gulf of Bahrain, an arm of the Persian (Arabian) Gulf formed by the mainland of Saudi Arabia and the Qatar Peninsula. The State, which consists of the main island of Bahrain and about 30 smaller islands, has a total area of 240 square miles (624 sq km)—slightly larger than the Isle of Man, or roughly one-fifth the size of Rhode Island.

The islands are low-lying—the highest point is Jabal Dukhan, on Bahrain Island, which is a hill 445 feet (134 metres) above sea level. Of the smaller islands, the most important are Sitrah and Muharraq, both close to Manama, the capital city on Bahrain Island. Muharraq is connected to Manama by a causeway, while Sitrah is separated from the main island by an extremely narrow strait that is dry at low tide.

Manama with 85,000 people, and Muharraq with 50,000 are the largest towns.

The islands form two groups, Bahrain itself and nearby smaller islands, and the Hawar group, which are closer to Qatar than to the first group. All of the islands are naturally barren and sandy with occasional oases—a considerable number of fresh-water springs exist in certain localities. Irrigation projects in recent years have greatly increased the amount of farm land.

For centuries, Bahrain had one known natural resource—the abundant pearl oysters found in its waters. Discovered in the 20th century, a second, far greater, resource—petroleum—is transforming the country from a barren waste to a productive zone of farms and factories, from a medieval principality to a modern welfare state.

Pottery and vessels made from steatite (soapstone) believed to be of Assyrian origin have been found in the tumuli.

2. HISTORY

BAHRAIN CONTAINS the remains of a very ancient civilization dating from the end of the third millenium B.C. Dilmun, as this civilization was called, was an important trading nation, at its height between 2000 and 1800 B.C. Dilmun, later called Tylos, was often referred to by the ancient Sumerians, Greeks and Romans. Babylonian, Assyrian and Roman records mention the high quality of the dates grown in Dilmun, as well as that of the pearls found in its waters.

Dilmun is now known to have been Sumerian in culture. Among the most characteristic artifacts of the Dilmun period are distinctive seals. The most spectacular remains of the past, however, are the tombs of the Aali Plain in the northern part of the island of Bahrain. There are well over 100,000 burial mounds there,

These giant tumuli, or burial mounds, on the Aali Plain are believed to be royal graves. The mounds enclose stone crypts containing skeletons, along with pottery and other artifacts.

Seals from the Dilmun period were a means of identifying property at a time when writing was known only to a privileged few. Many of them bear intricate designs representing gods, heroes and animals.

A clay pot containing over 300 Greek coins was among discoveries made in the 1970's at Qalat al Bahrain on the north coast of Bahrain Island. ⟶

varying in size from a few feet to 40 feet (12 metres) high. Some tombs go back to the middle of the third millenium B.C., others are as late as the Hellenistic Period (*circa* 300 B.C.).

During the 7th century A.D., Bahrain became part of the Islamic world and retained its Arabic culture despite later invasions and con-

quests. The Portuguese occupied the islands during most of the 16th century, and the Persians took control for most of the 17th. During the 18th century Bahrain came under the rule of the Khalifa family, tribal chieftains from the Arabian mainland. The Khalifa dynasty signed a treaty of friendship with

Coins found at Qalat al Bahrain bear the image and name of Alexander the Great.

At a press conference in August, 1971, the Prime Minister gives details of Bahrain's declaration of independence.

Great Britain in 1820. In 1861, Bahrain signed another treaty with Great Britain establishing the country as a British protectorate. This treaty, similar to those signed with other Gulf sheikhdoms and emirates, gave the British control over Bahrain's foreign affairs.

When the British announced their intention, in 1968, of abolishing their protectorate by the end of 1971, Bahrain joined in a scheme to unite with Qatar and the seven Trucial Sheikhdoms (now the United Arab Emirates). However, plans for the union did not materialize and in August, 1971, Bahrain chose independence for itself.

Bahrain joined the United Nations in 1971. Here the Foreign Minister of Bahrain chats with the late U Thant, then Secretary General of the United Nations.

The Emir signs a treaty of friendship with Great Britain following the abolition of the British Protectorate.

3. GOVERNMENT

BAHRAIN is a hereditary monarchy ruled by an emir. The present Emir, Isa bin Salman al Khalifa, ascended the throne in 1961 upon the death of his father. In 1973, after the abolition of the British protectorate, the Emir enacted a constitution which guaranteed civil liberties and created a parliamentary system on a trial basis.

The popularly elected parliament, or National Assembly, was dissolved in 1975, and the Emir has ruled by decree since then. The reason for dissolving the National Assembly, according to the Emir, was the presence in that body of members engaged in subversive activity. The government has announced its intention of restoring the parliamentary system in the future.

The Emir is assisted by a Council of Ministers appointed by himself. The Council was formerly responsible to the National Assembly, but now is directly under the Emir. A large proportion of the ministers belong to the Khalifa family.

For purposes of local government, Bahrain is divided into six municipalities, each governed by a municipal council, whose members are partially elected and partially appointed by the Emir. The small villages outside the municipalities are governed by officials called *mukhtars*, who are appointed by the Department of Rural Affairs.

Although they have a television set, this Bahraini father and his children seem to prefer reading.

4. THE PEOPLE

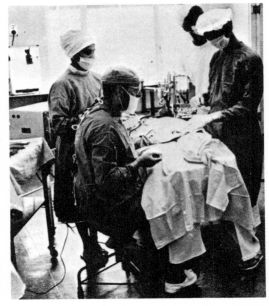

THE BAHRAINIS, who are of north Arabian stock with some Negro admixture, account for 80 per cent of the total population of 305,000. The remainder are Saudi Arabians, Indians, Pakistanis, Iranians, and Europeans, most of whom have come to Bahrain to work in the petroleum industry.

The native Bahrainis are about equally divided between the Sunni and Shiite sects of Islam, with the upper class and the city dwellers being mainly Sunni and the rural villagers, Shiite.

Bahraini surgeons and nurses perform an operation in one of the country's modern hospitals.

A visiting nurse attends a new mother in a rural village.

EDUCATION

Although many older Bahrainis are illiterate, the younger generations are among the best educated in the Middle East. In 1980, there were 62,000 students enrolled in primary and secondary schools, and over 6,000 in higher education.

There are two teachers' training colleges and a technical institute, all founded in the 1960's. In addition, numerous scholarships are available to Bahrain's students to pursue their education at universities in Europe, the United States and other Middle Eastern countries. These scholarships, which were first instituted in 1928, are provided by the government and by local voluntary organizations such as the Manama Rotary Club.

HEALTH

Free medical clinics run by the State Medical Service are available to all Bahraini citizens. The Medical Service was founded in 1925, when the government doctor was appointed. Since then, enormous progress has been achieved—for example, malaria has been eradicated, rural hygiene has been greatly improved, hospitals and nursing schools have been established, and progress has been made

towards elimination of such diseases as trachoma (an eye disease), otorrhoea (running ear) and tuberculosis.

SPORTS

Bahrainis are very sports-minded, and have ample facilities to play or watch the sport of their choice. Football (soccer) is the foremost sport, with 50 football clubs grouped under the Sports Association of Bahrain, and over 5,000 players—a remarkable number in view of the country's small population. Swimming is a sport increasing in popularity, followed by basketball, volleyball, field hockey and track.

WAY OF LIFE

Bahrain possesses a marked respect for its Islamic traditions, tempered by an adjustment to the needs of modern life. In contrast with Saudi Arabia, where rigid Islamic custom prevails, Bahrain has a relaxed society, where women work side by side with men, have equal educational opportunities and are not expected to go veiled.

The foreign visitor will find public night clubs, discotheques and bars, modern hotels, beaches, golf courses, cocktail parties, horse

The Long Distance Race is an annual event in sports-conscious Bahrain, where physical fitness is emphasized.

racing and tennis courts—a distinctly different atmosphere from the Saudi Arabian mainland a few miles off.

Culturally, little Bahrain has contributed several major poets to Arabic literature—Abu al-Bahrs in the 14th century, Mohammed al-Khalifa in the 19th and Ibrahim al-Arayedh in the 20th.

A broadcast is in progress on Radio Bahrain. Bahrain is the site of the Arab world's first earth station, inaugurated in 1969, and now sending radio communications to all parts of the earth.

The installations of the Bahrain gas field resemble an Impressionist painting when seen through a screen of burning excess gas.

5. THE ECONOMY

FOR CENTURIES pearl fishing was the principal economic activity in Bahrain. Then, in 1932, after several years of prospecting, oil was discovered. By 1938, the little island country was the 12th largest oil producer in the world. Since then the economic life of the country has been transformed.

Although Bahrain's importance as an oil producer was later eclipsed by the discovery of vast deposits in Saudi Arabia and elsewhere on the Gulf, the headstart that the country had enabled it to launch schemes for economic diversification and social betterment well before the other Gulf states. Beginning with building materials and the manufacture of soft drinks and ice, Bahrain then proceeded to manufacture paper, chemicals and clothing.

In 1963, the Bahrain Ship Repairing and Engineering Company was founded, to provide general repair facilities for ships of every tonnage plying the waters of the Gulf. The company's installations are the largest of their kind between Rotterdam and Hong Kong. One of the largest oil refineries in the Middle East was constructed at Sitrah. An underwater pipeline was built to the Saudi Arabian mainland and Saudi as well as Bahraini petroleum is now processed in the refinery.

The Bahrain Development Bureau, set up in 1967, undertook the construction of a huge aluminium smelter, using local natural gas as fuel. Major power and water supply projects now provide running water and electricity to most Bahraini homes as well as to industry.

A major factor behind the diversification schemes has been the expectation that Bahrain will be the first of the Gulf states to exhaust its oil reserves.

AGRICULTURE AND FISHERIES

Although the water supply is adequate, the soil of Bahrain is not very fertile. There is, however, a considerable production of dates, alfalfa, cereals, poultry, vegetables, cattle and fodder, and government agronomists are studying means of increasing yields. Formerly, dates and fish were the principal foods produced locally. The present range of crops is the result of diversification schemes.

The Bahrain Fishing Company, formed in recent years, is now a leading export industry, catching, processing and marketing abroad the prawns for which the Gulf is famous. The government is also seeking to revive the pearl fishing industry, which became defunct in the 1970's.

OUTLOOK

The civil war in Lebanon has indirectly benefitted Bahrain. The Bahrain International Airport on Muharraq Island, long a major stopover on flights between Europe and eastern Asia, has acquired much of the traffic formerly routed through Beirut. In addition, Bahrain is becoming a principal financial and communications hub of the Middle East. It is also developing as a tourist attraction with Concorde air flights from London now established. Every part of the main island is accessible by first class roads, thousands of trees have been planted under a government forestry scheme, and a resort complex is being built on the southwest coast.

Madinat Isa, a model city built close to the great burial mound field, is a showplace of the Middle East, and has served as a model for similar projects in other Arab countries. To Bahrainis, Madinat Isa is the Bahrain of the future—a blend of Arabic traditions and modern amenities.

In 1977, an agreement was reached with Saudi Arabia to build a causeway connecting Bahrain with the mainland. The economic advantages of this are great—Bahrain will be connected directly by highways with Europe and the rest of the Middle East. Many Bahrainis looked forward to the causeway with mixed feelings, as they saw it as a threat to their island way of life.

Cafe terraces along the banks of the Nile in Cairo.

Egypt

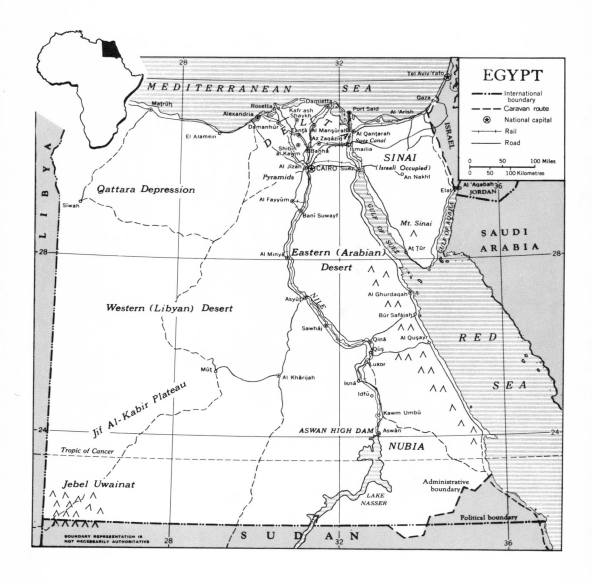

EGYPT

- · — · · International boundary
- — — — Caravan route
- ⊛ National capital
- +—+—+ Rail
- ——— Road

0   50   100 Miles
0   50   100 Kilometres

MEDITERRANEAN   SEA

Tel Aviv-Yafo
Maṭrūḥ
Rosetta
Alexandria
Damietta
Port Said
Gaza
Al 'Arish
Kafr ash Shaykh
El Alamein
Damanhūr
Ṭanṭā
Al Manṣūrah
Al Qanṭarah
Suez Canal
D E L T A
Shibin al Kawm
Az Zaqāzīq
Banhā
Ismailia
ISRAEL
SINAI
(Israeli Occupied)
Al Jizah
CAIRO
Suez
Pyramids
An Nakhl
Al Fayyūm
Bani Suwayf
Al 'Aqabah
JORDAN
Elat
Qattara Depression
Sîwah
LIBYA
Mt. Sinai
∧
SAUDI
ARABIA
Al Minyā
Eastern (Arabian)
Desert
∧
∧ ∧
Aṭ Ṭūr
GULF OF SUEZ
GULF OF AQABA
Western (Libyan) Desert
Asyūṭ
NILE
Al Ghurdaqah
∧ ∧
Būr Safājah
RED
Sawhāj
∧ ∧
Qinā
Qūṣ
Al Quṣayr
∧ ∧
SEA
Mūṭ
Al Khārijah
Luxor
∧ ∧
Isnā
Idfū
∧ ∧
Jif Al-Kabir Plateau
Kawm Umbū
ASWAN HIGH DAM
Aswān
∧
NUBIA
Tropic of Cancer
Jebel Uwainat
∧ ∧ ∧
∧ ∧ ∧ ∧
∧ ∧
LAKE
NASSER
Administrative boundary
∧ ∧ ∧ ∧ ∧
Political boundary
BOUNDARY REPRESENTATION IS
NOT NECESSARILY AUTHORITATIVE
28
S U D A N
32
36

At an irrigation ditch outside the village of Syndion in the Qaliub district, youngsters do their chores. A young girl rides a buffalo "side-saddle," as she guides it towards the water with a stick instead of reins. Even the toddlers at the right are busy washing pots.

I. THE LAND

EGYPT, THE LAND of the Pharaohs lies in the northeast corner of the African continent at the point where Africa and Asia meet. The Mediterranean and Red Seas form natural boundaries on the north and east, while straight lines which meet at right angles to each other form the western boundary with Libya and the southern boundary with Sudan. Egypt has an area of 386,900 square miles—about equal in size to Texas and California together, or more than three times the area of the British Isles.

Egypt has four main land regions—the Nile Valley and Delta, the Western Desert, the Eastern Desert, and the Sinai Peninsula, which has been occupied by Israel since 1967. The southern part of the Nile Valley, adjoining Sudan, is called Nubia.

In the Sahara region of Egypt one may see these curious formations called "nebkas." They are petrified mounds of vegetable origin which once clung to trees, and which have been sculptured into strange shapes by the weather.

THE DESERTS

The Western, or Libyan, Desert is part of the great Sahara and covers above two thirds of Egypt, averaging 600 feet above sea level. In the heart of the desert, the Jif al-Kabir Plateau rises to 3,000 feet, while in the extreme southwest the Jebel Uwainat mountains rise over 7,000 feet. This desert has vast depressions such as the Qattara Depression, which are several hundred feet below sea level.

The Eastern Desert, often called the Arabian Desert, is an extension of the Sahara east of the Nile. From the Nile Valley it rises gradually to a mountain range bordering the Red Sea, with peaks up to 7,000 feet high. Numerous dry

Market gardeners weed their crops in the rich soil of the Nile Valley.

The severe lines of the Temple of Deir Bahari at Luxor contrast with the cliffs behind it. Cliffs like this line the Nile Valley nearly as far as Cairo.

valleys called *wadis* intersect the Eastern Desert and give it a very irregular surface.

The Sinai Peninsula is separated from Egypt proper by the Suez Canal. It is flanked on the east by the Gulf of Aqaba and on the west by the Gulf of Suez, both of which are arms of the Red Sea. Geographically, the Sinai Peninsula is part of Asia rather than Africa. A mountainous desert, it contains Egypt's highest peak—Mount Jabal Katrinah, which is over 8,000 feet

Before the hostilities with Israel in 1967, the Suez Canal port of Ismailia was a haven for private yachts as well as commercial shipping.

Nile Delta. The two main channels are those of Damietta and Rosetta, named for the cities at their mouths. The Delta is a triangular area about 100 miles in length and 155 miles in width where it meets the sea.

Of Egypt's total area, only 15,000 square miles (less than 4 per cent) are habitable—a fact which through the centuries has dominated life in Egypt. Today 95 out of every 100 Egyptians dwell on the banks of the Nile—without the river there would not be an Egypt.

It is barely 100 years since the source of the Nile was discovered in the central African mountains, yet these mountains have provided Egypt with its water supply for untold ages.

Across Africa, rain-bearing winds from the South Atlantic blow thousands of miles in March and April and release their rain upon the central plateau and the highlands of Ethiopia,

and is the historic Mount Sinai on which Moses is said to have received the Ten Commandments from God. The Sinai Desert has more vegetation than either the Eastern or Western Deserts.

THE NILE VALLEY

The Nile flows from south to north, a green strip only six miles wide, until it reaches Cairo and widens into the fields and sand-spits of the Delta. Almost all of Egypt's farmland lies in this watered area. The Nile and its branches rise in east central Africa and flow north for 4,160 miles to the Mediterranean Sea. Much of the 960 miles of the Nile Valley in Egypt are lined with cliffs of granite, sandstone and limestone. North from Cairo the Nile divides into separate channels that fan out forming the

On the Nile at Aswan, palm trees, a white sail and calm waters provide the elements for a peaceful scene.

For centuries, water from the life-giving Nile has been raised into irrigation ditches by a system of buckets and levers. However, modern equipment is replacing such primitive methods.

to the south of Egypt. Countless streams pour down the hillsides, finding their way into rivers such as the Sobat, the Blue Nile, the White Nile and the Atbara. The Blue Nile and the White Nile join to form the Nile proper at Khartoum in the Republic of Sudan. Beyond this point, not one single tributary joins the Nile on its way to the sea!

THE ASWAN HIGH DAM

In 1902, in order to store the flood waters of the Nile, the Egyptian government completed the construction of a dam at Aswan. The dam was made higher in 1907, but eventually proved inadequate. It was decided that a new and much higher dam should be built south of the original one.

The first rock was blasted on January 9, 1960, by Egypt's President Nasser. Four years later the President activated another explosive charge which diverted the course of the Nile to allow work to begin on the main body of the dam. The new dam took 10 years to build and was completed in January, 1970.

The backing-up of the Nile waters by the dam resulted in the formation of Lake Nasser, which now stretches far to the south into Sudan. Its stored waters have made it possible to irrigate 1,000,000 acres of new land to the cultivated area of the country. An additional benefit from the dam is the vast quantity of electric power now generated by its hydro-electric plant, giving electricity to communities which had never before known it.

By mid-1975, however, Egyptian opinion was split over the Aswan High Dam. For one thing, it appeared certain that Egyptian industrial growth would require more power than the dam could produce. For another, some authorities claimed that the dam was having a bad effect on Egypt's ecology, as well as on famous monuments whose foundations have been weakened by the raising of the water table.

The Temples of Philae, on an islet in the Nile were partially submerged when the first Aswan Dam was built in 1902. The structures, dating from the Ptolemaic Period, were totally submerged in 1907 when the dam was heightened by 26 feet, except for the months of July and August when the water was allowed to run freely through the sluices of the dam.

The Administration Building in Port Said controls shipping in the famous seaport, which is no longer as active as it was before the closing of the Suez Canal in 1967. Port Said is at the point where the Canal enters the Mediterranean Sea.

THE SUEZ CANAL

Until it was closed in 1967, the Suez Canal was one of the two most important waterways in the world—the other being the Panama Canal. The canal is 100 miles long and connects the Mediterranean Sea with the northwestern arm of the Red Sea. It provides the shortest route for ships sailing between Europe and the Persian Gulf, Pakistan and India, and is also the shortest sea route between the eastern seaboard of North America and ports on the Indian Ocean. At least one quarter of all trade of the British Isles passed through the canal and more than a quarter of the ships using it were English.

The Isthmus of Suez, through which the canal runs, was once a channel joining the Mediterranean and Red Seas. When it dried up, a chain of salty lakes remained. The canal, which follows this chain, was the inspiration of a Frenchman, Ferdinand de Lesseps, who received permission to dig the canal from the Egyptian ruler, Said Pasha. The British were opposed, but work commenced in 1859 and the canal opened on November 17, 1869. A later Egyptian Ruler, Khedive Ismael, was part owner of the canal. When he ran short of money he sold his share to the British government, but Britain did not control the working of the canal until it occupied Egypt in 1882. In the beginning, the canal was not a success, but more ships began using it and some 11 years later, 485 ships had passed through its locks.

Egypt took over the canal in July, 1956, later compensating the former owners. However, during the Arab-Israeli war of 1967, Israeli forces occupied Sinai on the east bank and the waterway was closed. Many ships had been sunk in the canal during the hostilities and it was impassable—closing it was a mere formality.

In 1975, the canal was finally cleared of debris and re-opened to shipping. It was unlikely, however, that the waterway would soon regain its former importance. Since 1967, Persian Gulf oil has been shipped around the Cape of Good Hope in giant tankers. Not only are the tankers too big to use the canal, but shipment of oil around the Cape in them is more economical than using the canal.

Bedouins guide their camels over the desert wastes, a harsh environment but a familiar one, and one for which man and beast are well adapted.

CLIMATE

Egypt has a dry climate with hot summers—Cairo receives only about one inch of rain per year. The noon temperature in "high summer" may reach 110 degrees F., dropping sharply after sunset, so that the evenings are cool. The winters are healthy and pleasant with clear sunny days and cool nights. In winter, the temperature ranges from 55 to 70 degrees F. During April and May, hot storms called *khamsins* blow in from the south, filling the air with sandy dust.

FLORA AND FAUNA

There are not too many flowers in Egypt, since the Egyptians grow crops rather than decorative plants wherever the soil can be cultivated. However, in oases and in ground moistened by rain, wild flowers such as daisies have sprung up; orchids too are often found in wet desert spots. Cultivated flowers in Egyptian parks and gardens include lilies, jasmine, and narcissus. Other flowers are cultivated beneath the shade of elms, willows, cypresses and eucalyptus trees. The lotus, always highly prized (in architectural decoration throughout history), is still found in the Delta though never in the Nile itself.

Goose-grass, a wild plant with curling leaves and curved prickles on the stems, flourishes on the banks and islands of coastal lakes, and cacti grow in small amounts near Alexandria. The date palm is native, and at least 30 varieties of it are grown. The tree most frequently seen by the wayside and in villages is the acacia, or thorn tree of antiquity.

Snakes native to Egypt include the venomous Egyptian cobra and the horned viper; lizards are numerous. The hippopotamus, crocodile, ostrich and giraffe appear on ancient Egyptian friezes, but have vanished completely from the country.

Gazelles are found in the desert and hyenas, foxes, jackals, wild boars and lynxes in the Nile Delta. The desert hare is abundant in Fayyoum and the jungle cat frequents marshy regions of the Delta. In hills and the Nile Valley are various kinds of bats. Rats and mice are

The Semiramis Hotel in Cairo offers its guests a tree-shaded terrace on the bank of the Nile.

commonly found in the sand hills around Alexandria.

Nile fish, including very large perch and carp, are popular. At Lake Qarun, which is very salty, fresh marine species are stocked.

Moths, wasps and the praying mantis are common, but butterflies are rare.

NATURAL RESOURCES

In the cliffs bordering the Nile today are bountiful supplies of limestone and sandstone. For sculptors, harder stones, such as granite, alabaster and quartzite, are found in the river area. There are some deposits of iron ore, phosphate rock, and petroleum. In the Arabian desert, Upper Egypt and Nubia, gold deposits continue to be found.

CAIRO

Cairo with a population of 5,700,000, is a crowded city, where many languages may be heard on the streets, and shops display multilingual signs.

Cairo is a city where ancient and modern ways mingle, where skyscrapers face the Pyramids only a few miles away. The world's most ancient past is here alongside a vivid present. People of all types stroll the streets, some casually dressed, others in formal attire. Some stop at the sidewalk cafés to puff the traditional hookah pipe, while others rush on their way to work in commercial or administrative offices.

The Tower of Cairo is Egypt's version of the Eiffel Tower in Paris.

The visitor to Cairo is struck by the contrast between old and new. A good example of the old is the Mowsky, one of the famous bazaar districts of the city.

The formal Al Andalous Gardens provide one of the most serene settings in Cairo.

Tree-lined embankments and broad boulevards border the Nile in Cairo. The lions and pillars flank the entrance to the El Tahrir Bridge.

Cairo's skyline is going up and up as new buildings are all taller.

Women in modern dress are as numerous as old-style women in black dresses with long black scarves on their heads. Tucked away between fancy shops one may see a tiny restaurant where the proprietor is the cook. In the old part of town, near Cairo's most important bazaar, the Khan el-Khalil, the scene is like Ali Baba Land. The market's tiny lanes twist and turn into a maze of hundreds of small stalls and boutiques, some of them specializing in perfumes of the Orient, jewels and exquisite gifts. Their owners may be Turks, Syrians or Armenians. The bazaar is a gay place, where the usual means of conveyance are spirited little donkeys, light-stepping and quick, as they carry tradesmen and customers in and out of the market place.

In the market, the butcher who sells fresh

A felucca glides over the calm waters of the Nile against the tall buildings of modern Cairo.

meat, the baker who sells bread and the sweet pastries which Egyptians love, and the carpet maker, are grouped in special areas. Spices, groceries and all manner of produce and market goods, have separate places.

Egyptian ladies, often veiled, sit and select from rolls of cloth while telling the tailor what they need. The clothes-presser in the bazaar is unique—he clamps one foot on his large hot iron and guides it by means of a long handle; he fills his mouth with water before sprinkling it on the cloth!

At the edge of the Khan el-Khalil lies the Al-Azhar Mosque, noted for its university where more than 15,000 students devote their lives to studying the Koran. Behind the elegance of the palm-lined Nile Corniche (embankment) the memory of sultans and caliphs lingers in hundreds of minarets and mosques towering above and around palaces,

museums and luxury hotels. At the foot of the Moqattam (the cliff overlooking Cairo) is the Mosque of Saladin the Magnificent.

The tallest building in Cairo is the 30-storey Cairo Sheraton Hotel. Its rooms offer a spectacular view of the Pyramids.

Alexandria's Corniche Road follows the line of the artificial port. Beyond can be seen the breakwater which protects the port.

ALEXANDRIA

Alexandria, the second largest city in Egypt, with a population of approximately 2,260,000, is situated on the north coast, near the western mouth of the Nile. In ancient times, Alexandria was the greatest commercial city of the Mediterranean world and a focal point of learning.

Today it is still the chief port of Egypt, a great city markedly different in spirit and style.

Alexandria, where Cleopatra once reigned as Queen, is a handsome modern city with many high scholastic institutions, parks, fountains, libraries and marble monuments.

The first great public library in the world (created by Ptolemy, Cleopatra's father) was in

The needle-like spire of Ramleh Mosque rises above Alexandria.

Stanley Bay Beach is a popular cooling-off spot for Alexandria's cosmopolitan population.

Alexandria. It contained a vast collection of books written on papyrus, which unfortunately was lost when the library was destroyed by Christian fanatics in A.D. 391. Another Ptolemy built a great university and scholars flocked to it from near and far. The great mathematician Euclid taught at this university and it was there that the Bible's Old Testament was first revealed to the Christian world, translated from the Hebrew by 70 scholars. The Ptolemies built Alexandria's famous lighthouse, called the Pharos, which lasted 1,600 years, and was considered one of the Seven Wonders of the World.

In the port today, white sails jostle cruise ships and naval vessels, while fishermen step ashore to be hailed by Alexandrian housewives wanting fresh fish before it goes to the markets.

The city has several fine beaches where Egyptian tourists far outnumber those of other nationalities. In the heart of the city are the Zoo and the Greco-Roman Museum, with more than 40,000 antiquities, some dating from the 3rd century B.C. Among the ancient remains is Pompey's Pillar, 25 metres high, which was erected in memory of the Emperor Diocletian. A recent discovery is the Roman Amphitheatre, near the museum, with 12 marble terraces in a half-circle, the only one of its kind in Egypt. Another historical place is the tip of the north entrance of the port, which is where the Pharos lighthouse stood. There is now a museum there preserving all the naval heritage of Alexandria, sometimes known as the Pearl of the Mediterranean.

It is in summer that Alexandria truly comes into its own, when the streets and beaches flow

Modern murals in Alexandria's Marine Station depict scenes from Egyptian life.

Fishermen's boats are always to be seen in Port Said alongside big ships from all over the world.

with people streaming in from inland towns and rural areas for a day by the sea or the annual holiday. An international television festival is held each year as well as an annual film festival.

OTHER CITIES

PORT SAID

Port Said (pronounced Sy-eed) was an important commercial port until 1967, due to its position at the entrance to the Suez Canal at the Mediterranean end. After the closing of the canal, the city's importance declined, although large textile factories continued to produce fine woollen fabrics, and various small businesses catered to the needs of the local population. The fishing industry increased and occasional tourists still visited Port Said. The re-opening of the canal in 1975 fully restored the city's importance.

HELWAN

This small town, 32 miles from Cairo, noted for its fine climate, sulphur waters and beautiful scenery, is now reaping benefits from recent improvements. The sulphur spa, devoted to the cure of rheumatism and respiratory ailments, attracts world-wide visitors (as it did in ancient days). Helwan also has become important industrially with a huge complex, including military factories and iron and steel works.

EL ALAMEIN

Winston Churchill spoke of El Alamein as having the most beautiful climate in the world. Reached by train or bus direct from Alexandria, this city became famous in World War II as the site of a famous battle, in which the British turned back the German armies invading Egypt. It contains British, German and Italian cemeteries, where more than 8,000 soldiers are buried.

MERSA MATRUTH

Mersa, a small port on the Mediterranean west of Alexandria, is reputed to possess some of the finest beaches in the world. The sands are pure white, the waters clear and there are several good hotels and a youth hostel. Mersa Matruth was a port in Ptolemaic times, and the remains may still be seen. Nearby is the German General Rommel's hideout—a cave where he drew up his plans of battle in the North African campaign of World War II.

HURDAGAH

This Red Sea resort is a fashionable tourist rendezvous. It has mountains in the background and, in front of it, the clear waters of the Red Sea, where fish swarm among coral reefs. The warm sunny climate attracts countless visitors and campers. Hurdagah is situated 250 miles south of Suez and has become popular for under-water photographers, divers

Abou El Nomrous is a typical Egyptian village, not far from Cairo. In such communities, life has changed very little over the years—note the women carrying heavy burdens on their heads.

and fishermen. It has a fine Marine Life Museum with stuffed denizens of the deep, including decorative stuffed mermaids.

FAYYOUM

About 90 miles southwest of Cairo by rail lies Fayyoum, the largest natural oasis in Egypt. Water wheels and mills are to be seen everywhere in Fayyoum. Small streams and springs irrigate this desert garden, famed for its vineyards and citrus groves. Qarun Lake in Fayyoum is a mecca for sportsmen with its year-round temperate climate.

SUEZ

Suez, once a fishing village, lies at the southern entrance to the Suez Canal, overlooked by the barren peaks of the Sinai Peninsula and the arid sweep of Egypt's Red Sea coastline. New deposits of oil have been discovered in the area south of Suez but not in spectacular amounts. Nevertheless, the mineral resources of the countryside around it are being exploited and the city has a large oil refinery. Port Tewfik, which adjoins Suez is connected to it by a causeway and stands on a man-made island. Suez and its port, like Port Said, were inactive during the closing of the Canal, but have resumed activity since 1975.

TANTA

Tanta, a commercial town, with a population of about 100,000, is the capital of Gharbiya Province. It has a special significance to Moslems because of a famous saint, Ahmed al-Badwi, who dwelt a number of years in Tanta (though he was born in Fez, Morocco), and died there. Pilgrims visit his tomb to pray for health and prosperity.

The ancient Temple of Luxor lies close to the Nile bank. Note the obelisk at the far right and the mosque built within the temple walls by the Moslems of a much later period.

Murals such as this one to be seen at Luxor, often adorned the walls of ancient Egyptian tombs. At the top are hieroglyphics.

ASSIUT

Assiut, in Middle Egypt, is one of the most important provincial, commercial and educational hubs in Egypt. For centuries Assiut was visited by caravans from the interior of Africa, especially from Dharfur in Sudan, bringing the produce of the continent to Egypt. The city has since become one of the most progressive, with a higher standard of education than any other community of its size in the land, and it has its own university.

LUXOR

Farther south along the course of the Nile in Upper Egypt stands Luxor, a true resort town, taking care of thousands of visitors, who come to see the ancient remains in the vicinity. Nearby is the ancient site of Thebes, which was once the capital of the Pharaohs. Along the

The magnificent statues at Abu Simbel were saved from being flooded during the Aswan High Dam construction. A team of international experts co-operating with UNESCO dismantled the huge, brittle sandstone sculptures and moved them to a higher and dry location.

Human beings appear tiny beside the colossal statues of Abu Simbel.

grimness of the surrounding desert land. Its massive new High Dam adds to its importance. It is the last town before the Sudan border is reached. Since construction of the dam, Aswan's population has risen from 20,000 to 100,000.

Aswan has ancient origins as a frontier town, but its present prosperity dates from the old dam, built by the British in 1902 as the first major attempt to control the Nile. The new Kima fertilizer plant has added more prosperity to Aswan, and more development is planned. Within the area, the Pharaohs of Egypt obtained the pink granite used for their statues, tombs and monuments.

Elephantine Island, a short boat ride away, has a modern museum and an ancient temple. This island has been inhabited continuously for 5,000 years. One of the present-day inhabitants is the Begum Aga Khan, widow of Aga Khan III who has a villa there. The tomb of her husband is on the opposite bank of the Nile, dominating a desert height.

THE TEMPLES OF ABU SIMBEL

Farther south, the great rock-hewn Temples of Abu Simbel, built by the Pharaohs of Ancient Egypt between 1300 and 1233 B.C. stand as silent witnesses to a vanished age. The four seated figures of Ramses carved in the cliffs are each 66 feet high, miraculously protected from erosion by their sheltered position. The temples are dedicated to the God Ra, the Rising Sun, the Royal wife and the Goddess Hathor. These temples were almost flooded by the waters of the High Dam, but were saved in response to Egypt's appeal to UNESCO, the United Nations cultural and scientific agency. On September 22, 1968 the Egyptian government celebrated the completion of the rescue project, which had begun in 1963.

river bank is the Temple of Karnak, while on the western Nile bank lie the Valley of the Kings, the Valley of the Queens and the Tombs of the Nobles. The famous treasures of Tutankhamen were discovered here. Across green fields are the Colossi of Memnon, gigantic witnesses to the glorious past. In 1976, the Egyptian Government Antiquities Organization warned that the Colossi and other monuments at Luxor were endangered by changes in the Nile drainage pattern caused by the Aswan High Dam. A rising water table at Luxor was undermining the foundations of the monuments. Plans were launched to provide new concrete foundations for the gigantic twin statues.

Though Luxor is not large, it is a pleasing place, linked to Cairo by 400 miles of good roads.

ASWAN

The attractive town of Aswan stands at the edge of Nubia, forming a contrast with the

Egypt's two most famous monuments are the Sphinx and the Pyramid of Cheops at Giza.

2. HISTORY

PREHISTORIC EGYPT, in the days before written records began, has been revealed by archeological discoveries, wrested painstakingly from the layered silt brought down by the River Nile. Uncovered sites of ancient villages and cemeteries show that over a long period before recorded history, the swamps of the Nile Valley were cleared and settled by people from other parts of Africa and from western Asia. During this period, farming, the raising of livestock and the arts and trades of civilized life were developed.

ARCHAIC PERIOD

The record begins dimly, about 3100 B.C. with an Egyptian king who united the country from north to south as a single nation and made Memphis his capital. This king is referred to in later times as Menes, although modern scholars are not sure that this was his name. He was the founder of the First Dynasty and stands at the head of a line of Pharaohs who ruled over a civilized Egypt throughout 30 dynasties. Little is known of the Second Dynasty. During the

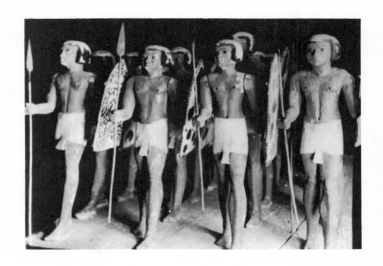

The Egyptian Museum in Cairo has countless artifacts from ancient Egypt, among them these figurines of warriors.

Third Dynasty huge tombs, called mastabas, were built, foreshadowing the pyramids of later periods. The ancient Egyptians believed in life after death and the dead were entombed with provisions for existence in the after-life. The elaborate tombs contained imposing rooms packed with furniture, equipment, tools and hunting weapons, and food and drink for the use of the deceased in the next world.

THE AGE OF THE PYRAMIDS

The Fourth Dynasty, which began with the reign of Snefru, was marked by the building of the pyramids. Each successive king built his own massive tomb in the form of a pyramid. During the time from 2700 to 2200 B.C., termed the Old Kingdom, 20 great pyramids were designed and built. The three most impressive were built at Giza, slightly north of present-day Cairo. These are the pyramids of the Pharaohs Khufu, Khafre and Menkaure. These monarchs are also known by the Greek forms of their names—Cheops, Chephren and Mycerinus. For several months each year, every able-bodied man was drafted to work in constructing these mountains of stone, which, incredibly, were completed within one lifetime and intended to stand for eternity. The pharaohs of this period were absolute rulers.

The civilization of this period was extremely high. The Egyptians were advanced in all the arts and sciences—their knowledge of geometry, for example, was remarkable, as evidenced by the precision of their architecture. They even employed cosmetics and furniture very similar to those in use today.

INTERMEDIATE PERIODS

From 2200 to 2050 B.C. Egypt fell into the turmoil of the First Intermediate Period, when warring families tried to gain the throne. The strife forced a decline in commerce and the arts. The Middle Kingdom (2050–1800 B.C.) saw Egypt, re-united under princes from the city of Thebes who ruled without the absolute power of earlier kings. At this time, Egypt carried out military campaigns in Nubia and in Palestine.

In the Second Intermediate Period (1800–1570 B.C.) the dynastic rulers grew weaker and Egypt was overwhelmed by the new technology of the wandering Hyksos, pastoral invaders from western Asia, who used horses, chariots, armour and superior weapons to subdue and dominate the Egyptians for over a century.

THE NEW KINGDOM

During the Early New Kingdom (1570–1300 B.C.) the Egyptians learned the methods of their conquerors and drove them back into Asia. Freedom and peace strengthened Egypt's economy under Queen Hatshepsut, who increased trade with Africa and saw to the con-

The Sphinx of Giza, on close examination, can be seen to have a broken nose. Thousands of sphinxes were built in ancient Egypt, but this one is the largest.

struction of magnificent temples and palaces. When her successor, Thutmose III, gained control of Egypt, his efforts were military in nature. Within 20 years he conquered Palestine, Syria and pushed Egypt's northeast frontier to the upper waters of the Euphrates River in Asia. This was the greatest triumph of Egyptian might, and it created an empire that survived for a century, making Thebes and Memphis political and cultural hubs of the ancient world.

At the close of the Early New Kingdom, Amenhotep IV began a worship of the sun's life-giving powers. He tried to establish a belief in one God, or Aton. He changed his name to Ikhnaton and removed his court from Thebes to a new capital at Tell al-Amarna. Ikhnaton's concentration on domestic affairs, led to neglect of the empire. Syria was lost to the Hittites, a people of Asia Minor, and Egypt itself was disturbed by revolts led by priests of the old religion. Ikhnaton's successor, King Tutankhamen, was forced by the priests to return to the worship of many gods.

Made of pure gold, this bust of the Pharaoh Tutankhamen has come down to us from the 14th century B.C. The discovery of "King Tut's" tomb in 1922 and the opening up of its perfectly preserved treasures threw new light on life in ancient Egypt.

FOREIGN CONQUERORS

During the Later New Kingdom (1300–1090 B.C.) Egypt again prospered, recovering lost territories and prospering in trade and building. King Seti regained Palestine and Syria, and his son—the famous Ramses II—fought the Hittites. But once again, Egypt was unable to retain its power as invaders came by

Goats nibbling on trees are depicted in this bas-relief (now in the Louvre in Paris) from the tomb of the 5th Dynasty Pharaoh, Akhouthtep.

sea from across the Mediterranean. Once again it lost its empire.

Now it was Egypt's turn to be dominated, first by the Libyans, then by the Assyrians, although during the Saites period (26th Dynasty) 663 to 525 B.C., Egypt was increasingly independent. In 525 B.C., the Persians forced the Assyrians out of Egypt, and in turn ruled it for 200 years. In 332 B.C. the Macedonian (Greek) conqueror, Alexander the Great, took over Egypt. After his death, Ptolemy I ruled, taking the title "King of Egypt." In doing so, he founded the Ptolemaic Dynasty, which lasted until the death of Cleopatra in 30 B.C.

This was a great period in Egyptian history. Arts and trades flourished and Alexandria, the Ptolemaic capital, grew into a hub of learning and religion for the whole world. The court of the Ptolemies was Greek in language and culture, although the common people continued to speak the Egyptian language and their ways were little changed. The language of ancient Egypt, which was written in hieroglyphics—or picture writing—belonged to the Hamito-Semitic family, which includes modern Arabic, Hebrew, Berber, Maltese and the languages of Ethiopia.

Egypt's prosperity eventually attracted the Romans, who conquered the country in 30 B.C., making it a Roman province.

If the statues at Abu Simbel show a marked resemblance to one another, there is a reason for it—they all represent the same Pharaoh, Ramses II, who lived in the middle of the 13th century B.C.

A silver tetradrachm from the reign of Cleopatra VII, Egypt's last queen, bears her portrait. Cleopatra has her place in history as the woman whose beauty captivated Julius Caesar and Marc Antony. Her hair style, shown on this coin, still is in vogue.

CLEOPATRA

The Romans had actually gained a foothold in Egypt in 80 B.C., when they assumed control of the city of Alexandria. Cleopatra, who became the queen of Egypt in 69 B.C. kept her throne by charming first Julius Caesar and then Marc Antony, whom she married. After the death of Caesar, a power struggle had arisen between his heirs, Marc Antony and Octavian. Antony and Cleopatra were defeated by Octavian in the naval battle of Actium in 31 B.C. and returned to Egypt where they both committed suicide in the following year. Their story is one of history's greatest romances.

ROMANS AND COPTS

The Romans and their successors, the Byzantines, ruled Egypt for over 600 years. During this period the Egyptians became Christianized, and developed their own branch of Christianity, the Coptic Church. Christian missionaries found the Egyptians very willing to embrace the new religion with its stress on self-denial, and the preparation for an after-life that promised to be better than that of the present. The Coptic Church flourished from 300 A.D. to 600 A.D., then weakened, as the

Byzantine rulers attempted to make the Copts conform to the main body of the Church.

In 639, the Arab war chief Amr ibn al-As invaded Egypt, capturing Alexandria in 642 and incorporating Egypt into the Moslem Empire. For 200 years, Egypt remained a province of the Arab realm. Most of the Coptic Christians were converted to Islam, and Arabic replaced the Egyptian language, except in the rites of the Coptic Church. In 969, the Fatimites from Tunisia, a rival Moslem sect, wrested power and made Cairo their capital, establishing the University of Al-Azhar.

During the Crusades, in 1169, the Caliph (ruler) of Egypt requested help from the Sultan of Syria. The Sultan sent his general, Saladin, who overthrew the Caliph, later becoming Islam's greatest leader by recapturing Jerusalem from the Christians. Saladin's Ayyubid dynasty controlled Egypt until 1250, when the Mame-

The Coptic church of Al-Moalaka located in the old part of Cairo, is built on the remains of a Roman gateway.

Cairo (seen here) is new compared to Alexandria, since its official founding date is A.D. 969. There were several earlier settlements, however, in or near the site of the present Cairo—one of them called Babylon. Babylon is said to have been built in 525 B.C. by emigrants from the famous Mesopotamian city of the same name. The Romans fortified Babylon and used it as a military headquarters. All that remains of Babylon today are its Roman walls.

lukes—Turkish and Circassian slaves who were trained as royal bodyguards—revolted and seized control of Egypt.

In 1517, the Turks marched into Egypt and made it a part of the Ottoman Empire. Nevertheless, the Turkish officials—*pashas*—left the governing to the Mamelukes who retained military and political power.

NAPOLEON IN EGYPT

By the end of the 18th century, Mameluke overlords were again firmly in the saddle. Their rule was harsh and economic conditions worsened due to oppression of the now steadily-declining Egyptian peasantry (*Fellahin*).

Such was the situation in Egypt when Napoleon Bonaparte landed near Alexandria in 1798 with an army of 40,000 men. France and Napoleon were then supreme in Europe, with armies stretching across the continent, and Napoleon's expedition was undertaken to sever Britain's vital line of communications with the East. Napoleon had said he came to Egypt as a friend of the Turkish Sultan to bring an end to the bad government of the Mamelukes and to try to stop the hardship which the people were enduring. Egyptians did not welcome him and Napoleon had to force his way without any help from the fellahin all the way to shore and from the sea to Cairo. He and his men had to forage for food while the Mamelukes prepared for war, and the viceroy of the Sultan fled to Syria.

The English Admiral Nelson searched for the French fleet, found it at Abukir and

to build up the economy. Mohammed Ali was not afraid to be ruthless and he used Egypt to achieve his ambitions, yet, in reaching his goal he benefitted the land, reorganized the government and made many improvements.

THE BRITISH INTERVENTION

In 1857 the French Suez Canal Company began building the Suez Canal to shorten the water route between Europe and India. The immense engineering undertaking was completed a decade later. In 1875, facing bankruptcy, the Egyptian government sold its share to Great Britain. In 1881, a revolt broke out to free Egypt from foreign control. To protect its investment, the British sent troops that

destroyed it. Napoleon was trapped with troops he could hardly feed. His only big victory was when he defeated the Mamelukes in a battle before Cairo, but was unable to capture their leader, Murad Bey. He stayed on in Egypt for another year until the Sultan of Turkey made war on him. He then sailed for France leaving General Kléber to carry on, but Kléber was assassinated a little while after. In 1801, the British made a military landing at Alexandria, then marched on to Cairo forcing the French to leave Egypt that year.

MOHAMMED ALI

A young Albanian officer, Mohammed Ali, appeared on the scene to take control. He had been sent by the Turkish Sultan to get rid of the French. In 1805, he was named the Governor of Cairo, and made order out of chaos with his firm rule. He is regarded as the founder of modern Egypt because of his efforts

Husain Kamil Pasha succeeded Abbas II Hilmi in 1914 and was given the title of sultan by the English. His reign ended with his death in 1917. His brother, Fuad, who succeeded him, took the title of king.

On the day the Suez Canal was opened, a long line of ships passed through it, carrying heads of state and other officials of the leading powers.

quelled the revolt. British arms remained the force behind the Egyptian government from then on.

In 1914, Egypt became a "protected country" under Great Britain, because the Turkish Ottoman Empire—of which Egypt was still technically a part—sided with the Germans in World War I. Britain occupied Egypt, protecting the Suez Canal, and using Egypt as a base for military operations. In 1922 the British granted Egypt independence. In 1936, aside from a force guarding the Suez Canal, Britain withdrew all forces from Egypt, but remained a strong power behind the throne.

MODERN EGYPT

During the Second World War, Italy and Germany invaded Egypt to capture the Suez Canal, but the British held out at El Alamein after bitter fighting. After the war, Egypt became a member of the United Nations, which in 1947 voted to establish a Jewish state—Israel—in nearby Palestine. Egypt immediately invaded Israel, but was defeated. In 1949, the United Nations established a cease-fire, but in 1950 Egypt blocked Israeli ships from using the Suez Canal and fighting broke out again.

In 1951 and 1952 rioting took place in Egypt over the failure to defeat Israel, the corruption of the King's Royal Government, and the continued British occupation of the Suez zone. On July 23, 1952, a group of army officers seized control of the government and one year later proclaimed Egypt a Republic, ending the power of King Farouk and the

On July 4, 1946, Britain withdrew its troops from Egypt (excepting the Suez Canal). Here on that day at the old citadel of Cairo, the British flag was lowered.

Montazzah Palace was the Alexandria residence of the late King Farouk of Egypt. It is now a museum containing many objects of art, as well as souvenirs and household effects of the monarch—including his son and heir's baby carriage.

Royal family, who went into exile. After a power struggle among the officers Gamal Abdel Nasser gained control and became prime minister. Life under King Farouk's rule had been attuned to the upper classes and the poor had suffered. Revolt was in the air throughout the land and Nasser was the spark.

In October, 1954, the British gave in to Nasser's demands and agreed to remove all their troops by June, 1956. In September, 1955, an agreement with Communist Czechoslovakia assured large imports of jet warplanes, rifles and tanks to Egypt. This tie with the Communist bloc worried the United States and other Western countries, but it spelled success for Nasser, who was elected President of Egypt in June, 1956.

the Suez Canal from its British and French owners. Nasser proclaimed that all tolls from the canal would be used to build the new Aswan High Dam.

During this period, relations with Israel worsened and Egypt continued to block Israeli ships from the Suez Canal and at the entrance to the Gulf of Aqaba, thus effectively cutting Israel's sea communications to the East. Israel protested and a war began on October 29, 1956. Israel quickly occupied most of the Sinai Peninsula. Britain and France, wishing to regain control of the Suez, demanded that Egypt and Israel stop fighting. Israel assented, but Egypt did not. After invasion of the Canal zone by English and French troops, resulting in the seizure of Port Said and Port Fuad, the United Nations stepped in and ended the fighting, stationing an International Force on the Egyptian side of the Sinai border with Israel and at Sharm el-Sheikh, at the tip of the peninsula.

In the Arab world, Nasser played a leading rôle. His countrymen had faith in what he did and, during the 1950's, Nasser became a leader of a movement for unity among Arab nations.

STOPPAGE OF THE SUEZ

One month after Nasser became President, the United States and Britain withdrew offers made in December, 1955 to help build a huge new dam across the Nile River near Aswan. Both these countries said Egypt was not strong enough economically to make the costly project a profitable venture. Egypt retaliated by seizing

An avenue lined with feathery palms leads to the former summer palace of King Farouk in Alexandria.

General Mohammed Neguib (middle), seen here on a pilgrimage to Mecca, was the first president of the Egyptian Republic. One of the leaders of the coup that overthrew the monarchy in 1952, he was replaced in 1954 by Gamal Abdel Nasser, who also was one of the leaders of that coup.

His propaganda from Cairo reached millions of Arabs, promoting freedom from Western influence and hatred of Israel. His friendship with the Soviet Union (which also wanted to end Western influence in the Arab world) brought Egypt enormous amounts of military aid and Nasser allowed a large Soviet force to be built up on Egyptian soil. The Russians also helped build the Aswan High Dam.

UNION WITH SYRIA

In 1958, political unrest and the fear of a Communist takeover in Syria led to the merging of Egypt with Syria to form the United Arab Republic, with Nasser as President of the new nation. Dissatisfaction set in among Syrians and, in 1961, just over three years after the United Arab Republic was formed, a group of Syrian officers rebelled and declared Syria an independent state. This was a great blow to Nasser, who tried to quell the rising with his troops, but on second thought withdrew them, accepting the loss of Syria. Egypt, however, retained the name of the United Arab Republic until 1971, when this name was discarded and the name of Egypt restored.

In 1962, Egypt took part in a civil war in Yemen, when the Yemeni army overthrew the king and established a republic. Royalist forces fought dearly to restore the monarchy, and Egypt sent troops to aid the republican rebels. Saudi Arabia opposed Nasser and helped the royalists. This campaign cost thousands of Egyptian lives, but nevertheless, Nasser was re-elected as president in March, 1965.

THE 1967 WAR

For reasons which have not yet become clear, Nasser now turned his attention to the Sinai frontier adjoining Israel. He requested the United Nations to withdraw their troops, closed the Gulf of Aqaba to Israeli shipping and massed his troops in Sinai. On June 5, 1967, war again broke out. Israel invaded Egyptian territory and made a massive strike which knocked out the Egyptian air force. The Egyptians fought back for six days, but Israel defeated Egypt, Syria and Jordan, occupying Sinai as far as the Suez Canal. With this battle Nasser lost face and offered to resign, but his countrymen had faith in him, insisting he stay on as their leader.

NASSER'S HERITAGE

Nasser resembled a lion chained when he no longer controlled events outside his world, and he was blamed for all the troubles in the Middle East. On September 28, 1970, Gamal Abdel Nasser died and all the Arab world mourned.

His achievements have lived on. He had changed the face of the Arab world. The night he overthrew the King on July 22, 1952, he had put on his army uniform, taken out his last savings, and given them to his brother to care for his family, should his plans to change world history fail.

Had he killed Farouk he would have become a hero instantly, but he saved the King's life, believing it was right, and let the glory of the revolution go to General Neguib—without drenching Egypt in blood.

ANWAR EL-SADAT

Nasser was succeeded by Anwar El-Sadat, who had been one of the officers in the coup that

Gamal Abdel Nasser led Egypt through the difficult decade of the 1960's, until he died of a heart attack in 1970.

overthrew the monarchy. Sadat's presidency began quietly, but gained world attention when he ordered the huge Russian military force to leave Egypt in 1972. The Russians left without protest, and it was clear that Egypt once more had a strong leader.

In 1972, Egypt entered into an understanding with Libya that the two countries would eventually be merged. This came about largely through the efforts of Libya's chief of state, Muammar Qaddafi—Egyptian support for the merger idea was less enthusiastic. Since then relations with Libya have deteriorated and such a merger appears unlikely.

In October, 1973, Egypt and Syria attacked Israel, claiming that Israel had struck the first blow. Unlike the 1967 War, the Arabs were well prepared, with Russian aid, and Egyptian forces surged across the Suez Canal into Israeli-occupied Sinai. Three weeks later the Israeli armies had driven them back and even had crossed the canal and were threatening Cairo. At this point the United States and Russia, to avoid a showdown, intervened diplomatically and a cease-fire was arranged, pending further resolutions of the recurring conflict between the Arab states and Israel.

By the summer of 1974, Egypt and Syria had signed agreements with Israel regarding the exchange of prisoners and the setting up of buffer zones, largely through the diplomatic skill of Henry Kissinger, the United States Secretary of State. Egypt also resumed diplomatic relations with the United States, which

work began, with United States aid, on restoring the Suez Canal.

The high point in improved relations, however, was President Nixon's visit to five Middle Eastern countries, including Egypt and Israel, in June, 1974. During his stay in Cairo, the United States President announced his intention of providing Egypt with United States nuclear reactors and the technical aid to operate them for peaceful purposes. This was to be but one phase of a broad agreement covering scientific and cultural exchange between the two countries.

Among the questions unresolved were the fate of the Palestinian refugees and the disposition of the Arab territories occupied by Israel in 1967.

The 1974 agreements and the re-opening of the Canal left Sadat free to concentrate on domestic affairs. He set as his main goal the liberalizing of the Egyptian economy, and the changing of Egyptian political and economic organizations to conform to Western standards. One example of this was the creation in 1976 of three distinct groups within Egypt's only legal political party, the Arab Socialist Union. These groups, called *minbars*, represent leftist, rightist and centrist factions within the party and presumably will serve as the nuclei of future separate parties, if and when the National Assembly and President Sadat decide that Egypt is ready for such parties.

In 1980, Egypt and Israel established formal diplomatic relations.

Modernization of transport is a main goal of the Egyptian government. A special effort is being made to replace steam engines with diesel and electric locomotives on the nation's railways. Seen here is a heavy repair workshop for diesel locomotives.

3. THE GOVERNMENT

A NEW ERA in Egyptian history came about with the revolution in 1952, setting out solid bases for a new life in Egypt. President Sadat aims to reorganize the government and the financial system in order to set the country on a sound path of reconstruction.

According to the constitution of Egypt, only one man can run for President. He is nominated by at least two thirds of Egypt's legislature and then approved by the majority of voters. The President may serve for an unlimited number of 6-year terms. He then may appoint one or more Vice-presidents and a cabinet, and may dismiss them and the legislature at any time. The Council of Ministers (cabinet) includes the Prime Minister and several vice-premiers and ministers. This council helps the President plan and direct national policy.

LEGISLATURE

In Egypt, the legislature, which is known as the National Assembly, has 360 members who serve 5-year terms. From each of 175 electoral districts, two members are chosen. The President appoints the remaining 10 members, but at least half of the National Assembly must be selected from among workers and farmers.

Originally the Assembly met for a minimum of 7 months each year, but while Egypt existed

Egypt has tried to settle some of its nomadic Bedouins in new homes in the northwest coast area. About 4,000 Bedouin families were supplied with food until they could harvest their first crops from their newly settled land. The food was provided by the World Food Program, a joint operation of the United Nations and the Food and Agriculture Organization (FAO). This Bedouin has just drawn supplies at Burg-el-Arab.

as the United Arab Republic there were longer periods with regular legislative meetings. Nasser ruled by decrees, backed by the law. President Sadat proposes to alter this procedure and replace it with more democratic methods.

JUDICIARY

Egypt was the first Arab country to abolish the Islamic law courts (known as the Mahkama Sharia) except for those handling certain questions of a personal nature. Special religious courts maintained by non-Moslems have also been abolished.

Egypt's penal and civil codes are based on French law and follow the French system. All

judges in Egypt are selected by the Ministry of Justice and the President. Egypt's highest court is the Court of Cassation which hears both civil and criminal cases. There are also Courts of appeal, trial courts and lower courts.

SOCIAL AND ECONOMIC POLICIES

Egypt is a "democratic socialist state" and its government is based on two documents, the National Charter of 1962 and the new constitution of 1971. The goals are Arab unity, freedom and socialism. President Sadat is encouraging all Egyptians above 18 years of age to register as voters. It is obligatory for all adult men to do so—those who do not are fined.

To speed up economic development the Egyptian Government with the aid of the International Labour Organization, is expanding vocational training. These young men are apprentices at the North Cairo Refrigerator and Air-Conditioning Training Centre.

GOVERNORATES (PROVINCES)

Each of the 25 Egyptian governorates is administered by a council acting under the guidance of a Governor, assisted by representatives of the central government from the Ministries of Education, Work, Supply, Treasury, Agriculture, Interior, Social Affairs, Education, Health, Transport and Labour. Other members of the council are selected from the members of the Arab Socialist Union.

Governorate Councils are responsible for the establishment and administration of public utilities and welfare services. They operate within the general laws of the state and within the terms of the policy laid down by the ministries of the central government.

At the next level the administration is carried out by a city council, made up of the local official comparable to a mayor, members from various ministries who are appointed by their departments, and active members of the Arab Socialist Union. The terms of service are the same as in the case of the governorates. City councils carry out the laws and regulations affecting the local public utilities, under the supervision of the appropriate government authorities.

The Governorate councils are responsible for all normal administrative functions. They control their own budgets, development plans, and other local projects which include hamlets. They also administer the former great estates. The councils organize health, cultural, social and workers' activities beneficial to the community—which are concerned with the daily life of the unit. This system of local administration aims at realizing greater efforts in general productivity.

An official government publication recently issued states: "The local government system has been introduced as a step towards the ultimate goal of the revolution: a socialist cooperative society. The participation of the people in the government system on various levels of the village, the city, and the governorate, fosters true democracy and self-reliance."

SOCIAL WELFARE

The most outstanding social and welfare plan carried out in Egypt is the establishment of rural development projects throughout the country. Libraries, new parks, schools, playgrounds, clinics designed to provide health, education, agricultural and social services have sprung up from both private and state initiative.

The villagers no longer need to seek opportunities in big cities, for the government has come to them with mobile schools, manned by instructors and professors of both sexes, primarily in the domestic science field, public health, arts and crafts and child welfare. Communal halls have been opened with night schools for young and old, who wish to catch up on the reading and writing they did not have the time or inclination for before.

A General Sports Union has been set up for government employees, and rural clubs for

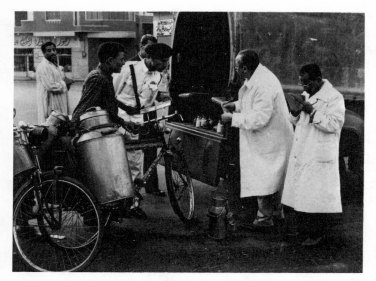

In a Cairo street, public health inspectors examine milk being delivered by bicycle.

youths have been established. Scouting is a deeply-rooted movement in Egypt, having a membership above 25,000. Government-sponsored summer and winter camps are also functioning, some as voluntary work camps for young people having free time, during which they can train and work collectively on development projects.

FOREIGN RELATIONS

President Sadat after taking office offered to open the Suez Canal to international navigation, if Israel agreed to begin the first stage of withdrawal from Sinai, under the auspices of the United Nations. However, Israel did not reply to these conditions, which were a test for peace in the eyes of Egypt, and nothing further was accomplished until the Kissinger negotiations of 1974. In re-opening the canal in 1975, Egypt indicated that Israeli ships would be barred from the canal pending a general Middle East settlement.

President Sadat represents his foreign policy as following the goals of freedom, friendship with the Western world and Arab unity.

In 1975, President Sadat accused Libyan head of state Qaddafi of organizing a plot to overthrow the government of Egypt. This and other incidents were part of a breakdown of good relations between Egypt and oil-rich and scantily populated Libya.

In 1977, President Sadat surprised the world by initiating talks with Israeli Prime Minister Menachem Begin, to which he invited other Arab chiefs of state, who declined. The discussions led to the signing of a peace treaty between Israel and Egypt in 1979. The results of Sadat's bold move remained to be seen, but it was apparent that Egypt had chosen a policy of leadership in world politics on its own terms.

Anwar El-Sadat, who became President of Egypt in 1970, has steered his country's foreign policy toward improved relations with the West.

A woman wearing the traditional "burqa" (left foreground) contrasts sharply with the Western dress of the crowd in Cairo's Al Tahir Square.

4. THE PEOPLE

MOST OF THE PEOPLE of Egypt are descendants of the ancient Egyptians with later admixtures of Greeks, Romans, Syrians, Arabs, Turks and Negroes.

At least 63 per cent of the 42,000,000 Egyptians dwell in the Delta. The remainder are concentrated in villages and small towns along the Nile Valley. This is where the Fellahin live and work as farmers, comprising the core of the Egyptian population, sturdy and diligent. Often they can become stubborn and go in for local feuds. There is little luxury in their lives, and they are slow to change.

From Cairo and other large cities, young professional men and women, experts in local dialects, have been sent to assist the more backward groups. Every day they go from farm to farm and house to house, teaching the mothers and fathers more practical and modern methods in agriculture, domesticity and how to bring up the babies in a simpler manner.

In remote areas, they have built outdoor stoves for cooking, adjacent to water wheels, replacing the single brazier which smoked up the entire dwelling of the family. How to mix milk formulas with powdered milk has been

Tea is popular in Egypt and these women of a Delta village have found a shady spot in which to enjoy it. Fellahin is the name given to such typical villagers and peasants in Egypt.

another lesson, eagerly accepted by the rural mother where refrigeration is not possible. The Fellahin still live very much as their forebears did in ages past, their diet principally bread, beans, strong tea, goat-cheese and onions, fish when available and only rarely meat.

THE BEDOUINS

Along the edge of the Eastern Desert far from the villages, the nomads known as Bedouins camp out in tents and still pursue their wandering way of life, by choice, al-

A village woman starts a fire in a mud-brick stove, using sugar cane stalks and dried cow-dung cakes (foreground) for fuel.

A woman of a nomad tribe waits outside a government health station with her ailing child. (UNICEF)

Cooking a meal in the desert is a casual and natural affair to the Bedouins.

Teen-aged boys as well as toddlers, children of re-settled Bedouin families, are adjusting to their new, non-nomadic life.

A young girl carries home a jug full of water from the canal.

These young Nubians are among the 45,000 of their people who were moved to new homes when the Aswan High Dam was built and their villages were flooded. (UNICEF)

THE NUBIANS

In the Aswan region, the Nubians are found —people of dark complexion, somewhat Negroid in appearance who speak the Nubian language. Nubian homes are neat and compact, characterized by domes of mud-brick. The women and children are friendly and take readily to visitors, whether government aides or foreigners.

THE COPTS

The Christian community is overwhelmingly Coptic and comprises one twelfth of the Egyptian population. For the Copts, their church is the focal point of their identity. They regard themselves as pure descendants of the ancient Egyptians. Greatly outnumbered by the Moslems, they feel a closeness within their own community. Each worshipper at the Coptic Mass holds the next person's hand so that "blessings are passed round." They are very numerous in Middle Egypt from Mallawi to a little south of Akhmin, and work as clerks, administrators and in manual trades. Nasser

though an effort is being made to settle them. They have camels, rifles and tools, work as they wish with a self-appointed leader, often assisting desert patrols.

The Bedouins are a carefree lot, enjoying whatever they do. Some say they are the purest Arabs of the land, rarely intermarrying and maintaining rigorous codes of morality. Highlights are the days when some new dam is inaugurated—Bedouin chiefs then accompany officials to the site, dressed in splendid regalia.

A Coptic priest is seen in the interior of the Church of Abou Serga in Cairo. Part of the church dates from the 6th Century A.D.

The construction of the Aswan High Dam caused the re-settlement of 17,000 Nubian families in new communities, such as this village in the Kom-Ombo area. The pigeon tower is a common sight in Egypt where these birds are raised in large numbers.

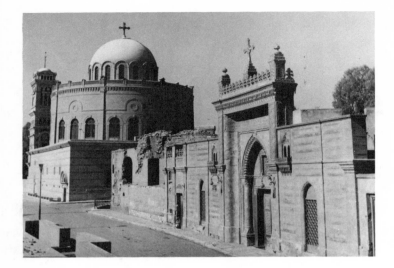

was friendly to the Copts and President Sadat carries on the policy of amiable relations with the Coptic Church.

ISLAM

Islam is no longer as militant as it was a thousand years ago. Modern Islam, and in Egypt this means Sunni, or orthodox Islam, teaches what might be called democracy in action. There is in reality no priesthood as the West understands it, but simply men, learned in the Koran or the Holy Book, and in the traditions of the Moslem faith. Rich and poor worship God side by side in their mosques, which are not only temples where they may worship the God-concept, but also community halls where people may gather to study the Moslem scriptures, and to talk about various problems.

EDUCATION

From the time of the Arab invasion in A.D. 640 until the middle of the 19th century, education was governed by the belief that the only essential was to memorize the Koran. Today, Islamic studies and Koranic teachings are important, but other subjects, such as mathematics, geometry and philosophy, have been introduced.

Progress was very slow, and the difficulty lay in the fact that until the revolution, Egypt was in the hands of invaders with governments whose leaders believed that the people could be

The Tree of the Virgin Mary at Matarieh figures in a traditional tale involving the mother of Jesus. Mary is a saint not only to Christians but also to Mohammedans, who regard Jesus as one of their major prophets.

The mosque of Mohammed Ali is one of Cairo's landmarks. Situated on a hill within the ancient citadel of Cairo, the mosque commands a splendid view of the city and the surrounding countryside.

Most Egyptians are devout followers of Islam. Whether in the cities or in the desert, prayer-time is a solemn moment, when the Moslem spreads his prayer rug and bends down, facing Mecca.

best controlled if they were not too well informed.

Since 1925, the Ministry of Education has tackled the problem, trained teachers and built new schools. Elementary, kindergarten, primary, post-primary and secondary schools came into being and four universities were established—at Cairo, Alexandria, Ain-Shams and Assiut. Cairo University alone has a student body of about 30,000.

The pattern of education today is based on a 6-year primary stage, a 3-year lower secondary and a 3-year secondary stage. After completing the latter and passing finals, enrolment in the universities is welcomed, or in any higher institute of learning. Government control over schools is rigorous, up to university level.

The University of Cairo at Giza was founded in 1908, nearly 1,000 years later than Cairo's Moslem University of El-Azhar.

In Egyptian kindergartens the children learn to read and write as well as play. (UNICEF)

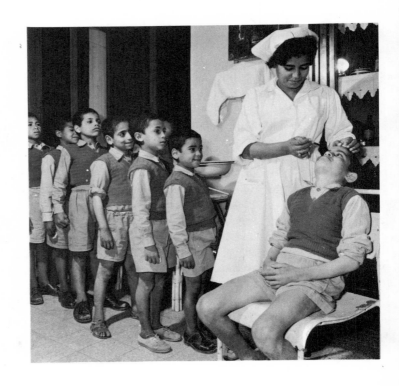

Regular health check-ups are held at a Cairo school for boys. (UNICEF)

Basketball is a popular sport with Egyptian schoolboys. (UNICEF)

Youngsters get practical training in farming methods at Delta Barrages, near Cairo. (UNICEF)

At the American University in Cairo, students from different countries find time for a little guitar music between classes.

These young ladies are learning to make cloth dolls in a handicraft class. (UNICEF)

Blind students, learning Braille, practice with pegboards at a special school in the Cairo suburbs.

The Manial Museum in Cairo houses art treasures of many different periods.

LANGUAGE

The history of the Egyptian language goes back well over 4,000 years, and it is actually the oldest recorded speech of any known language. It survived until some time after A.D. 1000, and forms a branch of the Afro-Asiatic (Hamito-Semitic) language family. It was thus related to Arabic, the present language of Egypt.

Middle Egyptian, late Egyptian and Demotic are phases through which ancient Egyptian passed. The last phase, known as Coptic, has survived as the ritual language of Egyptian Christians.

ANCIENT LITERATURE

Literary writings of ancient Egypt portrayed (for a great part) romances with historical or mythical backgrounds. Some were poems, some just letters, while others were collections of moral instructions, serving as school texts, copied by scholars and scribes. Preserved verses have been found on stone and bits of pottery and some on papyrus.

Many of the popular stories have lived on to this day, telling us of the life of Egyptians of other eras. One of the most noted has been the story of "Sinuhe" who was a fugitive from the Egyptian court and banished. He lived out his years in Palestine among the Bedouins, but feeling his end near, he appealed to the Pharaoh for a pardon which was granted and the story had a "happy ever after" ending.

A popular form of writing of ancient days were the so-called "Maxims and Instructions," wherein older people gave advice to younger ones, or a king told his heir how to rule wisely. Some of these are the Maxims of Ptahhotep, of Ani, and of Amenemope. These were learned by heart as part of a young man's education. They show similarities to Hebrew literature:

"If thou art one of those sitting at the table of one greater than thyself, take what he may give, when it is set before thy nose . . . laugh

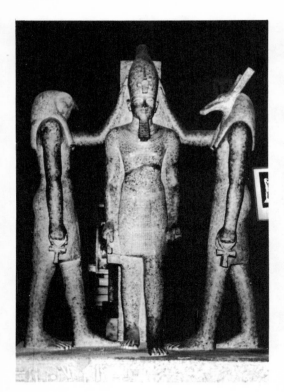

use the stone to decipher the ancient writing. It is now on view in the British Museum, London.

MODERN LITERATURE

Literature in the Arab countries has taken on considerable importance, due to the realization of both the Egyptian and other governments that it is necessary, not only for the spreading of culture, but also for the participation of the people in modern life.

Egypt has a growing publishing activity, state-sponsored in part.

One of Egypt's and the Arab world's leading writers, scholars and educators, Dr. Taha Hussein, blind from the age of 3, earned degrees from Al-Azhar University, the Sorbonne and Oxford. Author of numerous histories and works on philosophy and education, as well as essays and novels, Dr. Hussein supervised the translation into Arabic of all of Shakespeare's works. He died in 1973 at the age of 84, one day after receiving the United Nations Human Rights Prize.

FAMILY LIFE

Family life is close, but young couples now set up individual homes whereas they formerly lived under the parental roof. The young bride is often a trained worker whose ability is required in city offices, or who may teach school, work in a bank or in technical research. All professions and trades are open to the Egyptian girl of today. The double income enables the couple to live better and be entirely independent.

New apartment buildings have sprung up in the cities, as smart and practical as one would find in London or New York, and almost all have balconies. The skyscrapers are similar to New York's and many of the great hotels are

after he laughs and it will be very pleasing to his heart."

HIEROGLYPHICS

Hieroglyphic writing began in Egypt about 3000 B.C. At first it consisted largely of symbols or drawings representing objects and actions. Eventually some of these symbols were simplified and others came to stand for a sound rather than a concept. By the Middle Kingdom (2050–1800 B.C.), a form of writing called *hieratic* replaced the hieroglyphics for everyday purposes.

By about 400 B.C. a newer script, the *demotic*, came into use. Hieroglyphics, however, continued to be used for sacred writings until about A.D. 400, although by then almost no one but a few priests understood them.

The key to reading hieroglyphics was lost to the modern world until in 1799 some of Napoleon's soldiers found the "Rosetta Stone." This was a basalt slab with the same text inscribed in hieroglyphic, demotic and Greek characters. The French Egyptologist Jean-François Champollion (1790–1832) was able to

A rural nurse weighs the new baby during a visit to a village household. (UNICEF)

fancier. City shops are crowded with radios, television sets and the latest in electrical gadgets, and records. Egyptians would enjoy earning more money, but they too, have adopted the "buy now—pay later" system. The hospitality of the people is great, and English, French and Spanish are heard on thoroughfares mixed with Arabic. Western clothes predominate, but Arab robes (the woman's black cloak covering all of her) are still seen very often. Religious families still cover up their women for a stroll or a drive in town, while in the home they would still be wearing elegant dresses.

FESTIVALS

In ancient Egypt the season of reaping lasted from February to June. It was called *Shemu*, meaning "recession of the waters," and many of the customs related to it have not changed much to this day. When the tall stalks were of an equal height, gathering time commenced and the farmers cut off ears of grain, piled them in a rope net, left their knives behind and went off to rest. Refreshed, they would return and weigh the crop and enter the figures with ceremony in the official scribe's register. The grain was placed on elaborately panniered donkeys and sent to granaries to the sound of music. What was in excess of the country's need was sold (as now) to foreign merchants, "as well the brothers of Joseph knew," and earned for Egypt in Roman times, the title, "Granary of the World."

The ancient farmer's spirit was enthusiastic— he sang and danced while the water carrier brought cool drinks and musicians played. Prayers of thanksgiving were heard, and the family joined in, blessing the god of fertility. Even today, on farm doors, ritual offerings can still be seen hung up, fresh each day.

The Feast of the God, Osiris, was celebrated from one end of Egypt to the other, with dancing about his image. Songs of birth, death and rebirth were sung with joy and abandon while young men smiled at their future brides. Another deity was Sekhet, goddess of arable land. Her head bore a crown of flowers and plants, and she symbolized fertility. In the Temple of Amenhotep, 18th Dynasty, circa

A craftsman plies his needle as he makes tapestries with traditional Egyptian themes.

Nubian women are skilled in handicrafts. This woman is weaving a basket.

1398 B.C., Sekhet sits on the altar laden with food offerings.

Among the many festivals today, there is one dedicated to the "Scent of the Breeze." In Arabic it is called "Sham El Nessim." On the ancient Egyptian calendar, this was the day following the first full moon, believed to be the day the world was born.

This was also the day that Moses chose to lead the children of Israel out of Egypt, and thus this festival is closely associated with the Jewish Passover. Passover in turn is linked with the Christian Easter. Thus, the "Scent of the Breeze" is very precious to the Copts, but all modern Egyptians enjoy it, and the parks, gardens and fields are alive with games and laughter. Picnic baskets are laden at dawn with the same fare as the Pharaohs ate: hard-boiled eggs, fish and fruits.

An artisan works on a brass tray in Cairo's famous Khan el-Khalil Bazaar. Egypt is famous for its copper and brass wares.

Islamic architecture is well represented by the Ibn Tulun Mosque in Cairo.

NATIVE CRAFTSMEN

In all the bazaars, called *souks*, craftsmen work on brass, copper, ivory, silver and gold. They fashion trays, vessels of shimmering metals, goblets, boxes and trinkets, made as their forefathers made them. The technique

and painstaking work were learned during childhood at their father's knees. Truly when they sell a piece or two, they are giving part of themselves with it. One does not just buy in an Egyptian *souk*; a customer becomes a friend. He must have a tiny cup of Bedouin coffee (on a very hot day it could be an ice-cold soda), and no sale is consummated until the buyer is happy with his purchase. The warmth of the craftsman causes visitors often to buy more than they intended, but the ending is always the same. The craftsman in appreciation throws in some small gift, also hand-crafted, before the final "Mar-Salem," meaning "Goodbye."

EGYPTIAN FOOD

Eating to the people of the Land of the Pharaohs is a social event, not just a meal. One can find an Egyptian version of the quick lunch—the *sharwama* sandwich of sliced lamb—in Cairo and Alexandria, but real dining takes time, and food prepared with care. A meal starts with an assortment of smoked sardines, stuffed eggs, rich chopped meats served in tiny

The graceful mosque of Kannibay El-Ramah has intricate, richly detailed stone work on the dome and minaret, in contrast with the smooth surface of the walls and the simple arched windows.

Women of a Fellahin community in the Nile Delta learn how to make a milk formula under the guidance of an FAO home economics advisor (left).

rolls, and beans mixed with pure olive oil. The Egyptians eat a great deal of rice and mutton—yellow saffron rice, topped with boiled lamb is a popular dish. Sea food is taken daily and cooked with many pungent herbs and tomatoes. The egg is always a must. It has been enjoyed by Egyptians since time immemorial, for it symbolized the world to the Ancient Egyptians. Eggs are always served for breakfast.

Egyptians love highly seasoned foods and use a variety of native spices in preparation of most meat and fish dishes, whether it is bar-becued meat or an Egyptian herring. Stuffed vine leaves with rice are on all menus, and olives are always placed on the table along with the garlic, salt and pepper. The preferred drink (apart from milk for the children) is Egyptian beer, so cheap that everyone drinks it. At a celebration, heavily laden tables will have a gigantic loin of roast lamb, stuffed spiced chickens, *kebabs* and continuous supplies of hot flat rounds of baked bread. Meals in Egypt are festive with discussions, jokes and an exchange of ideas. Salads, fresh fruit and sweets round out the meal.

Malaria has long been a serious problem in many parts of Egypt. Here a World Health Organization eradication squad sets out to spray an area infested by malaria-bearing mosquitoes.

North of Cairo is the Arab States Fundamental Education Centre, where studies in rural community life in Arab countries are conducted.

HEALTH AND WELFARE

Along with developments in industry and agriculture, just about equal emphasis has been placed on improving health and social services. The once widespread poverty and ignorance in the country, particularly in rural areas, is being wiped out. The general state of health of the people is much better, especially in the very young, as a direct result of services of UNICEF, as well as of the national health and social security scheme now in effect. Free medical care is offered in government hospitals and clinics.

A class in basket weaving is in progress at the Sayeda Zeinab Neighbourhood Club in Cairo. (UNICEF)

Piles of grain wait to be threshed—either in the old way (foreground) with a team of oxen, or in the modern way, with a tractor (upper left).

5. THE ECONOMY

EGYPT THROUGH the centuries lived on its agriculture and even today the foundation of its economy is its 6,000,000 acres of Nile farmland. The national economy up until 1951 was wholly dominated by agriculture, which employed 58 per cent of working Egyptians and accounted for 80 per cent of national exports. Since then, commerce and industry have made important strides, under the direction of the government.

AGRICULTURE

Cotton is Egypt's most important crop and at least 70 per cent of it is for export. The country has been known as the leading nation in cotton production of the highest quality and since the time of the American Civil War (1861–65) when England could no longer obtain cotton from the United States and turned to Egypt.

Flat cakes of pressed cotton-seed are stacked in a warehouse. Later they will be distributed to farmers for use as fodder.

A farmer on his way to work in the fields plays a simple flute, an instrument that has changed little since ancient times.

Egypt has good crops of potatoes, millet, beans, rice, sugar cane, wheat and onions. Sheep, goats and cattle are raised for meat, fresh milk, and wool. All the villagers keep chickens for egg production. Buffaloes, horses, donkeys and camels constitute the working

In a cotton field, farm workers search for the eggs of the cotton leaf worm, a serious pest.

A farmer uses a barrow drawn by oxen to level off an irrigated rice field.

In Kalata village in the Delta, agricultural trainees inspect bee-hives. Kalata is a "classroom community" where trainees work directly with villagers.

A rice expert (right) provided by the United Nations (FAO) demonstrates transplanting methods.

At El Quasr near the northwest coast, a re-settled Bedouin girl picks olives in a grove owned by her father.

Rice experts inspect young plants at an agricultural experimental station.

Old and new means of power and locomotion contrast with one another as camels pass a new trench filling machine.

animals. With the advance of irrigation, wheat crops and rice crops have multiplied and are now as large as the cotton crops.

FISHERIES

The most important fisheries are for sardines off the Mediterranean coast and at the mouths of the Rosetta and Damietta branches of the Nile. The Delta lakes and Lake Qarun supply most of the remainder. Other fish caught in the lakes are several kinds of mullet, eel and sole. There is also a valuable sponge-fishing industry on the Mediterranean coast.

INDUSTRY

The most important manufacturing industry in Egypt is textiles. Fabrics produced include cotton poplins, shirtings and towelling, and fine woollens. (Egypt's wool is as fine as its cotton.) The weaves are attractive and the dyes and designs are handsome and modern.

Other consumer goods are footwear, furniture, nylon hose, stoves and all manner of tourist souvenirs, manufactured in the cities. Chemicals are produced in outlying districts, as well as cottonseed oil and fertilizers. Steel plants, cement and sugar factories are numerous.

At the Cairo Building Centre, trainee masons learn wall construction.

At the Metal Trades Training Centre in Cairo, a young apprentice operates a lathe.

TRADE

Until the beginning of the 20th century, Egypt was an agricultural land with a self-sufficient economy. This economy changed when cotton became an export crop, and foreign trade developed. Protective tariffs, initiated in the 1930's, encouraged the development of Egyptian industry, but exports of manufactured goods remained small and are even now limited chiefly to textiles and footwear. The traditional reluctance of the Egyptian to engage in foreign trade, in contrast to his aggressiveness on the tourist front, was overcome by the expulsion of European businessmen after the Suez conflict in 1956, and the urgent necessity for Egyptians to take their place.

Political differences with the West, particularly over financing the Aswan project and the seizure of the Suez Canal, altered Egypt's trade relationship with the free world, and made it more dependent on Communist countries, which by the early 1960's were supplying more than 30 per cent of the country's imports, the United States and Western Europe accounting for 48 per cent.

Egypt's exports include raw cotton, and its by-products including cotton piece goods (usually 80 per cent of total exports by value), along with rice and vegetables, phosphates, manganese ore, mineral oils, crude petroleum and Egyptian sandals. Egypt's chief trading partners are Russia, the Common Market countries, Japan and the United States.

A woman industrial hygienist checks on natural radiation in a mining area.

Cairo International Airport is Egypt's main point of entry by air.

The United States is still, however, the largest supplier of Egyptian imports, with wheat in the lead. Much of this wheat is imported into Egypt under the United States Food For Peace Plan.

TRANSPORT

Egypt has excellent railways with an extensive network covering more than 3,000 miles of track. Train services from Cairo to all the country's main points—Alexandria, Port Said, Suez, Luxor and Aswan—use modern rolling stock. First-class service on these routes is fast, punctual and enjoyable, with air-conditioning—a necessity when one considers the climatic conditions a traveller has to pass through, particularly in the inland areas.

Egypt in the past lagged behind in road building, but in recent years has surpassed other Arab lands in the construction of new highways for car travel. The oldest form of transportation in this land is still the River Nile and at least 13,000 vessels, from sailboats to big ships, use the Nile. The *dhows* and

feluccas with their picturesque sails add an Old World touch, although the majority of boats are motor-driven. In some places, however, there are large barges as flat as rafts, pulled by animals.

Camels are as popular as the Nile, carrying freight and passengers over desert sands. In the Sahara, the camel is king. Tribesmen consider camels as members of the family, calling each one by name.

Cairo International Airport, the chief airport of Egypt, is sufficiently large to handle the biggest and latest of jets.

Vocational training has been established on a nation-wide basis for all industrial trades. In the Automotive Training Centre in Cairo, an instructor demonstrates the repair of an engine.

At the Civil Aviation Training Institute at Embaba Aerodrome near Cairo, students receive practical training in air traffic control.

An FAO marketing expert examines Egyptian oranges packaged in the Province of El Tahrir.

COMMUNICATIONS

Egypt has the most powerful, comprehensive and far-reaching television and radio networks in the entire Middle East. Its broadcasting services are comparable to that of the most highly developed European countries. In fact the greater part of its radio broadcasting, which is conducted in more than 30 languages, including several African dialects, is devoted to transmission to foreign countries.

Television in Egypt began in July, 1960, and television broadcasts are transmitted 24 hours a day. There are stations at Mansoura, Alexandria and Aswan, and secondary stations in Kasseassin Boche, Maghagha, Minia, Mallawi and Kusiya. The State controls the radio and television services.

CINEMA

A variety of American, English, French and Italian films are shown in all the main cities. Going to the films is a popular pastime of Egyptians. Egypt has an old-fashioned film-making industry, whose productions are distributed to the rest of the Arab world and East Africa, where they are extremely popular whenever shown.

Omar Sharif, the film star, studies his hand during a bridge tournament in his native Egypt. In chess and bridge circles he is as well known for his prowess in these games as he is known to film-goers for his cinematic rôles.

The Nile Hilton Hotel overlooks the river in Cairo.

PRESS

Egypt has 40 daily newspapers, chief among which are the long established *Al-Ahram*, *Al Gomhouria* and *Al Akhbar*. All publications of the press were taken into public ownership by presidential decree in 1960, and now belong to the Arab Socialist Union, as the body representing the people. *Al-Ahram* is the most influential paper and is regarded as the voice of the government, besides offering the fullest news coverage. It has also a wide circulation in other Arab lands.

Since the early 1960's, the Middle East News Agency has grown and developed a national news agency—with services in Arabic and English. Its headquarters are in Cairo, and it has overseas offices in Europe and most Arab capitals, as well as exchange and co-operative agreements with several noted foreign news agencies.

TOURISM

Egypt is a country of natural hosts, or at least it seems so when the Egyptians meet you with warm smiles as you arrive in their homeland.

Tourism once again ranks high as a great aid to Egypt's economy. It fell off after the Israeli Wars, but now it has surged upwards, and hotels of all classes are full the year round, especially in Cairo. In earlier years it was considered very fashionable by the English to visit Egypt. Now Cairo and Alexandria are crammed with American tourists. Nevertheless, English cruise ships still make Alexandria an important stop on their round-the-world schedules. Airlines from all over the world bring tourist and businessmen travellers, and all of Egypt is their itinerary.

Every city and many a village has a Bureau of Tourism, often staffed with young, tri-lingual girls in modern dress.

Egypt looks forward to the day, in the near future, when tourism will be its second most important economic activity.

*The snowy peaks of Haji Umran, near the Iran-Iraq border,
are popular with skiers in February and March.*

Iraq

This gate, a replica in miniature of the famed Ishtar Gate, stands at the entrance to the ruins of ancient Babylon. The original structure was built of kiln-baked bricks cemented with pitch. It was so solid it survived the razing of the city by the Persians in the 6th century B.C. and the subsequent erosion by natural elements that eventually levelled most of the surrounding walls.

INTRODUCTION

THROUGHOUT ITS LONG history, Iraq—formerly Mesopotamia—has justifiably been called "the cradle of civilization." Here, at the very dawn of mankind, some 2,000 generations of Neanderthal men are believed to have spanned 60,000 years. Here, where according to tradition the Garden of Eden was located and the Biblical flood took place, some of the most significant scenes in the drama of man occurred —the invention of the wheel, the first use of the plough, the beginnings of mathematics and pictographic writing. During the lifetime of two mighty civilizations, Assyria and Babylonia, Iraq was the site of such marvels as the Tower of Babel and Nebuchadnezzar's Hanging Gardens of Babylon. Here the prophet Daniel translated the handwriting on the wall and foretold the fall of Belshazzar's mighty kingdom. Here history's most intriguing story-teller, Scheherazade, spun her wondrous thousand and one tales for Harun-al-Rashid, the great caliph whose only equal was Charlemagne.

Against this vast canopy of history, Iraq witnessed and survived the passing of many other empires, races, and cultures; Sumerians, Persians, Greeks, Romans, Arabs, Ottoman Turks, and British all played their brief parts upon this exotic stage.

Today the oldest habitat of man stands on the threshold of a new historical era. Since gaining its independence in 1932, Iraq has overcome countless obstacles to take giant steps toward progress. One of the richest oil-producing nations in the world, it has set aside 70 per cent of its oil revenue for new construction and development. Although the imprint of poverty still lies bold and heavy upon part of the population, although there is much internal strife and dissension after the third military *coup d'état* in 10 years, Iraq, rich in history and natural resources, ambitious and forward-moving, now looks toward a future as brilliant as its past.

The legendary site of The Garden of Eden and Adam's Tree of Knowledge is located here at Al-Qurna, where the Tigris joins the Euphrates.

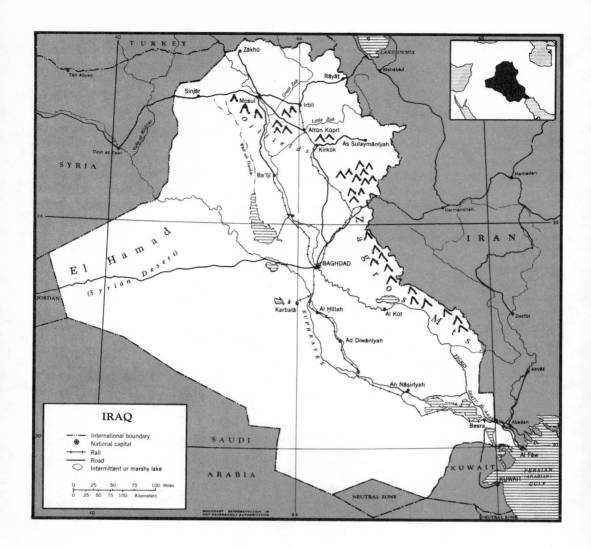

IRAQ

International boundary
National capital
Rail
Road
Intermittent or marshy lake

0   25   50   75   100 Miles
0 25 50 75 100. Kilometers

BOUNDARY REPRESENTATION IS
NOT NECESSARILY AUTHORITATIVE

The north of Iraq is cool and hilly, unlike the rest of the country.

1. THE LAND

THE REPUBLIC OF IRAQ, with a total land area of approximately 175,000 square miles, is slightly larger than Sweden. It is bounded on the north by Turkey; on the east by Iran; on the south by the Persian Gulf (known to the Iraqis as the Arabian Gulf), Kuwait, and Saudi Arabia; and on the west by Jordan and Syria.

The country's previous name, Mesopotamia, means "land between the rivers," indicating the outstanding physical aspect of the country— the presence of the two river valleys of the Tigris and the Euphrates. The wide, flat alluvial plain that is formed in central Iraq where the two river valleys merge is economically the richest and most fertile area of the country. Beyond this great plain, there are striking contrasts in topography and vegetation.

The steppe desert that follows the whole course of the Euphrates in the west and southwest is flat, dry, and featureless. Covered with lifeless-looking vegetation and sun-bleached protruding shale, it is an area so desolate and uninviting that even a rattlesnake would feel lonely there. A part of the great Syro-Arabian desert, this area extends for hundreds of miles into the heart of Arabia.

In northern Iraq, a swift river meanders through the gorges and canyons that it has carved out of the rock over countless centuries.

In the north and northeast, a rolling plain beside the Tigris is filled with cornfields and orchards and fields that are ablaze each spring with wild narcissus. The plain gradually rises in a series of parallel folds to the snowcapped peaks of the rugged Zagros mountain range that separates Iraq from Iran.

At the south end of Iraq, the broad marshlands where the Tigris and the Euphrates flow together are considered one of the most strange and forbidding regions of the world. It is a seemingly endless landscape of shallow lakes, swamps, narrow waterways, and dense thickets of canebrake. It is populated by marsh dwellers, who are sometimes called "the people of the reeds," and who follow an age-old pattern of existence.

WATERWAYS

An Iraqi writer once said that, while Egypt has only one mighty river to sustain its agriculture and its people, Iraq has the Tigris and the Euphrates—two Niles. For centuries, these two rivers, like the Nile, have been carrying silt to the valley they traverse, enriching the fertility of the land and providing irrigation for crops.

Both rivers have their sources in Armenia, the Tigris (1,150 miles long) to the south of Lake Van, the Euphrates (1,780 miles long) near Mount Ararat. When the rivers emerge from the Taurus mountains of Turkey and flow into Iraq, they are separated from each other by 250 miles of open plain. While the Tigris flows southwards, the Euphrates takes a southeasterly direction. As they near Baghdad, they very nearly converge, being only 20 miles apart, but they soon diverge again. At Qurnah, 60 miles to the north of Basra, their waters mingle to form a wide, majestic river that did not exist in antiquity—the Shatt-al-Arab. Ocean-going vessels enter Basra, Iraq's only important seaport, over this broad, navigable waterway.

With its cool waterfalls, mountain views, and wooded valleys, Rawandooz, in the mountainous northern region, is a vacationland and summer resort area.

In Basra, the confluence of the Tigris and Euphrates rivers form the Shatt-al-Arab River. Shaded by feathery date palms, the 120-mile-long Shatt-al-Arab flows toward the Gulf, forming part of the Iraq-Iran border.

Baghdad straddles both banks of the Tigris River, with 6 bridges providing connecting links for vehicular and pedestrian traffic. This is a view of the Al-Shohada Bridge.

An ancient device, known as the Euphrates Wheel, is used for raising water from the river to irrigate fields along the banks. The giant water wheels dot the river all the way to the Syrian border.

Above the region of Baghdad, both the Tigris and the Euphrates flow in well-defined channels with retaining valley walls. Below Baghdad, however, the vestiges of a retaining valley disappear, and the rivers flow over a vast open plain with only a slight drop in level—in places merely 8 or 10 feet in 100 miles. One remarkable feature is the change in relative level of the two river beds—water can be led from one to the other and this possibility, utilized by irrigation engineers for many centuries, still remains today. At the same time, however, the courses of both rivers can suddenly alter. A flood may break the wall of the levee and water then pours out onto the low-lying plain, inundating many square miles of territory. The Tigris, in particular, used to break its banks almost annually. People in Baghdad, which straddles both sides of the great river, still recall the devastating flood of 1954 which took countless lives and caused $50,000,000 damage to the city. As a protection against floods, barrages have been thrown across the rivers, a continuing project since 1956.

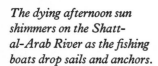

The dying afternoon sun shimmers on the Shatt-al-Arab River as the fishing boats drop sails and anchors.

A freighter plows its way up the Shatt-al-Arab River to the port of Basra. Because of the heavy volume of trade, a new port was constructed at Umm Qasr which will eventually relieve Basra of more than 450,000 tons annually.

FLORA AND FAUNA

The date palm, often referred to as "the eternal plant," is considered one of the oldest tree species used by man. There is archaeological evidence that the ancient Sumerians and Akkadians who lived in Iraq about 3500 B.C. used date palm fronds to thatch the roofs of their dwellings. Today, there are about 35,000,000 date palms in the country—climatic conditions there are ideal for date-growing. Over 80 per cent of the world's supply of dates comes from the region extending along both banks of the Tigris and the Euphrates, from Ana and Samarra down to the Gulf. Basra

Since the date palm's fruit supplies an important source of revenue to their country, many Iraqis, understandably enough, refer to it as "the tree of life."

has the most extensive date palm groves in the world, automatically fed with fresh water when the water level in the river rises twice a day due to the back-up effect of the tide. There are about 450 varieties of dates, only about four of which are commercially significant.

The mountains of the northern part of the country are covered with gall oak, juniper, Oriental plane trees, walnut, willow, tamarisk, sage, and milk-vetch. The alluvial and marsh areas in the south are rich with reeds, box thorn, buttercups, rushes, and saltbrush. The desert areas are covered with rockrose, stork's-bill, and catchfly, which bloom for a brief period in the spring and provide pasturage for the sheep, goats, and camels of the nomadic tribes. Orange and lemon trees are grown extensively in the shade of the date palms throughout the central and southern parts of the country.

The traditional beasts of burden are camels, oxen, water buffalo, and horses. Large flocks of sheep are raised in the north for their wool and skins. Wild animals include hyenas, jackals, foxes, wild cats, brown bears, wild boars, and a few leopards and wolves. Herds of graceful gazelles are found in the steppes, wild goats in the mountains.

Game birds include wild ducks, geese, black partridge, bustards, and sand grouse. There are various species of birds of prey including vultures, eagles, and buzzards. Storks are a common sight in Baghdad and elsewhere in Iraq. They build their nests on the trees, roofs of private houses (considered good luck), and even the domes of the mosques; their migration marks the beginnings and ends of the four seasons. The Tigris, Euphrates, and Shatt-al-Arab rivers abound in fresh-water fish that constitute an important part of the main diet of the Iraqi people.

CLIMATE

Iraq has rather hot, dry summers with the highest temperatures occurring from June to September, but winters, although cold at times, are generally mild and sunny. The ideal times of year to visit the country are in the spring and autumn.

A comparatively long winter is usual in the mountainous northeastern area of Iraq, with the temperature falling below the freezing point between December and February. Heavy snowfalls in the mountains attract thousands of winter sports enthusiasts.

The ghostly Eternal Flames, fed throughout the ages by gases seeping through cracks in the earth's crust, flicker in the dusk at Baba Gurgur, not far from the Kirkuk oil fields. Reputedly, this is "the fiery furnace" into which King Nebuchadnezzar threw the three Hebrew youths, Shadrach, Meshach, and Abednego, and from which they emerged unharmed. During World War II, the ground fires had to be smothered to prevent Axis planes from targeting the oil fields. Today, they provide convenient camp fires for wandering shepherds and their flocks.

In the mountainous northeastern region, a comparatively long winter is usual with temperatures falling below the freezing mark between December and February.

Rainfall is scant over all the country except for the northeast where 15 to 25 inches occur annually—enough to grow crops without irrigation, unlike the rest of the country where farming is entirely dependent upon irrigation from river water. Rain falls mainly in the winter, spring and autumn.

NATURAL RESOURCES

Although ancient artwork and writings refer to the exploitation of metals in early times, Iraq today has very few mineral resources, aside from its vast oil reserves. Recent geological sur-

veys have shown, however, that there are some usable deposits of iron ore, copper, sulphur and sulphur compounds, bitumen (a source of asphalt), dolomite, gypsum, and marble. The recent find of a salt dome near Basra may replace the solar evaporation method that is now being used at al-Faw.

Oil greatly compensates, however, for the lack of other minerals. One of the leading oil-producing countries of the world, Iraq's proven reserves of crude oil are roughly estimated at 9,000,000,000 metric tons. Primary oil fields are at Kirkuk, Naft Khaneh, Ayn Zalah, and Butmah near Mosul. Under an agreement with Russia and France signed in December, 1967, rich new fields are being developed in southern Iraq.

CITIES

Although Iraq is one of the first places where men came together to live in cities, the large cities of the country today, far from looking ancient, are extremely modern in appearance. After first having been destroyed in successive barbarian invasions, they declined under centuries of Turkish rule. Only since the emergence of Iraq as an independent state after World War I, have they had a chance to grow again.

BAGHDAD

The largest city of Iraq, Baghdad is a true metropolis, housing nearly one-fourth of the country's people. The present population of over 3,000,000 equals that of the city at the height of its glory in the Middle Ages—yet in the intervening centuries the figure dropped to a low of 14,000 (in 1638).

Old Baghdad lay on the west bank of the Tigris only; the modern city occupies both banks, and spreads far into the surrounding countryside. Handsome and spacious in design, with a network of broad avenues connecting all quarters of the city, Baghdad presents a Western, or international appearance with its great blocks of ultra-modern office buildings and brick houses.

Located at the crossroads of the ancient caravan routes between Europe and Asia, the city is once more a hub of commerce and transport—where camels and horses once streamed in and out of its limits, jet planes, motor vehicles and railway trains now do so. Modern river boats ply the tree-lined Tigris banks, past rich farmlands and attractive villas,

Rashid Street is the oldest thoroughfare in Baghdad. All of the old buildings at the right are to be razed to make way for new offices, such as the structure in the background.

Bank Street in Baghdad is well-named—all of the buildings on this street are banks.

In a time-lapse photograph of Baghdad by night, the traffic on the rain-swept street around Al-Tahreer Square takes on the appearance of gleaming, uncoiling snakes.

stable than the Euphrates—less given to shifting its course—although flooding is a constant danger.

BASRA

Founded by Caliph Omar in A.D. 36, Basra was originally eight miles from its present location on the Shatt-al-Arab—the river having shifted its channel in the meantime. Although 75 miles from the sea, Basra receives ocean-going vessels and is Iraq's chief port. A major item of export from Basra are the dates produced in the vast palm groves around the city. Old Basra was a focal point of Arabic culture in the days of Harun-al-Rashid; today the city is a major commercial hub.

to unload at the city's busy wharves. Baghdad's survival and return to greatness is in large measure due to the fact that the Tigris is more

In the Andalus Gardens in Basra, graceful pavilions, trees, flowers, and splashing fountains are all conducive to quiet meditation.

The style of this old house in Basra is now considered to be outmoded. The majority of homebuilders in the large cities prefer simpler, more modern dwellings with the latest conveniences.

MOSUL

The chief city of northern Iraq, Mosul is situated on the right bank of the Tigris, opposite the site of ancient Nineveh, once the proud capital of the Assyrian Empire.

Modern Mosul owes its prosperity to the oil fields of the surrounding countryside. But long before that, cotton weaving was the city's mainstay. Perhaps not many people know that muslin, a household word in English, is derived from the name of this city. In the Middle Ages, Mosul was famous for its fine cotton cloth, which we know as muslin. Even today weaving is an important activity in Mosul.

OTHER CITIES

Set amid oilfields, farmlands and pastures, Kirkuk, largest city of the Kurds (Iraq's chief minority), is built upon a "tepa," or mound, covering the remains of earlier settlements going back as far as 3000 B.C. Karbala, on the edge of the desert in central Iraq, is one of the great pilgrimage places of Shi'ite Moslems, for it contains the tomb of their chief saint, Husein, grandson of Mohammed. The gold-domed tomb, with its three tall minarets, dominates the city.

The leaning minaret of the Nuri Mosque in Mosul was built in 1172.

Iraq's greatest treasures and proudest possessions are the crumbling ruins of past civilizations. In an effort to stay time's inexorable hand, the Department of Antiquities has a continuing plan of restoration and preservation.

2. HISTORY

ALTHOUGH THERE ARE numerous references in the Old Testament to the great empires that once flourished in Mesopotamia, it has only been within the past 30 years or so that the country's key rôle in the saga of civilization has become fully known. The discovery of the huge Shanidar Cave in the Zagros Mountains in the early 1950's shed the first light on the country's prehistory. Archaeologists have unearthed seven Neanderthal skeletons from various depths of the excavation; one of these is believed to be about 60,000 years old. At a time when much of Europe was still covered by great glaciers, prehistoric man, a solitary, homeless hunter, wandered nomadlike over what is now Iraq, Iran, Turkey, and Syria, hunting wild beasts and gathering wild plants.

When, after countless centuries, man ceased his roaming and learned how to build his own dwelling, cultivate crops, domesticate the wild beasts, and live amicably with other men in hamlets and villages, civilization was at last born. Judging from the rich and ofttimes astonishing archaeological discoveries unearthed in Iraq, it, more than any other land or region of the world, fully merits being called the "Cradle of Civilization."

THE FIRST CITIES

Sometime in the fifth millennium B.C., the farmers of northern Mesopotamia—known as Ubaidians—deserted their villages and emigrated southward to the Tigris-Euphrates plain that stretched from present-day Baghdad down to the Gulf. It must have been a bleak and dismal region, but the rivers and marshes teemed with fish and waterfowl, and the natural, fertile, silt-covered levees were ideal for the type of simple agriculture pursued by the early farmers. Here they planted their precious seeds and built villages and towns of mud brick, giving their settlements such names as Lagash, Ur, Eridu, and Kish.

The crops and the cities thrived, inviting the envy of the Semitic nomads inhabiting the Syrian desert and the Arabian peninsula to the west. Some came as invaders in search of booty, others as peaceful immigrants. The mingling of the Ubaidian and Semitic cultures, and the ensuing productive era, laid the cornerstone for the world's first true civilization. About 3500 B.C., the Sumerians arrived on the scene to become the builders of that civilization.

The problem as to the real origin of the Sumerians has never really been solved. It is not known whether they came from another country or if they represent another layer of population of prehistoric Mesopotamia. What is known is that their influence over the Ubaidians and the Semites was to influence the future course of humanity.

Bab al-Wastani, the ruins of Baghdad's last remaining fortress-like gate, is now being used as a museum for ancient arms and weapons. Originally, there were four such gates leading into the city.

THE SUMERIANS

The land came to be called Sumer and, under a succession of powerful kings, heights of material wealth and political power were achieved. With the riches born of agriculture, trade routes were established for the first time and caravans laden with barley and textiles left the cities of Sumer for Asia Minor and Iran, returning with timber, stone, and metals.

Perhaps it is because of this trading and the need for some sort of record of shipment that led to the invention of writing. The first written words, crude symbols etched with a stylus on clay tablets and known as pictographs, are inventories of sacks of grain and were probably used as a crude type of shipping tag.

This is an example of Sumerian cuneiform. Writing, perhaps more than any other human invention, made civilization possible. Over 5,000 years ago, the Sumerians refined crude symbols (pictographs) which they had been using to record inventories, into a complex script that was more capable of expressing abstract ideas. Employing over 700 different symbols, the cuneiform later yielded to the alphabetical writing of the Phoenicians.

The characters so produced are called cuneiform, meaning wedge-shaped, since the stylus left an imprint in the form of a wedge. Early in the third millennium B.C., Sumerian scribes improved the cuneiform by using symbols phonetically, and making it possible to spell out any word in the language.

Although Sumer was a small country—a little less than the area of Belgium, it eventually was composed of no fewer than 13 politico-religious units known as "city-states." The

This finely sculptured bronze head, on display at the Iraq Museum in Baghdad, is believed to represent Sargon of Agade, who established the first Semitic dynasty in Mesopotamia about 2370 B.C.

bitter and almost incessant struggle for supremacy among the rulers of the city-states was one of the major factors for the ultimate decline of Sumer. At the beginning of the 18th century B.C., the Babylonians won ascendancy and 1,500 years of Sumerian dominance in Mesopotamia drew to a close.

HAMMURABI

Hammurabi, King of Babylon, moulded the rival cities into a unified state, mainly by overwhelming his rivals and destroying them one by one. A formidable war leader, he was also a skilful diplomat and a humane ruler with a deep concern for the welfare of his subjects. He displayed an unusual respect for the traditions of the country he had conquered and, under his reign, the fundamental way of life in Mesopotamia was very little altered.

A grey stone statuette of Dudu the Scribe, unearthed at Tellu (ancient Lagash), dates back to 2600 B.C. and is now on display at the Iraq Museum in Baghdad. When cuneiform writing was important, trained scribes such as the dignified Dudu were in great demand as secretaries, book-keepers, accountants, and archivists.

Among the artifacts discovered in the royal tombs of Ur is this harp (restored). The ancient Sumerian city of Ur, which was flourishing by 3500 B.C. and is identified in the Bible as the home of Abraham, was uncovered and identified by archaeologists in 1852. Over the centuries, the sediment deposited by the Tigris and Euphrates rivers has driven back the headwaters. Ur, once a seaport, is now 150 miles inland.

Hammurabi's passion for justice led to the issuing of his famous Code of Law "to destroy the wicked and the evil, that the strong may not oppress the weak." Although the terrible Law of Retaliation—an eye for an eye, a tooth for a tooth—may seem cruel to modern minds, Hammurabi's Code includes many other laws that are amazingly close to the concept of 20th century justice. This is especially true of the laws dealing with family affairs, property, and the protection of women and children. Although the Code was until recently believed to be the world's oldest, modern investigators have discovered an earlier one codified by one of Hammurabi's Sumerian forerunners, King Ur-Nammu, the founder of the third dynasty of Ur (2050 B.C.).

Hammurabi sought to establish a kingdom that would have foundations "as firm as those of heaven and earth," but after his death in 1708 B.C., his empire began to crumble almost immediately.

In 1600 B.C., the dynasty came to an inglorious downfall under the invasion of the Indo-European Hittites of Anatolia (Asia Minor). The Hittites were interested only in plundering the land and, when they finally withdrew to their homeland, they left Baby-

Their huge eyes symbolizing awed adoration of the gods, their hands clasping libation cups used in religious ceremonies, these gypsum figurines are the work of the Sumerians of the early Dynastic Period. They served as mute stand-ins at the altar for worshippers who were too busy to attend the votive rites.

With flowered tunic and neatly curled hair and beard, the Assyrian King Assurbanipal pursues his quarry with bow and arrow in this bas-relief sculpture unearthed from his ruined palace at Ninevah. By the 7th century B.C., *Assurbanipal reigned over an empire extending from Egypt to Iran.*

lonia weak, drained, and fair prey to any conqueror. The Kassites, also a non-Semitic people, swooped down from the Zagros Mountains to seize control. They were to rule for the next 425 years. Aside from an archive of diplomatic correspondence unearthed in 1887, archaeologists as yet have not been able to shed much light upon the Kassite period in Babylonia.

THE STOLEN GOD

The last of the Kassite kings was overthrown in 1170 B.C. by the Elamites of Iran. The conquerors plundered Babylonia, taking back with them to Elam as spoils of war such important national treasures as the famous stele (upright stone) inscribed with Hammurabi's Code and a gigantic statue of Marduk, Babylonia's chief

god. The humiliation and anger of the Babylonians over the loss of their deity caused them to rally quickly from this disaster. A new native dynasty was set up, and one of the rulers, Nebuchadnezzar I, rid the land of the garrisons left behind by the Elamites. He then attacked Elam itself and returned in triumph with the statue of Marduk.

Despite this bright note, however, the 10th and 9th centuries B.C. could be called the Dark Age of Mesopotamia. Floods, famine, civil wars, invasions by a number of Aramaean tribes from Syria, and a succession of ineffectual rulers made the land of Sumer easy prey to the Assyrians, whose fortunes, on the other hand, had soared so spectacularly that they were ready to embark upon a policy of ruthless conquest. Assyria's climb to power would ultimately make it master over nearly all the Middle East.

Around 745 B.C., Tiglathpileser III, the Assyrian monarch who was most responsible for leading his country to its first era of prominence, struck and captured Babylon, at the same time relieving that city from the pressure of the encroaching Aramaean tribes. For the next 200 years, a succession of warrior kings ruled with cruelty and rapacity, inspiring a series of massive revolts throughout the Assyrian empire. The Medes of the Iranian Plateau—a young and, until then, little known people—joined with the Chaldeans of Babylon and succeeded in toppling the Assyrian giant. A line of Chaldean kings ushered in the Neo-Babylonian period which, though lasting only 75 years, was the most brilliant and glorious in the history of Mesopotamia. The monarch most responsible for this dazzling renaissance was Nebuchadnezzar II.

This ivory plaque, carved in relief with gold and carnelian inlays, is one of the many art treasures unearthed by archaeologists at Nimrud. It dates back to 710 B.C.

By virtue of its unique artistic beauty, this ivory head, dating from 720 B.C., has been christened the "Mona Lisa of Nimrud" by archaeologists. It was recovered from a well in the palace of Nimrud.

The Prophet Isaiah predicted that glittering Babylon, "the Glory of Kingdoms," would crumble into desolation. Some 4,000 years later, the ruins of King Nebuchadnezzar's spectacular city, a short drive from Baghdad, still bear mute testimony to its greatness. Visitors to the site can see the foundations that remain of the Hanging Gardens, one of the Seven Wonders of the Ancient World; the banquet hall where Belshazzar saw the handwriting on the wall; and the famed Ishtar Gate (middle of photo, see page 80) adorned with baked clay bas-reliefs of sacred animals.

THE HANGING GARDENS

In re-building Babylon, King·Nebuchadnezzar created one of the mightiest cities of antiquity, as well as one of the most beautiful. With its massive fortified walls, magnificent palaces, and lofty temples, it straddled both sides of the Euphrates, the two sides of the city being connected by a stone bridge, the first ever known. The royal palace dominated one end of the city, surrounded by a massive notched wall. High above the palace setting were the official gardens of the king—the famed Hanging Gardens of Babylon, one of the Seven Wonders of the World. Built for the King's wife, Amytas, a Mede, so that she would not miss her mountain home, the gardens were kept green by an ingenious irrigation and water supply system. This masterpiece of engineering had its continuous water supply pumped from a well with a triple shaft, to irrigate the thousands of varieties of trees and plants brought from every corner of the vast empire.

Soaring 300 feet above the other half of the city was another wonder of the ancient world—the Tower of Babel. The restoration of the original Tower, referred to in the Book of Genesis, had been begun by Nebuchadnezzar's father. When Nebuchadnezzar took over, he told the royal architects to raise the top of the Tower that it might rival Heaven itself. Although no longer standing, the Tower represents to this day, an enduring symbol of the vanity of man's ambitions.

THE PERSIANS

In 550 B.C., Cyrus the Great, founder of the Achaemenid dynasty ascended the Persian throne. Cyrus' powerful army overran practically the whole of the then known world, seizing Lydia, Chaldea, Syria, Palestine, and the Greek communities of Asia Minor. In the autumn of 539 B.C., the Persians attacked Babylonia. After a series of internal disorders and weak monarchs who had succeeded the brilliant Nebuchadnezzar, the Babylonians almost welcomed the conquest. For while their last king, Nabonidus was a liar, madman, and heretic who blasphemed the god Marduk by rebuilding the temple of Sin in Harran, the Persian Cyrus was a generous, benevolent prince who respected and even encouraged the cults, traditions, customs, and religions of his conquered terrritories.

Under Cyrus and his successors, Cambyses and Darius I, life along the Tigris and Euphrates resumed its normal course. Matters took a turn for the worse, however, when Darius' son, Xerxes, came into power. Obsessed with the desire to crush once and for all the revolts of the troublesome Greeks in Asia Minor, Xerxes united the armies of 46 nations. In order to finance the military expeditions of this formidable war machine, Xerxes heavily taxed his subjects. The cost of living in Babylonia doubled without a corresponding increase in wages. In addition, the Persian court had to be supplied with food during four months of the year and the palms of the Persian satraps, who headed the local administrations, had to be heavily greased. Xerxes also sought, unlike his forbears, to "denationalize" the country. He forbade the worship of any deities other than those of Persia, and the Babylonian language was to be replaced by Aramaic. Whenever

Before the Arch of Ctesiphon, not far from Baghdad, a blind minstrel plays an ancient native instrument that resembles a violin. Originally established as a camping ground by the Parthian kings in the first century B.C., Ctesiphon prospered until it became the capital of the Sassanids. The impressive structure, said to be the largest arch made of bricks in the world, survived the disastrous flooding of the Tigris River that in 1887 destroyed most of the original building.

Two symbols of the old Iraq meet for a fleeting moment—an old woman in a burqa and an old "kora" (brick kiln) that is no longer in use. The burqa is a garment covering the entire body, with a sort of latticed "window" over the face. It was once worn by all Arab women.

revolts sprang up, they were brutally and cruelly repressed. The empire began to crumble physically, too. The magnificent buildings, left unattended, showed signs of disrepair; canals became silted-up and much of the land reverted to desert.

ALEXANDER THE GREAT

The days of Achaemenid rule were numbered when, in 333 B.C., a powerful league that represented the union of Greece and Macedonia was formed. An army under Alexander the Great defeated at Issus a Persian army that had been weakened, infiltrated, and corrupted by Greek mercenaries. In October, 331 B.C., Alexander again defeated the Persians at Gaugamela, a victory that opened the road to Babylonia and Persia. The Persian troops stationed at Babylon submitted without fighting, and Alexander made a triumphal entry into the city.

Realizing—like Hammurabi and Cyrus before him—that he could never control an empire composed of "a hundred different nations" unless he courted and won the hearts of his conquered subjects, Alexander made sacrifice to the great god Marduk and immediately began the awesome task of rebuilding the temples. After his conquest of Egypt, he proposed to make Babylon and Alexandria the twin capitals of his far-flung empire. He wanted to make the Euphrates navigable down to its mouth, with a great port to be built at Babylon and another at the mouth of the river. But Alexander's grandiose scheme was never to be. On June 13, 323 B.C., he died in Babylon at the age of 32, probably of malaria.

Since Alexander's heir was not yet born and his brother was young, weak, and mentally retarded, the power fell into the hands of his generals. Babylon changed rulers several times until, after a successful military junta, Seleucus, chief of Alexander's Macedonian cavalry, took charge.

Historians believe that a daughter's treachery led to the destruction of the ancient city of Hatra around 250 A.D. The daughter of King Daizan betrayed her father by revealing to his enemy, the Sassanid king, Sapor I, the secret of the talisman which protected the well-guarded city. After sacking and razing Hatra, Sapor, shocked by the lady's disloyalty to her father, ordered her to be tied to the tail of a horse and dragged to her death.

The Seleucid dynasty exercised a fruitful influence over Mesopotamia for the next two centuries, especially in the areas of art and architecture. But, unable to make the choice between the Oriental controlled economy and the Greek system of free enterprise, the Seleucids were not strong enough to provide the leadership that was needed.

Around 223 B.C., the empire was wrested from them by the Parthians, a warlike Persian tribe of nomads who considered it a disgrace to die of natural causes. After 400 years in power, the Parthian dynasty was eventually undermined by its very successes; it crumbled through the sheer weakness produced by luxury, corruption, intrigue, and civil wars.

Very little is known about life under the Sassanids, who ruled from A.D. 227–636. What is known is that about this time many of the ancient cities of Mesopotamia were buried beneath the sand of the desert and the silt of the valley. With them perished one of the oldest and most remarkable civilizations of the ancient world.

THE ABBASID CALIPHATE

The rule of the Sassanids was broken by the Arab conquest in A.D. 637, led by the Abbasids, an Arabic family descended from Abbas, uncle of the prophet Mohammed. The era of the Abbasid Caliphate (750–1258) was one of magnificence. In 762, Caliph al-Mansour founded the fabled city of Baghdad. The original city was round, with three consecutive enclosures—the ruler residing within the innermost enclosure, the army within the second, and the people within the outermost. The Round City, the capital of the Caliphate, was to become a cosmopolitan and international hub of the medieval world.

The Abbasid Caliphate represents—to the Western mind in particular—all that is exotic and alluring about the Middle East. This was the age of the intriguing story-teller, Scheherazade, of the fantasy of *The Thousand Nights and a Night*, when Sinbad the Sailor set off on his seven magical journeys and Aladdin fought off the Forty Thieves. As for the fifth Abbasid caliph, to whom Scheherazade spun her nightly tales, Harun-al-Rashid was considered to be the greatest monarch of his time with, perhaps only one equal—Charlemagne, the great king of the Franks.

The prosperity and luxury of the Abbasid Golden Age produced an intellectual awakening that extended in its impact far beyond the borders of the Tigris and the Euphrates. Arabic

An outstanding example of Abbasid architecture, the Mustansariyah College in Baghdad was founded by the Caliph Al-Mustansir in 1232. It originally was comprised of four law sections representing the four orthodox Sunnite sects. After 1533, teaching ceased in the great college, the fabulous library of 80,000 books disappeared, and the building was abandoned and fell into a sad state of disrepair. In 1945, the Government of Iraq's Department of Antiquities took over the building and is responsible for its extensive structural restoration.

In the 9th century, Caliph Mu'tasim, son of the great Harun al-Rashid, lavished a great deal of time and money on building Samarra, a new capital to replace mighty Baghdad. But the glory of this magnificent city of palaces, artificial lakes, gardens and, pavilions, proved to be fleeting. Caliphs who succeeded Mu'tasim moved back to Baghdad after 40 years, and Samarra fell into ruins. This is a view of the remains of the city walls.

One of the main attractions in Samarra is this ancient minaret built by the Abbasid Caliph al-Mutawakkil (A.D. 847–861). Its design is based on the ziggurat, a staged tower in which each storey is smaller than the one below it. Starting at the base, a ramp spirals around the main solid column of the minaret, making five complete turns and ending at a small circular watchtower. The tottering walls in the background once enclosed the rectangular courtyard of what is believed to have been the largest mosque in the world.

numbers and the decimal system were introduced, as was algebra. The great doctor, Avicenna, produced what was to be the standard medical text throughout Europe, and the Orient as well as the Arab world. Maimonides, philosopher and court physician to the great Saladin, dealt with baffling religious and metaphysical problems that were to influence Jewish and Christian religious thinkers profoundly.

Ambassadors were exchanged with many lands, trade and commerce were conducted on an enormous scale, and delegates were even sent to China and India to establish trade relations. They returned bearing fabulous gifts as tokens of Eastern good will. Baghdad was an open market for all merchants and every kind of goods. Like Sinbad, the native traders ventured by sea and land to distant countries and thus played a major rôle in the empire's prosperity. Their ships sailed to China for silk and porcelain, to India for fragrant, precious spices, to Zanzibar and East Africa for ivory and gold.

In the 13th century, Baghdad was overrun by the Mongols and the Abbasid Caliphate came to an end. Iraq was, in the concert of nations, a country of very little importance for the next 600 years. In the 16th century, it was conquered with very little effort by the Ottoman Turks. Centuries of Ottoman neglect and crushing poverty followed.

EUROPEAN PENETRATION

Although some of the European nations had long been in contact with Iraq through their commercial interests in the gulf area, it was not until after 1831, when Turkish control of Iraq was very weak, that signs of more rapid European penetration appeared—such as steamboats on the rivers in 1836, telegraph lines from 1861, and a number of proposals for railways. By 1869, Iraq had been set on a course from which there was to be no retreat. A newspaper, military factories, a hospital, schools, municipal and administrative councils, comparative security on the main routes, and a reasoned policy of settling tribesmen on the land—all testify to the advent of reform in the

neglected land. The measures of improvement introduced between 1831 and 1914 must indeed be viewed as belated and hardly adequate—the Iraq of 1900 differed very little from that of 1500—yet a process of fundamental change and emergence from Ottoman autocracy had begun which nothing could reverse.

The outbreak of World War I in 1914 heralded a new era for Iraq. The Western Allies declared war on Turkey, and negotiations began between the Allies (who were becoming increasingly aware of the untapped potential of the Middle East) and Arab nationalist leaders. The Arab leaders promised to revolt against the Turks, and Britain and its allies then

The portico of the Abbasid Palace in Baghdad is a fine example of Islamic architecture. The ruins of the old citadel have been partly restored and are now used to house an important collection of Arab relics.

promised to recognize the independence of all Arab countries. The collapse of the Ottoman Empire raised Iraqi hopes for freedom, but in 1920 Iraq was declared a League of Nations mandate under British administration.

The exchange of one colonial master for another rather than the promised independence fanned the already fervent flame of Arab nationalism. A series of riots and rebellions ensued and lasted for nearly a year. Finally the British granted Iraq a form of national government composed of a council of ministers chosen from among prominent Iraqis and headed by the Emir Faisal as King. Thus, in 1921, a modern Arab state was born.

The acquisition of statehood was only the first step in Iraq's long and arduous struggle for independence. In 1922, Great Britain and Iraq signed a treaty establishing 1932 as the year of termination of the mandate and as the time of independence for Iraq. Not only did Iraq

achieve independence in that year, but its stature as a sovereign state was greatly enhanced by its admission to the League of Nations.

King Faisal died in 1933. His young son and successor, Ghazi, was killed in an automobile accident in 1939. Until the accession to the throne of Faisal II, upon attaining his majority in 1953, his uncle acted as regent.

REVOLUTION

On July 14, 1958 the Iraqi Army overthrew the monarchy and proclaimed Iraq a republic. A number of leaders of the old régime, including King Faisal II and Prime Minister Nuri-al-Sa'id, were killed. Power was transferred to a Council of Sovereignty exercising presidential authority and to a cabinet led by Brigadier Abdel Karim Qasim with the status of Prime

The Monument of Liberty in Baghdad commemorates the Revolution of 1958 that ended the constitutional monarchy and established Iraq as a Republic.

Minister. Since the revolution, the political atmosphere in Iraq has been relatively unsettled, with various groups, including the Communists, vying for influence. From the outset, the Qasim régime reversed the pro-Western posture of the Government. In a brief period, Qasim concluded economic agreements with the Soviet Union and other Eastern European nations.

The Qasim régime was replaced in February, 1963, by the Socialist Baath Party which was unable to consolidate its power before it was ousted in November of the same year. Colonel Abel Salem Arif, who had played a leading rôle in the 1958 revolution, was declared President. He formed a new cabinet comprised of army officers and moderate elements, including independents and non-party experts.

In 1966, President Arif was killed in a helicopter crash and was succeeded by his brother, General Abdel Rahman Arif. Political and economic difficulties posed a threat to Arif's régime. Discontent was registered among almost every important segment of Iraq's population—the army, the students, the unions, and the middle class. There was also a growing animosity between the Kurds of the North and the Arabs in the rest of the country. The nation's unrest was attributed to such factors as frustration over a lagging economic development, opposition to continued political rule by presidential decree, bitterness among the militants who wanted the régime to follow the lead of the Egyptian president, Gamal Abdel Nasser.

On July 17, 1968, a Revolutionary Command Council headed by Major General Ahmed Hassan al-Bakr staged a bloodless *coup d'état*. The council, all members of the right wing of the divided Iraqi Baath Socialist Party, assumed control of the Government. President Arif left for London.

The long conflict with the Kurds seemed to be on the way to a solution, when the Iraqi Government announced the granting of Kurdish autonomy on March 12, 1970. Henceforth, it was proclaimed, Iraq was to be officially composed of two nations—Arabs and Kurds. President al-Bakr promised that one Iraqi vice-president would be a Kurd and that Kurdish would be an official language along with Arabic. All of these changes were to be worked out in the drafting of a new constitution.

A provisional constitution was put in effect in July, 1970, and in 1971 a "National Charter" was drafted as the basis for working out a new permanent constitution. In March, 1974, the Iraqi Government launched a decree establishing Kurdistan as a region with limited local autonomy. The Kurdish leaders refused to accept the decree, declaring that its terms fell far short of the promises made in 1970. The possibility of civil war seemed greater than ever.

At the heart of the problem was the fact that Kirkuk, the chief city of Kurdistan, lies in the middle of one of Iraq's richest oilfields. The Iraqi Government seemed reluctant to grant too much freedom to a region of such vital importance to the national economy.

In 1974, the Kurdish leaders called for all-out war against the Iraqi government. The Kurds at first held out with the aid of arms from Iran. However, in 1975, Iran signed an agreement with Iraq cutting off aid to the Kurdish rebels, and this broke the back of the rebellion. By 1976, all Kurdish resistance had ceased.

In 1979, Ahmed Hassan al-Bakr was succeeded in the presidency by Saddam Hussein. The Baathist party remained in power, however.

Panoramic view of Baghdad, capital of Iraq, with the Cheik Adb-el-Qadir el-Gailani Mosque in the foreground.

3. THE GOVERNMENT

THE DAY AFTER the bloodless *coup d'état* that ended with the Baath (Socialist) Party taking control of the Government of Iraq, President Ahmed Hassan al-Bakr and his newly formed Revolutionary Command Council announced a new 26-man Cabinet that included several military officers who had assisted in the take-over. These young officers were conservatives who were not in full agreement with the Arab nationalist and socialist policies advocated by other members of the Baath Party, which, although opposed to the Baath extremists who rule in adjacent Syria, was nevertheless to the left of the military. A little more than two weeks after their appointment, the officers were ousted from the Cabinet, indicating to the world the sharp swing to the left in the policy of the new régime.

Three early decrees of the President and the ruling Revolutionary Command Council demonstrated a philosophy of puritanism coupled with suspicion of foreigners. A decree on foreign marriages stated that any citizen who wed a non-Arab would no longer be eligible to work for the Government or a state-controlled enterprise, a severe penalty indeed in a country where previous régimes nationalized most businesses and industries. A second decree saw the Government taking control of Al Hikma University in Baghdad from the American Jesuit priests, an action that had become necessary, according to a Government spokesman, because Al Hikma's operation was "contrary to Iraqi planning for higher education." A third decree, aimed at assuring "adherence to Islamic and Arab moral codes," outlawed miniskirts and "hippie" haircuts.

THE PROVISIONAL CONSTITUTION

The Iraqi Constitution of 1925 was abolished in 1958 when the Iraqi army overthrew the monarchy that had governed since shortly after World War I. Iraq was proclaimed a Republic and a new provisional constitution was drawn up, vesting legislative and executive power in the Cabinet, which functioned with the approval of a three-man Sovereignty Council. The Presidency—more of an honorary post until

President Arif made it an office of political power and substance—was vested in the Council. Each Cabinet minister has legislative power within his jurisdiction. The National Assembly, the legislative organ of the Government, consists of members elected in a general election, but until the termination of the provisional constitution, legislative powers are actually exercised by the Cabinet.

Iraq is divided into six judicial districts: Baghdad, Mosul, Basra, Diyala, Hilla, and Kirkuk. The Court of Cassation is the court of highest recourse from the civil courts; it sits in the capital and consists of not less than 9 permanent members and 6 delegated members. In addition, there are Courts of Appeal, Courts of First Instance, and Peace Courts, as well as Sharia Courts to deal with religious matters.

INTERNAL PROBLEMS

The "Kurdish problem", as it is known in the Government, dates to the summer of 1961 when the Iraqi Army and Kurdish irregulars fought with varying intensity in the north. The fighting was brought to a formal end with the announcement of a cease-fire in June, 1966. At that time, the Government announced a 12-point conciliation plan. It included decentralization of the Kurdish provinces, recognition of the Kurdish language, amnesty for the Kurds, the surrender of arms by the Kurds, reconstruction of the devastated area, and resettlement or re-establishment of the Kurdish refugees from the war area. In 1970, Kurdish autonomy was recognized and, in 1974, limited autonomy was granted to Kurdistan, but not on terms satisfactory to the Kurds. Even though the ensuing rebellion was put down, the Kurdish problem was not put to rest, and the prospect of future disturbances in Kurdistan remained.

The 1975 agreement with Iran, which cut off Iranian aid to the Kurds, also provided for settlement of a boundary dispute over the Shatt-al-Arab River.

FOREIGN RELATIONS

In his first-anniversary address, President Ahmed Hassan al-Bakr paid warm tribute to the Soviet Union and other countries of the Communist bloc, stating that "there can be no non-alignment between world imperialism and our international friends." Earlier that month, the Soviet Government had agreed to provide Iraq with long-term loans totalling about $120,000,000; over half of this amount is to be used to develop a rich oil field in southern Iraq.

In April, 1969, Iraq became the first Arab nation to extend full diplomatic recognition to East Germany. In appreciation, East Germany provided a loan to finance 13 industrial projects in Iraq, the loan to be repaid not in cash but in products to be produced by the industries developed by the funds. In July of the same year, Poland announced that it would invest a large sum to help develop the rich sulphur deposits in north central Iraq.

Iraq, like the other Arab nations, has never recognized Israel and considers itself to be in a technical state of war with that country. This has been the major deciding factor in Iraq's foreign policy. At the time of the June, 1967 Arab-Israel conflict, Iraq, claiming that the United States and the United Kingdom had assisted Israel's war effort, broke off diplomatic relations with both countries; United States interests in Iraq are now represented by the Government of Belgium. Iraq also broke relations with the Federal Republic of Germany when the West Germans began selling arms to Israel.

In inter-Arab affairs, Iraq has staunchly supported Arab unity as well as such proposals as an Arab common market. Yet, in 1973, Iraq placed a strain on relations with the adjacent state of Kuwait by claiming two islands belonging to Kuwait.

By 1980, Iraq, along with other Arab states, had cooled somewhat in its relations with Russia and the Soviet bloc and had increased contacts with the West.

Mothers bring their children to play in the courtyard of the Cheik Adb el-Qadir el-Gailani Mosque in Baghdad.

Kurdish men perform a native dance. The Kurds are a hospitable, fun-loving, and vigorous people, but because of their periodic revolts and demands for political independence, they have been a source of constant concern for Iraq's new régime.

4. THE PEOPLE

ACCORDING TO A 1979 United Nations esti-mate, the population of Iraq is close to 12,700,000, composed of several ethnic groups. The Arabs constitute about 80 per cent of the total, while the Kurds, the largest and most important non-Arab group, constitute about 15 per cent. The density per square mile varies from 12 in Al-Dulaym to 64 in Baghdad pro-vince. Compared to Turkey's 126 persons per square mile and Great Britain's 599, Iraq has a thinly spread population.

The nature of the country inevitably deter-mines the distribution of its people. Nomadic tribes roam the deserts south and west of the Euphrates, while the Jazirah Bedouins and other semi-nomads graze their flocks on the pastures of the steppes and highlands. Many of the villages shelter as many as 2,000 people. Some 20 towns have a population of over 10,000. Baghdad, Iraq's capital and largest city, has (with its suburbs) an estimated popula-tion of 3,000,000, this bustling city is the country's major shipping point, and rail and air terminus.

Mosul, the hub of communication and com-merce in the north, is the second largest city

A group of women of a nomadic Kurd tribe tend to the children and the cooking. The Kurds have occupied northeastern Iraq since before 2000 B.C.

with a population of 330,000; it was once known for its fine cotton goods, called muslin from a corruption of its name.

The largest city in the south is Basra (300,000); because of its location on the Shatt al-Arab River, 75 miles from the gulf coast, Basra is Iraq's main port. Kirkuk (175,000) is the great oil capital of the north; its oil fields are linked by pipeline to the Mediterranean port of Tripoli in Lebanon.

Other cities derive their fame and position in the life of the country from their religious connections; the holy shrines of Kerbala and Najaf count 339,692 and 138,321 inhabitants respectively.

A woman from the village of Fadhilia near Mosul poses in the fanciful garb traditional in that area of the country.

Despite the stern appearance of this Arab chieftain from Jezira in the north of Iraq, the nomads are known for their hospitality to strangers. Seldom can a visitor continue on his way without first stopping for a cup of tea.

This young boy of Akra lives in one of the houses built along the terraced hillside. The architectural style, peculiar to the north of Iraq, affords every occupant a view of the surrounding countryside.

This old man is one of the thousands who specialize in the production of silverware in exquisite designs. He is one of the unusual Sabaean community found in Iraq and parts of Iran.

In order to combat a housing shortage in busy Baghdad, the Government is planning and building a number of low-cost residential colonies (above). In size and shape they resemble the old mountainside homes (below).

LANGUAGE AND LITERATURE

Arabic, the official language of Iraq, is the language of the overwhelming majority of the people. The languages of certain people—such as the Assyrians—indicate an original connection with ancient, now extinct, religions or ethnic groups not necessarily native to Iraq. The Assyrians speak a surviving form of Syriac, a Semitic speech replaced by Arabic in much of the Middle East. Two main dialects of Kurdish, an Iranian tongue, are spoken by the Kurds. Chaldean, which is believed to be based on ancient Babylonian, is spoken by certain Christian groups living around the city of Mosul. An Iranian dialect is spoken by the Lurs, while the Turkomans speak a Turkish dialect. English is widely spoken and understood.

Since writing was invented by the Sumerians, it is natural that the literature of ancient Iraq has greatly affected the entire Western World. Certain themes in the Bible's Book of Genesis—the Creation, the Garden of Eden, the Great Flood, the Cain and Abel rivalry, and the Tower of Babel—can all be traced to Mesopotamian literary antecedents; the Sumerian literary device of the formal lamentation for the destruction of a city—dating to the 21st century B.C. when the city of Ur was razed—

Kurdish women love gay costumes, mixing brilliant hues of yellow, blue, red, and green with little regard for harmony.

After the lute, the ancient "al-qanoun" is the musical instrument most loved by Arabs in general. Orientalists compare it to the Western piano, in that it is capable of reproducing identical permanent notes. It is played by running thumbs and forefingers, to which metal strikers are attached, over the instrument's 78 strings.

The interior of the Martyr's Mosque in Baghdad is considered by many to be a splendid example of the blending of Eastern and Western artistry and craftsmanship.

most certainly influenced the Book of Lamentations; the Song of Solomon had an earlier counterpart in Sumerian love songs, while many of the psalms in the Book of Psalms are reminiscent of Mesopotamian hymns.

Scholars have lately uncovered many writings that show that the Greeks, too, were influenced by the Mesopotamians, whose myths and epics have their counterparts in *The Iliad, The Odyssey, Aesop's Fables*, Plato's *Dialogues*, and the poetry of Hesiod.

Ancient Mesopotamia's major contribution to world literature is undoubtedly the Akkadian *Epic of Gilgamesh*, dating to the time of Hammurabi. Some 3,500 lines long, the epic poem narrates the exploits of Gilgamesh, an early ruler of Erech, who, despite his many courageous feats of daring, could never achieve his goal —earthly immortality.

The book most familiar to Western readers, however, is *The Thousand Nights and A Night*, the Arabian Nights entertainments that found a wide audience after it was painstakingly translated by Sir Richard F. Burton in 1885. Although the book has inspired countless plays, motion pictures, and novels, modern readers have evinced impatience with Sir Richard's tortured, too-literal prose and lengthy explanatory annotations.

RELIGION

The predominant and official religion of Iraq is Islam, its followers making up about 95 per cent of the total population, almost equally divided between the Sunnite and Shi'ite sects. Most Westerners are not aware that there are different Moslem denominations just as there are different Christian denominations. The spread of Islam after its founding by the prophet Mohammed was phenomenally rapid in the 7th and 8th centuries and it was soon dominant from Spain to India. The split between the Shi'ites and the Sunnites occurred in the 7th century.

The latest of the three great monotheisms, Islam drew upon the other two, Judaism and Christianity, with Abraham and Jesus in its list of prophets preceding Mohammed. The message of God to Mohammed was transmitted by the angel Gabriel and is known as the Koran, the sacred book of Islam, which contains an immense body of laws and regulations to be followed by the faithful. Since the Koran forbids the making of any images of God (Allah), the magnificent mosques of Iraq—of which the Kadhimain Mosque in Baghdad is probably the most splendid example—are decorated only with abstract designs.

The largest group of non-Moslems is made up of 300,000 Christians, who belong to various Oriental sects. Some 100,000 native Christian "Chaldeans" joined in the 19th century, under the influence of Roman Catholic missions, to form the Uniate churches which are connected with Rome. There are about 30,000 Syrian Catholics, about 4,000 Roman Catholics and Orthodox Armenians, and some Jacobites, a sect denying the human nature of Christ.

Although at one time there were over 100,000 Jews living in Baghdad, nearly all of them left Iraq to move to Israel in the early 1950's; about 2,500 Jews remain in Iraq today.

Other interesting religious minorities are some 60,000 Yazidis in the north, and 12,000 Sabaeans, self-styled followers of John the Baptist who are world-famed for their exquisite silverware. Both of these sects relate to pre-Christian cults in their belief in good and evil forces controlling the world, and both have acquired some Moslem and Christian elements.

One of the busiest thoroughfares in Baghdad is Al-Jamhuriya Street. A new building can be seen in the background while the old Catholic Church of St. Joseph is at the right. There are approximately 360,000 Christians in Iraq today, forming the largest of the minority communities.

An Assyrian church in Baghdad. These Assyrians —who are not descended from the ancient Assyrians —are actually Nestorians, members of a heretical sect that broke away from the main body of Christians in the 5th century A.D.

Visitors arriving in Baghdad by air are afforded a magnificent view of the golden domes and minarets of the Mosque of Kadhimain, a few miles north of the city on the west bank of the Tigris. Two important Imams—Moslem religious leaders—are entombed in the golden mausoleum.

In the Government's battle against illiteracy, the future welfare and prosperity of Iraq is in the hands of its young people, such as these school children dutifully adding their sums at the Kindergarten School in Mosul.

EDUCATION

In 1958, when the Republic was established, the illiteracy rate was about 80 per cent. Since then, with a marked expansion in education, this figure has been brought down to about 50 per cent.

Illiteracy is being combated on several levels. At the primary stage alone more than 1,500 new elementary schools have been opened within the past six years. Education is compulsory on this level and is free for both primary and secondary schools. The primary schools provide a 6-year course at the end of which the student must pass an examination to be admitted to secondary school. The secondary schools have a 3-year intermediate course followed by a 2-year course in preparation for entrance to college.

Higher education was introduced into Iraq in the 1920's, and in 1958, Baghdad's various colleges were united to form the University of Baghdad. One college is open to women only, while the College of Agriculture accepts men only; all others are co-educational. All higher education is free. At certain colleges, however, the student, in exchange for government-paid tuition, must devote a specified number of years to government service. Three of the newest universities are located in Mosul, Arbil and Basra.

The Government also provides its youth with vocational training at more than 40 vocational secondary schools with courses in agriculture, business and home economics.

In an art class, Iraqi schoolgirls shape plasticine to produce their artistic impressions of the world around them. The girls in the foreground have included the familiar date palm in their creative efforts.

Grain samples are scrutinized under microscopes by two students of the College of Arts and Sciences in Baghdad.

A first-year student at the Technical Training Institute in Baghdad is intent on workshop practice on a lathe. The Institute, with the assistance of the United Nations Development Programme, is training technicians at a post-secondary level for industry and Government services, as well as teachers for vocational and technical schools.

ARTS AND CRAFTS

Astonished at the number of art exhibits scheduled the year round in Iraq, one British art critic reported that the country's production of artists is second only to its production of dates.

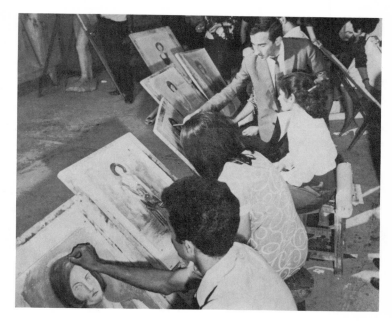

Pottery from various eras of Iraq's rich history is on display at the Iraq Museum in Baghdad. Archaeologists can deduce a great deal from pottery—the dating of other objects discovered around it, the level of technology achieved by its makers, etc. Earthenware has often been called "the alphabet of archaeology."

A walk through the fascinating bazaars of Baghdad affords the visitor the sight of bearded artisans fashioning gold and silver into delicate filigree, a skill that has been handed down over the centuries from father to son with true Oriental fidelity. In the busy Copper Market, craftsman tap-tap-tap their hammers, raising an ear-splitting din as they produce gleaming, useful household and decorative articles from imported copper. One item made principally for desert sheiks who entertain hundreds of followers, or hostesses who give lavish parties, is the copper *ghoum-ghoum*, a coffee pot that weighs 8 pounds and holds 3 gallons. The artistry of the Iraqi craftsman is also evident in hand-made rugs and quilts, almost always in vivid shades of orange, red, green, yellow and purple.

The arched interior of a sheik's house is constructed entirely of reeds, with a single naked light-bulb providing an odd note of modernity.

A woman of the north puts the finishing touches on one of the many clay jugs that she has fashioned on her pottery wheel.

This statue, symbolizing the Iraqi woman, stands in the Public Gardens of Baghdad.

Hand-crafted jewellery and elaborate embroidery distinguish the fashions worn by the women of northern Iraq.

The Sarsank Hotel, in the north near Mosul, is a popular summer resort. Its architecture strongly resembles the fortress palaces of ancient Mesopotamia.

Holiday makers relax around the pool of a Baghdad hotel. Although everything else is as up-to-date in modern Iraq as it is in the West, the current political régime takes a dim view of mini-skirts, hippie haircuts, bikinis on men, and two-piece swim suits on women.

Pilgrims often spend the night in the courtyard of the Cheik Abd el-Qadir al Gailani Mosque in Baghdad. Here a woman prepares the evening meal on portable, charcoal-burning stoves.

RECREATION

The national sport is football (soccer). The game is so popular that the stadium in Baghdad recently had to be enlarged to accommodate the growing crowds of enthusiasts. Skiing in the snow-clad mountains of the north is a sport that is gaining popularity.

FOOD

Iraqi cuisine is rich and varied, ranging from the traditional *kebab* to the internationally famed fish dish, *samak masgouf*. The preparation of the *masgouf*, especially in Baghdad, is a picturesque ceremony in itself. The fish, fresh from the Tigris, are cooked right on the river bank in the evening. For many visitors, the sight of the bonfires dotting the bank and twinkling in the darkness is as unforgettable an experience as the taste of the *masgouf* itself—crisp at the edges, white and succulent inside.

Other popular dishes are *quzi* (stuffed roasted whole lamb) and *kubba* (minced meat, nuts, raisins and spices). Arab coffee, brewed very strong and bitter with a thick sediment, is the national drink. Tea and lemon tea served in small glasses is also quite popular, as is *lebn*, a local drink that resembles yoghurt. In Arabic, the word *arak* means "sweat, juice," a reaction not untypical of the unwary soul who lightly samples this potent liquor distilled from dates.

Three main railway lines radiate to all parts of Iraq from the Mosul Railway Station in Baghdad. The tall towers supporting the building's superstructure are symbolic of the ancient "Six Pillars of Strength" guarding the approaches to the peak of Haji Umran in the northern Zagros Mountain range.

5. THE ECONOMY

ALTHOUGH IRAQ DOES not have the same impelling reasons for rapid industrialization as do countries with a surplus population too large to be supported by agriculture, it has, in recent years, begun a vast process of development in every economic field. However, the Government has been aiming at an industrial development that will not be so accelerated as to outrun the available supplies of skilled workers. Iraq's estimated work force is 3,000,000, of which agriculture uses up more than half; the largest single industrial employer is the oil industry.

INDUSTRY

The Government is encouraging the careful selection of industries to be developed on the basis of domestic resources and domestic markets. Under the Detailed Economic Plan for 1962–67, industrial plants were allocated a large share of funds. At present, apart from oil—which stands in a category by itself in the country's economy—Iraq has few industries of any major importance, although new industries are constantly being encouraged and developed.

The "pause that refreshes" for these ladies of a sewing factory in Baghdad is the lunch hour. In manufacturing, the total employment in Iraq is less than 100,000. These women have abandoned the traditional, as have many Iraqi women today.

Workers build a brick wall that will be tested with a Universal Testing Machine. In order to promote the use and improve the quality of local building materials, particularly limestone and brick as well as reeds, to strengthen concrete, the Government has established a Building Material Research Centre in Baghdad.

Bricks were invented in Iraq, where the first attempt at a building code was introduced by Hammurabi around 2000 B.C. These new clay bricks will dry in the sun for two to three weeks.

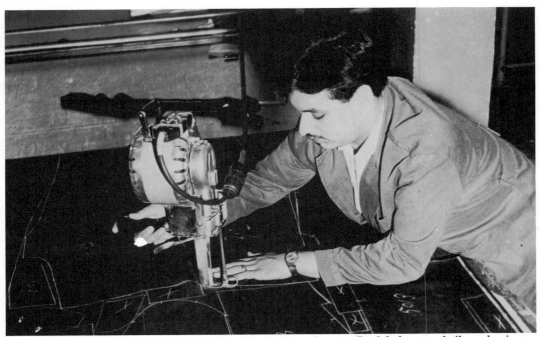

In the mid-1960's, 11 factories—including this clothing plant at Baghdad—were built under international cooperation agreements. The industrial policy of the government has encouraged state-ownership for heavy industries and the participation of private capital in the production of consumer goods.

In recent years, the state has built a number of factories, including a bitumen plant south of Mosul which produces 60,000 tons of asphalt annually; a large textile factory at Mosul, equipped with 644 looms producing 25,000,000 square yards of calico from locally grown cotton; and two cement factories, each with a daily output of 350 tons. A shoe plant at Kufa opened in 1962, and a cigarette factory at Sulaimaniyah began production in 1961. Under international co-operation agreements, 11 factories were also built, including a steel mill and an electrical equipment factory at Baghdad, textile and clothing plants, a drug factory at Samarra, and an agricultural machinery plant at Mussayib.

The industrial policy of the Government includes state-ownership of heavy industries and the participation of private capital in the production of consumer goods. Tax exemptions are offered to new industries if 90 per cent of the employees are Iraqi—in some cases extended to citizens of other Arab nations.

Iraq has received foreign economic assistance from a number of sources, principally in the form of loans. In 1969, the new régime received economic aid in the form of long-term loans and investments from the Soviet Union and other countries of the Eastern bloc. This aid is expected eventually to bring about a large annual increase in income to the Iraqi economy.

On a hillside outside Baghdad, workers arrange their new bricks to dry in the sun.

A state-built textile plant in Mosul is equipped with 644 looms and employs 1,200 workers.

The Tigris River is harnessed outside Baghdad by the Al-Hinia Dam to provide irrigation and hydro-electrical power.

This worker is protected by recent legislation, which regulates minimum wages, working hours, compensation for injuries, disease, loss of life, and weekly and annual holidays. All government departments and most shops and businesses are closed on Friday.

OIL: THE KEYSTONE OF THE ECONOMY

The oil industry, the principal source of Iraq's wealth, providing most of the capital for all state and municipal industries, has aptly been described as the keystone of the Republic's economy.

The first oil production began in 1927 and, by 1980, total crude oil production amounted to nearly 112,000,000 metric tons. Operations are conducted by the Iraq Petroleum Company and its associated company, the Basra Petroleum Company, as well as the Mosul Petroleum Company. The main oil field is located at Kirkuk, with other fields at Naft Khaneh, Ayn Zalah, and Butmah, near Mosul.

Oil constitutes such a major part of Iraq's foreign trade that the official statistics are calculated in two segments: all external trade with the exception of oil—and oil, standing alone and accounting for about 80 per cent of the foreign exchange.

Up until 1969, the Iraq Petroleum Company, controlled by British, United States, French,

and Dutch interests, had a monopoly on the export of Iraqi oil. This long-time dominance suffered a set-back when the Soviet Union, with its long-term loans to Iraq, for the first time got a toe-hold in the oil-bearing Gulf

Iraq Petroleum Company employees at work in the company's Engine Re-Conditioning Workshop at Makinah Depot. The oil industry is the largest single industrial employer in Iraq.

At the Basra Petroleum Company's deep-sea terminal at Khor Al Amaya, two oil tankers are loaded.

area, which until then had been the exclusive domain of the big Western oil companies. A large part of the Russian loan will be used to develop the North Rumeila oil field in southern Iraq, near Basra. North Rumeila was taken away from the Iraq Petroleum Company in 1961, but the field was never developed because of lack of funds. It is known that there are oil deposits of about 20,000,000 tons at North Rumeila.

In 1972, Iraq nationalized the Iraq Petroleum Company.

Under the Iraq Petroleum Company's housing scheme for its employees, the Company finances the construction of attractive low-priced modern dwellings, such as this example in Kirkuk. Any IPC employee from ordinary worker to section chief is eligible to buy one for a 10 per cent down payment.

Oil was discovered in Iraq on October 14, 1927, in Kirkuk. As so often happens in the Middle East, the event was violent and unexpected. Shortly after midnight, a worker decided to lift the drilling bit from a 1,500-foot hole to clean the cuttings. What came up with the bit was a gusher spouting gas and oil 140 feet into the air. It took ten days to cap the well that was gushing 80,000 barrels of oil a day, and creating a swift-flowing black river more than 100 feet across. A new era began that day for all of Iraq.

TRADE

Because of Iraq's basic lack of extensive industry, it must import such items as iron and steel, internal combustion engines, boilers, machinery, and automobiles and parts.

Exports reflect the agricultural complexion of the economy, being comprised of such items as barley, straw and fodder, raw wool, livestock, hides, skins, and seeds.

What would be a trade imbalance for Iraq is remedied, however, by the export of oil and dates, the revenues from these two items alone being sufficient to pay for the needed imports of machinery and equipment.

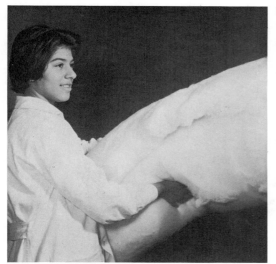

Iraq's exports—cotton (shown here), raw wool, barley, dates, livestock, hides and skins—reflect the agricultural complexion of the country's economy.

THE SMILING CROPS

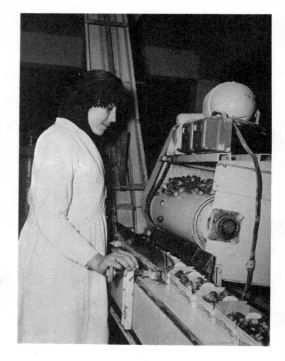

According to one historian of the period, the soil of ancient Iraq was so fertile that when tickled it "smiled a crop." The historian Herodotus testified that the country's agriculture was unrivalled anywhere in Asia or Europe, claiming that the blade of the wheat plant was often four fingers in breadth, and the height of the millet so incredible that he dare not mention a figure for fear of being branded a madman.

Today, as it was in ancient times, Iraq's agricultural livelihood and welfare is contingent upon the Tigris and Euphrates rivers.

Iraq's present policy calls for the building of dams and reservoirs to tap the full potential of the Tigris and the Euphrates rivers for flood control, hydro-electric power, and irrigation.

An Iraqi farmer poses with the traditional beast of burden, a water buffalo. Despite the fact that the country has much land for pasture and forage crops with which to build up sturdy herds, Iraq is exceptionally poor in livestock. In order to combat tuberculosis and other diseases that affect both sheep and cattle, the Government recently set up an Animal Health Institute near Baghdad.

Pumps are used extensively along both the rivers for irrigation. They are generally privately owned but are controlled by a licensing system. On the Tigris 1,250,000 acres are watered by pumps; on the Euphrates, 500,000 acres. The Government has begun a much-needed plan of river control, directed towards southern Iraq since the northern regions are rain-fed and, on the whole, not suitable for irrigation. Four new dams and barrages provide ample security against devastating floods, as well as water for hydro-electric power and irrigation. Altogether, the full utilization of the waters of the two rivers by means of dams and reservoirs now completed or under consideration will add some 4,500,000 acres to those already under cultivation, nearly doubling the area of cultivated land in Iraq.

Shortly after the Revolution in 1958, the Government instituted a new land reform project that provided for the break-up of large estates and the distribution of land to subsistence farmers and landless workers. The largest holding now permitted on flow-irrigated land is 600 acres, and on land watered by rainfall, 1,200 acres. The primary aim of the land reform was the creation of some 50 villages, each with 50 or 60 families of small landowners with an improved standard of living, who can contribute to the nation's agricultural output through better farming methods. More than 50,000 families actually received land under this scheme, and jobs were provided for about 35,000 agricultural workers.

The largest and most successfully grown crop in Iraq is barley, followed by wheat, lentils, vetch, linseed, cotton, tobacco, rice, and sesame. The date palm supplies an important source of revenue since Iraq's 20,000,000 date palms of bearing age provide about 80 per cent of the world's date supply. Approximately 400,000 tons of dates are produced annually.

Camels in the desert.

Jordan

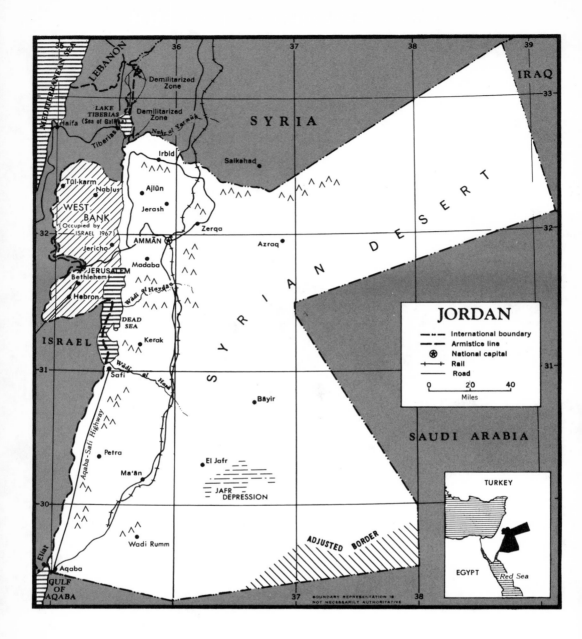

Near Wadi Rumm, in southern Jordan, camels are heading for a waterhole after the day's work.

I. THE LAND

The Hashemite Kingdom of Jordan is bounded on the north by Syria, on the east by Iraq, on the southeast and south by Saudi Arabia, and on the west by Israel and by the Israeli-occupied West Bank region, part of Jordan until 1967. Jordan proper, which lies east of the Jordan River, has an area of 35,000 square miles (88,000 sq. km.), while the West Bank area has about 2,640 square miles (6,600 sq. km.). The total area of Jordan is about the same as that of Indiana, or of Scotland and Wales combined. Jordan's short 17 miles (27 km.) of coastline lies in the southwest on the Gulf of Aqaba, an arm of the Red Sea. The city of Aqaba, the only port, plays a large part in the economic life of the country.

SURFACE FEATURES

Jordan has four major geographical regions—the East Bank Uplands, the West Bank Uplands, the Jordan Desert and the Jordan Rift Valley. The Desert, located in the territory of the East Bank, taking up about four fifths of its space, is part of the Syrian Desert. Its northern part is composed of volcanic lava and basalt, and its southern part of sandstone and granite, partly eroded by wind. The East Bank Uplands overlook the Rift Valley and have an altitude of between 2,000 and 3,000 feet (600 and 900 metres) increasing in elevation to about 5,750 feet (1,725 metres) in the south. Outcrops of chalk, sand, limestone and flint extend to the

Young visitors on the shore of the Dead Sea read about where they are in English and Arabic.

extreme south, where igneous rocks predominate. Many valleys and streams circulate east, west and north while south of Al-karak, seasonal streams run east into a low region known as the Jafr Depression.

The Jordan Valley, almost 1,300 feet (390 metres) below sea level at the Dead Sea, is the lowest point on the surface of the earth. As it travels south, the Jordan River drains the waters of the Sea of Galilee, the Yarmuk River and the valley streams of both plateaus, into the Dead Sea. Actually a lake, the Dead Sea is 45 miles (72 km.) long by 10 miles (16 km.) wide— its waters are far saltier than the ocean.

The West Bank Uplands, known for centuries as the Samarian and Judean Mountains, have an average height of 3,000 feet (900 metres) above sea level. Several large valleys cut into them and drain west towards the Mediterranean; the valleys draining east are shorter, many consisting of deep gorges with soils both thin and poor, though occasional rich alluvial deposits are found among the hills.

In the Dead Sea area, a farmer carries home brush which he has gathered— with the help of his donkey and camel.

A Bedouin and his grandson stand on the summit of Mount Nebo. Their light, loose clothing protects them from the brilliant desert sun and allows cool air to circulate close to their bodies.

CLIMATE

The climate of Jordan is generally arid, varying from a pleasant Mediterranean type in the western part to desert heat in the east. Jericho, on the West Bank, 492 feet (150 metres) below sea level, ranges in temperature between 61° and 90° F. (15.6° and 32° C.) while in Amman, the monthly temperatures range from 44° to 87° F. (7° to 30° C.). The prevailing winds throughout the land are westerly to southwesterly. The short cool winters (very pleasant) have an average rainfall from 16 inches (40 cm.) in the north to 4 inches (10 cm.) in the south, while the Jordan Valley has about 8 inches (20 cm.) a year. In the Uplands, frost and snow occur in small amounts, but this seldom happens in the Rift Valley.

NATURAL RESOURCES

Jordan is fortunate in having a number of mineral resources, including huge deposits of limestone and phosphates, as well as iron, phosphorus, manganese and copper. Recently discovered minerals of importance include barite, quartzite, gypsum (used as fertilizer) and feldspar. Countless brightly hued marbles are quarried and used for decoration on pottery and on new buildings.

THE JORDAN RIVER

The Jordan River is revered by Christians, Jews and Moslems alike, and it is in its waters that Christ was baptized by St. John the Baptist. The Jordan has often been an international boundary and since 1948 has marked part of the frontier between Israel to the west and Jordan to the east, from a few miles south of the Sea of Galilee to the point where the Yabis

Modern electronic equipment is being used in the search for mineral resources.

In the Baq'a Valley, abundant water for irrigation is now being extracted from wells. The water runs off the surrounding mountains into the sandy soil to a depth of almost 250 feet (75 metres), where it is held by a vast bowl-shaped formation of hard rock.

composed of papyrus, water lilies and other pond flowers once filled the area, which was drained in the 1950's to form agricultural land.

Projects have been planned that embrace the waters of the entire basin. A proposal is being considered to maintain the level of the Dead Sea by channelling in salt water from the Mediterranean—at the same time using the flow to generate hydro-electricity. Because of the Arab-Israeli tensions, only a partial use of Jordan's waters have been made. Syria and Jordan look to the future construction of an irrigation and hydro-electric dam on the Yarmuk River, which forms a small part of their border before entering the Jordan.

River flows into it. Since 1967, however, when Israeli forces occupied Jordanian territory on the West Bank, the Jordan River has served as the cease-fire line as far as the Dead Sea. While 223 miles (357 km.) in length, its course meanders, and the beeline distance between its origin and the Dead Sea is roughly 124 miles (200 km.).

At one time the Greeks called the river the Aulon, the Hebrews knew it as al-Yardon but to the Arabs it is still thought of as ash-Shariah, meaning the Watering Place. The river has three principal sources, all of which rise at the foot of Mount Hermon. The longest one is the Hasbani, rising in Lebanon at a height of 1,800 feet (540 metres). From the east in Syria, flows the Nahr Baniyas, and between the two is the Dan, with its sparkling fresh water. These three rivers join together in the Hula Basin, into which other streams flow, the most noted being the Enot Enan. Dense vegetation

Concrete conduits cut down on the evaporation of the water they carry and help to make the desert bloom.

The ancient art of falconry, hunting with trained hawks, is still practiced in Jordan.

FLORA AND FAUNA

Flowering plants found in Jordan include poppies, roses, anemones, tamarisks and buckthorn.

There are about 35,000 acres (14,000 hectares) of forest in Jordan, most of it growing on the rocky highlands of the East Bank. In spite of heavy wood-cutting by villagers and heavy grazing by Bedouin flocks of sheep, the forest trees have not been thinned out as much as might be expected, due to the reforestation scheme commenced in 1948 by the Jordanian government. Predominant types of trees are the Aleppo and Kermes oak, the Palestine pistachio, and the Aleppo pine tree. Olives grow wild in many places, and the Phoenicia Juniper grows in the areas of lesser rainfall. The grasslands offer lean fare to the livestock, while on the East Bank they have been depleted to make way for land now devoted to olive and fruit trees. To increase the fertility of the pastures, artesian wells have been dug.

The wildlife of Jordan includes animals of

Goats graze on the slopes of Mount Nebo, where Moses once stood and looked upon the Promised Land.

The city of Amman spreads out over seven hills.

Ancient Amman has grown modern rapidly in recent years—many new residential quarters like this have been built.

both African and Asian types—jackals, hyenas, foxes, badgers, along with mongooses and jungle cats (the last named in the reeds along the Jordan River). Gazelles and other antelopes are common in the desert. Until fairly recent times the lion and the leopard stalked their prey on Jordanian soil, but these great cats are now extinct there.

A curious creature is the hyrax, small in size, resembling a rodent, but it has hoofs, can climb, and is considered by zoologists to be more closely allied to elephants than to any other animal group.

Birds are numerous, including quails, swans, cranes and cuckoos. The brown-necked raven is a characteristic bird of the Jordan Valley and the Palestine sunbird is typical of the Dead Sea area. Because of the dry climate, water-loving amphibians are few, but reptiles abound, including many species of snakes and lizards. Insects and their kin are very numerous in the dry regions, especially scorpions and locusts (which have attacked crops since Biblical days).

AMMAN

Long before recorded history, primitive people dwelt among the hills of Amman, enjoying the cool waters of its many springs. Instruments of flint have established their presence from Paleolithic times. Amman, later known as Philadelphia, was known in 1200 B.C. as Rabbath Ammon, having been the capital of the Ammonites who fought with the biblical Kings of Israel.

Amman today is a modern city and among the fastest growing of national capitals. Its population has increased from 20,000 in 1920 to 615,000 today. Amman is famous for its 7 hills, its hotels, good food, archeological sites and friendly people.

Glimpses of ancient times linger in the long, winding bazaars where just about everything is sold. The bazaars contrast with shops and boutiques of ultra-fashionable design. Historic sites rival those of Europe—among the most impressive is the 2,000-year-old Roman Theatre

The Roman Theatre in Amman has a seating capacity of 6,000, and is still in use for festivals, concerts and other events.

The pool at the Philadelphia Hotel in Amman is a popular spot on a warm day.

Business as usual goes on in Amman's busy streets, in spite of the upheavals and privations caused by the tense situation in the Middle East.

facing a well-known tourist hotel, the Philadelphia. Guests at this hostelry are aware that a few steps away lies a trip back into time. The theatre, built in three tiers into the semicircular curve of a hill, seats 6,000 spectators and is used today for outdoor festivals and orchestral concerts.

Other antiquities include the Citadel and its fine museum containing relics of the city's ancient history. On a hill in the middle of Amman are the remains of a Roman temple to Hercules, a Byzantine Church and an Ommayyad palace from the 8th century A.D.

Development in the capital has exceeded expectations. Amman has a fine race track where camel racing is enjoyed as much as horse racing. Tennis clubs, swimming and glider clubs exist, while entertainment at the various hotels headlines performers of international reputation.

Several years ago Jordan's modern university opened its doors in the environs of Amman. Buildings of note are the two palaces where King Hussein lives and works. The Basman, a stately edifice, houses the royal offices—here the King receives visitors, confers with his cabinet and more often than not stays late to complete the countless tasks always awaiting him. He dwells on the outskirts of Amman but holds official functions at the Ragadan Palace, the original Hashemite residence, where Hussein's grandfather, Abdullah, lived as Jordan's first ruler. Abdullah's tomb, a magnificent triple-arched shrine, is behind this palace. The

Camel racing as a sport attracts enthusiastic crowds to the race track at Marka, just outside Amman.

main street of Amman is King Hussein Street, in the heart of the city, a busy thoroughfare lined with modern buildings.

Modern Amman has fine hospitals and clinics, modern cinemas and an increasing number of factories producing cement, electrical apparatus, textiles, paper products and aluminium utensils. Food and tobacco-processing are among its most important industries.

Participants in a camel race enter the track at Marka. Racing camels are a special type—slender, light and fast.

This ancient double gate survives from the days when Amman was a walled city.

The graceful minaret of the Hussein Mosque towers over the heart of Amman.

JERASH

Known as the "Pompeii of the East," Jerash (in ancient times called Gerasa) is a 45-minute drive from Amman. Once it was a great city under Roman jurisdiction in the 2nd and 3rd centuries A.D., but later it decayed. The Jordan Department of Antiquities has dug it out of centuries of sand and debris, revealing hundreds of stately columns, a triumphal arch and other splendid ruins. Jerash was one of the renowned stops on the ancient caravan routes. All the treasures of the Orient found a market

Roman steps and columns (1st and 2nd centuries A.D.) lead up to the site of the early Christian cathedral at Jerash (4th century). At the top of the stairs is a shrine dedicated to the Virgin Mary and the archangels Gabriel and Michael.

The Nymphaeum, or Temple of the Nymphs, at Jerash was a sort of public fountain and temple combined. Water gushed out of holes in the lower niches into a tank. It dates from A.D. 190.

here. Silks, spices and precious stones used as barter brought immense wealth to its citizens.

Jerash was the epitome of luxury in its day and Roman generals and wealthy townspeople enjoyed a life filled with expensive pleasures.

In the 2nd century A.D. Jerash entered its golden age. New buildings and lavish architecture were the order of the hour and Jerash attained the rank of an independent colony in the 3rd century. It only declined when the

The columns of Jerash rise spectacularly from the arid plain.

The forum at Jerash (seen here) stood at the end of a mile-long colonnaded street. Archeologists now believe that Jerash was far larger than at first supposed.

Romans themselves declined. Earthquakes in the 8th century hastened its end, and by the 13th century, the sands of the desert had swept across it and the ruined city was no more. Arabs passing through spoke of it as the "ruins of Jerash." Only a humble Arab village remained in our time when excavations and reconstruction began.

The paving blocks of the Roman Forum at Jerash are still in excellent condition.

A mosaic picture map of Jerusalem in the 6th century A.D. is one of the attractions of Madaba. The inscriptions are in Greek characters. Madaba was first mentioned in the Bible, in Numbers 21, as an Amorite town that was seized by the Moabites.

HADRIAN'S ARCH

The Roman Emperor Hadrian wintered in Jerash in A.D. 129–30, while making plans on a grand scale for the town. He built his own triumphal arch far away on the outskirts leaving part unfinished, suggesting that he meant the finished town walls to meet at his arch.

MADABA

Madaba lies just a 30-minute drive from Amman on rising ground in the middle of a plain where many battles were fought. An Ammonite town, it dates from the Middle Bronze Age and is noted for its Byzantine mosaics. One of the highlights is a 6th-century mosaic map of Jerusalem, the oldest map of the Holy City in the world. Embellished with

mosaic pictures of monasteries, people, boats and plants, the map is preserved in the Greek Orthodox Church of Madaba. Other fine mosaics have been transferred to Madaba's small museum, where one can see depictions of Greek hero Achilles, the goatlike god Pan, and Bacchus the god of wine, along with exhibits of Roman jewels and utensils.

Madaba is just east of Mount Nebo, from the top of which Moses had his first view of the Promised Land. From this peak one can see the Jordan Valley and the Dead Sea, and on a clear day it is possible to see the spires of Jerusalem in the distance. Madaba reached its heights between the 5th and 6th centuries A.D. It was destroyed by the Persians in A.D. 614. Then it was occupied by the Arabs. In 747, an earthquake caused it to be abandoned until the early 19th century, when 2,000 Christians from Kerak settled there.

The vast Crusader castle at Kerak stands on a towering height above the Dead Sea. It was the southernmost fortress of the Crusader dynasty that ruled Jordan in the 12th century.

KERAK

Over the Mountains of Moab from Madaba lies the town of Kerak, a Crusader outpost of the 12th century. Its castle-fortress, one of the most renowned in all the Middle East, was built by the Crusader leader, Godfrey of Bouillon. Kerak lay across the trade routes that led from Arabia to Egypt and the Mediterranean. Stripping the caravans laden with brocades, ivory, spices, metals and jewels became a vital source of income for the Crusader military outposts. Saladin, the Saracen or Moslem leader, made numerous attempts to storm the castle, finally succeeding after starving out the defending Crusaders and took the great fortress in A.D. 1188.

Tales of Arab chivalry still remembered took place at Kerak. During the wedding feast of Humphrey of Toron, a Crusader knight, and Isabel, sister of Baldwin, Saladin attacked the castle. The mother of the groom sent a gift of provisions, along with a message informing Saladin of the wedding. He replied, thanking her for the gift, while asking which tower was the bridal suite so that his soldiers would refrain from attacking it.

Kerak became an important and prosperous place in the later Middle Ages. When the Turks conquered the Middle East, they restored the castle, and, in spite of later neglect, it is still a historic and majestic sight, set in beautiful surroundings.

High above the valley floor at Petra are the ruins of cave dwellings.

The Siq is the narrow, winding passage through towering cliffs that leads to ancient Petra.

Known as the Urn, this huge finial ornament tops off one of Petra's largest monuments, the Monastery. Visitors are often challenged to climb it.

PETRA

This stronghold of an early Arab people, the Nabataeans, is the chief attraction of Jordan. Petra was part of a forgotten past until it was discovered by a Swiss explorer, Burckhardt. He brought it to light in 1812, after hearing tales from guides about the ruins of an old city lost in the mountains. He induced the guides to take him there, by telling them of a sacrifice he was pledged to make at the reputed tomb of Aaron, which lay beyond Petra.

So bewildering was the glory of what he beheld—a noble city carved out of the mountain rock, statues from the Roman and Hellenistic eras, spacious cave dwellings half in

The Treasury is one of the finest of the amazing buildings at Petra. Note tiny horsemen in foreground.

At Petra, the ruins of a Roman theatre can still be seen.

ruins, everything cut out of sandstone—that he was overcome. After he proclaimed his discovery, archeologists from all over the world flocked to it and were amazed at the grandeur and wealth of the still livable edifices. They recognized an art, a craftsmanship and a miracle of planning rarely achieved. The rough roads and rugged transport of those days deterred travellers, but today Petra, easily accessible over excellent roads, is but a 3-hour ride from Amman by car via Wadi-Musa's Police Post (reminiscent of the French Foreign Legion). Horses are obtained here for the fantastic narrow passage leading to the lost city, though jeeps can get through part of the way. The passage is an adventure in itself, for towering mountain walls block out the light and the sudden burst of daylight is blinding as one emerges from the Siq (which is the name of the passage) and beholds Petra.

The soft hues of the rock formations of Petra have given it the name of the "Rose red city, half as old as time." Many of its great tombs and caves are now occupied by Bedouin families. The softness of the sandstone did not allow for detailed sculpture, so the Nabataean artisans

Jordanians entertain tourists inside one of Petra's caves.

At Petra, a narrow stairway hewn out of solid rock leads to a flattened mountain top. Here is a huge altar of smoothed rock, called the "High Place," where pre-Christian Nabataeans made sacrifices.

devised a different method, a wider and more flowing style, reflected in the carved façades. The Place of Sacrifice, where religious ceremonies were performed and prisoners were sacrificed, is well preserved, and the Halls of Justice and the Monastery are giants of architectural beauty.

The Urn Tomb at Petra was used by a Nabataean cult of the dead. Note the people at the right.

Grim hills devoid of vegetation overlook the boom port town of Aqaba.

The Water Ski Festival at Aqaba takes place against a background of purple mountains.

At Aqaba, the resort area is totally separate from the busy port.

AQABA

The road to lively Aqaba is the road to the Red Sea, since the city is situated on the Gulf of Aqaba. Aqaba is Jordan's only seaport, set against the rugged background of stark mountains, but the city itself is a scene of golden beaches, blue waters and flowers everywhere. At first sight, it appears to be mainly a tourist spot, for happy youngsters crowd the waterfront, bathers relax on the fine, warm sands, sailboats skim back and forth and all water sports seem to be the order of the day.

Aqaba was a place of importance long before water skis and scuba diving arrived, long before it became known as a winter resort, or famous for its Water Festival. Aqaba is the Hashemite Kingdom's outlet to the outside world of international trade. Its history can be traced back to King Solomon, when ore from the copper mines of the region was smelted in furnaces which took advantage of the winds always blowing from the north to keep their fires hot. Commerce flourished with Egypt and the small town had a busy life.

The city came into importance again in the later Middle Ages under the Mamelukes, whose last Sultan's name is still engraved on the town's ancient gateway, the Sultan Qansah el Ghuri.

Before the new docks for large vessels were built at Aqaba, passengers had to wait to be taken by launch back to their steamer at anchor in the bay.

The pink sands and black hills of Wadi Rumm sheltered the English adventurer, Lawrence of Arabia, and his Bedouin allies and served as the base from which they raided the Turkish outposts in World War I.

WADI RUMM

Wadi Rumm, the Valley of the Moon, between Petra and Aqaba is Lawrence of Arabia country. Among the deep sandstone cliffs of the Valley the British adventurer, Lawrence, helped the Arabs in the desert fight against the Turks in 1917. The mountains here are black, standing upon pale pink sands, and here falconry is still practiced by the Bedouins. The falcons are trained for months on end, and later are sold to the wealthy princes of Saudi Arabia.

The new highway to Wadi Rumm ends at the entrance to the Valley and is replaced by a primitive road which jeeps and camels can traverse with ease. Sweeping vistas provide miles and miles of scenery so breathtaking

that one feels humble among the immense plateaus partly covered with green desert scrub, where the mountains are overwhelmingly beautiful in the haze of the day and awesome in the clear blue night. In this landscape the filming of *Lawrence of Arabia* took place.

Large boulders here and there bear inscriptions centuries old. Bedouins on camels and young boys herding long-haired black goats are part of the scenery, as are the glimmering camp fires of travellers. Tourists can now enjoy desert camping at Wadi Rumm and the delights of food cooked over open fires by Bedouin guides, who know where to find overhanging rocks in the shade and gushing streamlets to quench thirst. A grand finale awaits campers at the Camel Corps Police Fort, where the Desert Legionnaires receive

Tourists at Wadi Rumm enjoy an open-air meal.

visitors with traditional black coffee, filling up the cups until everyone is satiated.

OTHER TOWNS

At Ajlun, the Castle of Saladin stands on the highest ground, at whose foot sprout luscious pomegranate trees and groves of figs. Pine and oak forests line the way to Ajlun, where Jordanians trek to enjoy picnics on a day's outing and a view of the Jordan Valley.

On the Jerash Road, north of Ajlun, lies the large commercial city of Irbid, near which is a mound covering the remains of a village dating back to 3,000 B.C.

About 30 miles (48 km.) north of Irbid, in the valley of the Yarmuk River, are hot sulphur springs, used for health baths. Many tourists visit here and residential and bathing facilities are set in an attractive background.

The old cities of the West Bank, under Israeli administration since 1967, include Bethlehem, Jericho, Nablus and Hebron.

Bethlehem and its famous Church of the Nativity were under Jordanian rule until 1967. A Christian Arab woman is kissing a silver star set in the floor of the grotto beneath the church.

JORDAN ◈ **163**

Heavily fortified, Kharana Castle was built by the Ommayyads mainly to protect their caravan routes, although like all their castles, it was luxuriously appointed inside.

VILLAGES

The villages of Jordan range from those with 50 to 100 inhabitants to large ones with up to several thousands. The average Jordanian village is a compact settlement with houses close together, each built of stone with a courtyard surrounding it. In the smaller villages the dwellings are of one storey, and made of mud brick.

Castle Amra is the best preserved of the Ommayyad desert retreats.

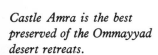

A pierced stone window suggests the former luxury of the Hisham Winter Palace of the Ommayyads, dating from the 8th century.

DESERT CASTLES

A little known attraction of Jordan are the desert castles set amidst trees in the eastern part of the land, most of them used by the Ommayyad Caliphs around the 8th century A.D. Their main residence was in Damascus, but the Caliphs enjoyed life in the desert and would move with their entire entourage back to the land of their original Bedouin ancestry, to regain the pleasures of the simplicity and spaciousness of desert life.

The castles were created to house the Caliphs and their families and followers, and their concubines too. Dancing and music were the chief indoor amusements and vast pools, elaborately decorated with heating pipes, can still be seen, where the family spent hours relaxing between feasts and sports.

In the castle known as Kharana, 62 miles (99 km.) east of Amman, deep in the desert, are huge and mysterious basalt blocks and a mosque dating from the 13th century. Azraq now lies in the heart of a great National Park and reserve. Its enchanting oasis pools have yielded evidence of Paleolithic settlements, 200,000 years old.

Castle Amra, built in the early 8th century, 20 miles (33 km.) from Azraq, is considered the best preserved. Hunting scenes, figures of Victory, Philosophy, Poetry, even saluki dogs and Islam's enemies are shown on the numerous frescoes on the Castle's walls. Castle Mushatta, the nearest one to Amman, though covered with fine carvings and much delicate detail, was never completed. However, the gigantic remains reflect how ornate the Ommayyads' taste could be. Castle Hallabat, originally built in the reign of the Roman Emperor Caracalla (A.D. 198–217) as a fortress against raiding desert chiefs, is still well preserved.

Near Ajlun, Castle Qalat al Rabadh, a true Arab structure, has fortified double gates. Built by a governor of Saladin's near Ajlun to protect the Arabs from the Crusaders, it is not an Ommayyad Castle. Once it was part of a chain of bases and flying pigeon-posts that could flash news from the Euphrates to the Nile between dawn and dark. In 1927, the Department of Antiquities cleared its moats, gates and towers, and several deep wells inside the castle are in use today.

The Kidron Valley outside Jerusalem is one of the holy places which were under Jordan's control until 1967, and whose disposition remains to be settled. In the foreground, surrounded by terraced olive trees, is the Church of All Nations, which marks the spot where Jesus prayed before his arrest.

2. HISTORY

ANCIENT CONQUERORS marched across the land that is now Jordan, and each in turn left behind traces of their presence. From the east came Assyrians, Babylonians and Persians. Philistines, Hittites and Greeks appeared from the north and west. From the west also came the Romans and the Egyptians, and from the south finally came the Arabs, who stayed to make Jordan part of the Arab world.

Excavations at Jericho, in the disputed West Bank region, have shown remains of a civilization at least 8,000 years old.

Wadi Musa, near Petra, is a village on the site of a well which is believed to have been used by Moses.

EARLY HISTORY

Since ancient times, the huge deserts of the Arabian Peninsula have been the home of Semitic peoples. They were shepherds and, as their tribes grew larger and the deserts drier, they moved north in search of water for their flocks. Among them were the Canaanites, who reached the shores of the Mediterranean. All along the coastline and in the Jordan Valley, they built small cities.

The movement from the Arabian Peninsula during the Bronze and Middle Bronze Ages also included the Ammonites, Amorites, Moabites and Edomites, all familiar to readers of the Bible as ancient enemies of yet another Semitic people—the Israelites.

ISRAELITES

The Patriarch Abraham pitched his tribal tents at Hebron in the land of Canaan, where he and his family prospered. Later on there was famine in Canaan and the descendants of Abraham struggled to reach Egypt about 1700 B.C. At that time, Egypt was under the rule of desert invaders, the Shepherd Kings,

or the Hyksos, who developed the war chariot.

About 1560 B.C. the Egyptians rebelled and regained control of their land, expelling the Hyksos. Moses, from the family of Abraham, emerged as a leader of the Israelites and led them from slavery in Egypt, across the Red Sea. For 40 years they wandered in the desert until Moses lay dying. His last act was to point out the rich Jordan Valley ahead of them. They crossed the Jordan, took Jericho and other Canaanite towns and established themselves in Palestine.

About 1000 B.C. David, one of the Children of Israel, became king, made great conquests and established Jerusalem as his capital. His son Solomon beautified Jerusalem and built the Temple there. In 586 B.C. Nebuchadnezzar, the Babylonian king, destroyed Jerusalem and took 50,000 Israelites into captivity in Babylon, where they remained until 538 B.C. when Cyrus of Persia captured Babylon and sent the Jews back to Jerusalem. In 333 B.C. Alexander the Great of Greece conquered Syria. Two hundred years later the Romans occupied Syria, Jordan and Palestine, and in the 1st century B.C. installed Herod the Edomite as King of the Jews. During Herod's reign, Jesus was born in Bethlehem.

The Monastery, one of Petra's most imposing structures, was built in the 3rd century A.D. as a pagan temple, and later was used as a Christian church.

NABATAEANS

The Nabataeans who first inhabited Petra amassed fortunes in the 5th century B.C., because their land lay close to the Syrian-Arabian border trade routes, and they collected large tolls from caravans for safe passage. They used their wealth to glorify their capital and named it Petra, which means "The Rock."

In later years the Nabataeans came under the Empire of Alexander the Great and his successors.

The Grecian Empire tumbled under pressure from Roman legions who tried in vain at first to capture Petra, though in the end its people had to pay tribute to Rome. In A.D. 107 Petra became part of the Roman Province of Syria. The Emperor Trajan built the first great road passing through Petra, connecting Syria with the Red Sea. Petra prospered beyond its dreams. As the Roman Empire declined, this route was abandoned in A.D. 300 and Petra lost much of its importance.

Christianity came to Petra in the next century but fewer caravans crossed its path. Decline set in and by the time of the Arab conquest in the 7th century, Petra was deserted.

PERSIAN OCCUPATION

About the year A.D. 600 the Persians won Syria and Palestine from the Eastern Roman or Byzantine Empire, which had acquired these territories through the break-up of the Roman Empire. In the end, in 614, they captured Jerusalem, massacred many of the people and pulled down all the Christian churches. The Persian occupation lasted less than 20 years until the Byzantine Emperor Heraclius came to Jerusalem, bringing with him several of the holy relics the Persians had taken away.

ISLAM

Islam, the religion of the Prophet Mohammed, was introduced into Jordan in the 7th century by Arab invaders. This happened after the Arabs, impelled by the new faith of Islam, swept out of the deserts of Arabia and defeated the Byzantine forces in A.D. 636. An era of peace and prosperity followed and Jerusalem's Famous Dome of the Rock (still standing today) was built by one of the Ommayyad Caliphs, Abdul Malak Ibn Marwan. Successors of Mohammed, the Caliphs were both spiritual and earthly leaders of the Arab realm. The Ommayyads, an Arab dynasty whose capital was Damascus, ruled from there for 100 years.

CRUSADERS

In A.D. 750, the Abbasids, a rival group, fought and conquered the Ommayyads, moving the Caliphate to Baghdad. Late in the 11th century, they lost control over Jordan and Palestine, which fell to the Frankish, or Western European, Crusaders. The aim of the Crusaders was to restore the Holy Land to Christian rule. After Jerusalem fell into Crusader hands in 1099, following fierce warfare, the Crusaders built castles, north, west and south, to control the caravan routes, and also built thousands of churches and Christian shrines.

SALADIN

Once again Arab armies, those of Saladin and the Ayyubites, came to power and overthrew the Crusaders in 1187 in the Battle of Hittin near the Lake of Tiberias. The Ayyubite soldiers commanded the area until the Mamelukes from Egypt took over. The Mameluke Sultans had aided in crushing the Crusaders and they now ruled in Jordan and Syria, forcing out all the Crusaders.

The interior of the Dome of the Rock in Jerusalem is richly ornamented in the Moslem style. One of the most holy shrines of Islam, this great mosque came under Israeli administration in 1967. Control of it is one of the many touchy problems still unresolved in the Arab-Israeli confrontation.

Jordan's famous Arab Legion was trained by a legendary Englishman, General John Bagot Glubb, known as "Glubb Pasha." One of the results of his efforts is the unusual sight of a Jordanian soldier piping "Retreat" on a true Scottish bagpipe.

TURKISH DOMINATION

In the meantime, invaders from Central Asia had conquered much of the Middle East. One group, the Ottoman Turks, had occupied Anatolia and parts of Persia. By 1516, they had annexed Syria, Jordan and Palestine. The Ottoman Turks, although they had adopted Islam, reigned as cruel lords for 400 years. It was 400 years of hate, corruption and neglect. They seized power, collected taxes, imposed restrictions, denying the people health and medical care, and education. Jordan, Palestine and Syria were poverty stricken and their inhabitants lived like slaves. The only development of worth made by the Turks was the Hejaz Railway which ran from Turkey to Aleppo in Syria, over to Damascus, down to Amman and ended in Medina, the Moslem pilgrimage city in Saudi Arabia. Turkish occupation of Jordan lasted until the end of World War I in 1918.

WORLD WAR I

As early as 1914, the Hashemites (direct descendants of the Prophet Mohammed) aspired to regain independence from Turkey. Sherif Hussein, a Hashemite who was Emir of Hejaz (the part of Arabia including the holy cities of Mecca and Medina), undertook the task of appealing to the Ottomans for self-rule. His appeal was in vain, and persecutions of the Arabs by the Turks resulted. Sherif Hussein, through his sons, contacted the Allies and an Arab revolt against the Turks was planned, to take place in 1916. Within 3 months after the revolt began, the Arab forces led by Hussein's sons forced a surrender from the Turkish garrisons with the exception of the one at Medina.

An independent Arab state was formed in Hejaz and Sherif Hussein was proclaimed King. After this event thousands of Arabs from other countries joined the Arab armies and fought on the side of the Allies, led by Emir Faisal, a son of Hussein, who captured Aqaba in July, 1917. This army also aided the British Army in Palestine by cutting off Turkish communications along the Hejaz Railway. Later all of what is now included in Jordan and Syria was conquered by the Arabs and British together.

FORMATION OF TRANS-JORDAN

Emir Faisal established an Arab government in October, 1918, at Damascus. Britain and France then declared their intention of dividing Syria, Palestine and Trans-Jordan into French and British spheres of influence. In July, 1920, French forces advanced from Lebanon, occupied Damascus and expelled Emir Faisal. Quarrelsome peace negotiations followed and two documents came to light which caused great shock to the Arabs.

This water trough is fed by a spring which the Bedouins call "Lawrence's Well," after the English desert hero, who often camped near the spring.

SECRET AGREEMENTS

The first document was the Sykes-Picot Agreement made secretly in 1916 between the French and the British. The second document was the Balfour Declaration in which the British said they "looked with favour" upon the creation of a "national home for Jewish people" in Palestine.

This appeared to be unbelievable to the Arabs and a double blow to them. They discovered that they were not going to have complete Arab independence and learned that the Arab Middle East was to be divided, according to the Sykes-Picot Agreement into a French and a British Mandate.

Trans-Jordan had been administered by the Arab government in Damascus. In October, 1920, Emir Abdullah (another son of Hussein) arrived at Ma'an, a town in southern Jordan, at the head of an Arab force. In response to the wishes of the people of Trans-Jordan, the Emir entered Amman in March, 1921, and established an Arab government there.

THE NEW STATE

Britain did not wholly relinquish control of Trans-Jordan, however. A British resident, with a staff of British advisers, was installed in Amman and remained there until after World War II. During the war Trans-Jordan actively supported the Allies, through its army, the Arab Legion. Emir Abdullah was proclaimed King in 1946 and a new constitution replaced the old one. The country at long last had full sovereignty.

On May 15, 1948, Britain relinquished its mandate over Palestine and the new state of Israel was proclaimed, formed from parts of the mandate. Immediately the surrounding Arab states attacked the new nation. These countries were allied in the League of Arab States, formed in 1945, including Egypt, Syria, Lebanon, Iraq and Trans-Jordan.

After the cessation of hostilities between the Arabs and the Jews in Palestine in 1949, the Jordanian Parliament representing Central Arab Palestine and Trans-Jordan, approved the union of these two regions, forming one country. The new state was called "The Hashemite Kingdom of Jordan." Of the two regions, Palestine was then known as "West Bank" and the other, Trans-Jordan, became the "East Bank" of today. The holy city of Jerusalem was divided in two by the armistice demarcation line of 1949. The newly formed government of Jordan, at its first parliamentary session in 1951, drew up a constitution.

THE ASSASSINATION

In 1951, King Abdullah, on a visit to Jerusalem accompanied by his grandson, Prince Hussein, went for prayers to Aqsa Mosque. There he was assassinated, apparently by Arab terrorists, while the young prince was unharmed. The shock to Jordanians was so great, a crisis existed during which time Abdullah's son Talal was crowned King. Because of ill health, King Talal later abdicated and was succeeded by his son, Hussein, then 17 years old.

King Hussein, in military uniform, is ready to make a radio speech shortly after ascending the throne of Jordan.

The courage and informality of King Hussein (here at the wheel of one of his many cars) has won the support of the Jordanian people.

HUSSEIN'S REIGN

Three times, after Hussein ascended the throne, Egypt and Syria went to war with Israel—in 1956, 1967 and in 1973. In all these encounters, the Jordanian king managed to keep Jordanian participation to a minimum. Hussein's rule has been jeopardized by the presence of large numbers of Palestinian Arab refugees in the East Bank area of Jordan. His attempts to curtail their activities have brought him close to being assassinated more than once.

Due largely to Hussein's leadership, Jordan by 1975 was among the most stable nations of the Middle East. This stability led dozens of large foreign firms to open offices in Amman.

Palestinian Arab refugees wait outside a clinic in a refugee camp near Amman.

King Hussein and Crown Prince Hassan (second from right) join in a dance with enlisted men of the Jordanian Army.

3. GOVERNMENT

THE CONSTITUTION of the Hashemite Kingdom declares Jordan to be an hereditary monarchy under the King, who has powers over the legislative, executive and judicial branches.

THE KING

King Hussein, born in 1935, first son of King Talal, selected by his father to take his place while still a minor in 1952, formally ascended the throne of the Hashemite Kingdom in 1953.

Years later, King Hussein told about his grandfather's assassination in his biography. One could sense the sorrow in his remarks. The mental shock had prepared him for a possible similar attempt, and therefore he resolved to live his life to the fullest each day, knowing it could well be his last.

Apart from his courage the King is a sports enthusiast—he flies his own plane, is an amateur radio operator, enjoys miniature car racing and all forms of water sports. Like other fathers he takes his children on picnics, is

King Hussein is an enthusiastic pilot and usually flies his own plane.

Hussein chose his youngest brother, Prince Hassan, who was proclaimed Crown Prince of the Hashemite Kingdom on April 1st, 1965.

THE LEGISLATURE

The legislature is composed of two branches, both of whose members are notables of the Al-Ayan clan, selected by the Prime Minister, who in turn is chosen by the King, subject to parliamentary approval, as is the cabinet. The King wields final powers over the legislature, however. Elections for deputies are held every 4 years. Political parties are banned, but all men 18 years of age or older may vote, provided they meet certain legal standards; excepted are the men of the royal family. About 75 per cent of the eligible citizens vote.

proud of their efforts and will not allow them preferential treatment because they are of royal blood—they must earn their credits, prizes and high marks.

Though the monarchy is hereditary, the King may select whom he wishes for his heir, provided he is of the same royal blood.

The cabinet acts and supervises the work of the different sections of the government and establishes general policy. In the years previous to 1957 (when parties were banned), there were numerous political parties, including the Moslem Brotherhood, Communists, Arab Ba'th, Socialists, the Liberation Movement and the Community Party, but their membership was very limited.

Ladies of the royal family include (left) Princess Alia, only child of King Hussein's first marriage, Princess Basma (middle) and (right) his second wife, Princess Muna (from whom he is now divorced).

Crown Prince Hassan of Jordan (right) and his guest, the Crown Prince of Bahrain, drink orange juice at a meeting. Notice the engraved hilt of the golden sword, always worn tucked in a leather belt.

JUDICIARY

Judges for the judiciary are appointed (or dismissed) by royal decree and the judiciary is constitutionally independent of the other branches. There are three classes of courts. The first consists of regular courts, including magistrates courts, courts of the first instance and courts of appeals and cassation in Amman, which hear appeals from lower courts. The con-stitution provides for a Special Council which interprets laws and passes on their con-stitutionality.

The second category is made up of religious courts for both Moslems and non-Moslems; these have jurisdiction over matters of a personal nature such as marriage and divorce. The third category consists of special courts, such as land, government, property, municipal, custom and tax courts.

The Queen Mother, Queen Zein (left) is revered by Jordanians as the mother of their very popular King.

Camels of a desert patrol rest while Camel Corps police visit a Bedouin tent.

SOCIAL AND ECONOMIC POLICIES

Jordan is in the midst of a struggle for power in a whirling mass of Middle East problems, bounded by Israel, an enemy that would prefer to be a friend on the West, and by Syria and Iraq (who are not so friendly to Jordan) to the north and east. Within Jordan's own borders there are tensions and cliques and different ideologies (which exist throughout all Arab lands) and the struggle between them often erupts. The Jordanian government attempts at all times to foster loyalty and seeks to accelerate social changes. Schemes have been initiated to raise the standard of living, with better housing, free education for all and increased medical care. The government strives to offer alternatives to the leftist aims and theories that are just beginning to affect the Arab world. In spite of jealousies and constant intrigues, not to mention the influx of refugees, social improvements have proceeded in an uninterrupted manner.

GOVERNORATES

Jordan is divided into 8 administrative units called governorates, which in turn are divided into districts and sub-districts. The Minister of the Interior chooses a worthy official to head each governorate. Generally it is a local

At Amman's Roman Theatre a match is in progress between a Jordanian Army boxer and a member of a visiting group from the United States.

Another of the pilgrimage sites in the disputed West Bank region is the Mount of Temptations, near Jericho, where Christ is said to have fasted 40 days and 40 nights, after he was baptized in the Jordan. Halfway up the Mount, a Greek Orthodox monastery is built around the cave where he fasted.

citizen of high repute who has earned his position as "a son of the people." In this manner he is looked upon as a tribal father. His word is obeyed and his advice sought. In the cities, the mayor and his elected council take care of the local affairs. It is surprising to note that in the West Bank, despite the Israeli military occupation, the former municipal councils are almost all in operation, continuing their manner of administration as before.

THE ARMY

The most striking thing about Jordan's armed forces is that there is no conscription— no one is forced to join. Young Jordanians consider it a privilege to join. Many youngsters today from tender school ages join the army as reserves. Each of King Hussein's two young sons, at the age of 9, took two years of training, just like any Jordanian soldier (after school hours).

It is estimated that 60,000 soldiers serve in all branches of the armed forces of Jordan. The Air Force, though small, is equipped with modern jet aircraft, developed from the Arab Legion, originally taught by British officers. The King is Commander-in-Chief.

RELATIONS WITH ISRAEL

The Jordanian Government has never given up hope of regaining the West Bank and the pilgrimage places which attracted thousands of foreign visitors and provided financial gain. King Hussein has no peace plan to offer for their return. He relies on the United Nations and especially the United States for help in this direction.

Hussein's policy, both foreign and domestic, has been one of general solidarity with the Arab world. He has avoided friction with Israel, as shown by his action in suppressing the Palestinian guerrilla forces in his land. The Israeli occupation and the refugees pouring

Palestinian Arab refugees filled the Muascar Camp in the Jordanian sector of Jerusalem in 1961. All of Jerusalem has been under Israeli administration since the 1967 War.

between the East and West Banks, and discussions have been held with West Bank leaders relating to joint planning.

To the outside world, the occupied West Bank of the Hashemite Kingdom appears to be sealed off to Jordanians in the East Bank. In the beginning of the occupation, this was so. For quite some time now, all a Jordanian or any Arab residing in Jordan, as well as foreign residents, has to do is to apply for a permit to visit the West Bank and families and friends. It is as easy as buying a railway ticket and the results make for happiness on both sides of these man-made barriers.

OUTLOOK

into Jordan contributed to the rise of extremist Palestinian guerrilla organizations. The destruction by Israel of many communities on the East Bank by shelling and air attacks indeed led to the civil war in 1970 and 1971, in which Jordan's army expelled the guerrilla fighters with a great deal of bloodshed.

By mid-1974, the climate was healthier, with a feeling in Jordan of greater internal security and business confidence. There are even some business transactions going on

The challenges affecting the nation are still enormous. The Israeli war and its aftermath created social and economic furor. Subsequent events forced thousands of people living on the eastern side of the Jordan Valley to move to the highlands in order to seek protection from casual air and ground attacks from the Israelis. Jordan is determined to handle these disruptions by absorbing refugees and devoting greater efforts to normalize the daily life of its citizens within its borders.

At El Jafr, Bedouins have been settled in permanent farming communities— quite a change from their former nomadic life.

Old and new are blended in this scene—a woman in Western dress still wears a veil, as she passes new shops being built in traditional Arab style.

4. THE PEOPLE

MOST OF THE 2,800,000 people of Jordan are Arabs, speaking Arabic. In addition to the classic Arabic written language, there are various dialects differentiated by local accents and inflections. About 12 per cent of the people are Christians, and the rest are Moslems. Besides the Arabs, there are small numbers of Circassians, Turcomans, Armenians, Kurds, White Russians and approximately 220 Samaritans, remnants of an ancient Jewish sect from Biblical times, who live in Nablus, on the West Bank. At least 200 Druzes live in and around Amman. The Bahai-Persians—about 200 of them—live in the Jordan Valley. The Circassians are a Sunni Moslem group numbering about 10,000, descendants of an immigrant group from the Caucasus. The Turcomans, a non-Arab community, inhabit the village of Rammun near Jerash.

These ethnic groups present a picturesque diversity in dress, related to the secular background.

Jordan is a country of youth—more than half the people are under the age of 19 years.

Bethlehem on the West Bank, now under Israeli control, was part of Jordan when these refugee children were photographed there.

REFUGEES

The influx of refugees has altered the population map of Jordan, affecting its social, political and business life. There were approximately 700,000 in 1966, and 350,000 more refugees arrived after the Arab-Israeli war of 1967. Many have since acquired Jordanian citizenship and make significant contributions to the country's welfare, having uplifted themselves out of the refugee camps. Thousands live in Jordan's 29 refugee camps, part of them in huts and tents, but a good number have small, sturdy houses within the camp areas. Schools,

Many of the refugees on the West Bank prior to 1967 lived in crude shelters such as this one at Hebron.

A tidy refugee camp adjoins well-tilled fields in the Baq'a Valley.

clinics and other health facilities are built around the camps. Teen-aged refugees are taught useful trades and the young girls specialize in fine needlework. Since the inhabitants of the camps by and large insist on returning eventually to their homes, they are classified as "displaced persons who resist efforts at resettlement." As such, they are supported by the United Nations Relief Agencies for Palestine Refugees in the Near East.

The largest of all refugee camps in Jordan is Aqabat Jaber, which houses 32,000 people, including these women going to and from a well. It is usual for the women to carry all types of vessels neatly balanced on their heads.

JORDAN ◊ 181

Bedouin tents are still a common sight in Jordan.

The male members of a Bedouin family are ready to receive visitors—the women remain out of sight.

Bedouin hosts instruct a guest from the city in the proper method of eating "mansaf."

A Bedouin woman and her donkey stop at a waterhole at Q'a Disi.

BEDOUINS

The Bedouins of Jordan are among the most picturesque of all its people. Their home is the desert, stretching from Syria and Iraq in the north, to the dimly marked Saudi border in the south. Besides being crossed by ancient caravan routes the desert is dotted with oases and wells from Azraq to Wadi Rumm—here the Bedouin is still king.

There are three principal Bedouin tribes—the Beni Sakhrs, the Huywaytats and the Sirhans. Once they were all cattle drovers, but now some of them have added sheep and goats to their flocks. All three tribes share the traditions of desert life, which are chivalry, courage and hospitality.

They have the greatest reverence for King Hussein. In his biography, Hussein describes them:

This Bedouin at El Jafr owns a house now—but he prefers to live in a tent nearby with his sons, while his wife occupies the house.

Jordan's famous Camel Corps patrols the vast desert areas, aiding tourists and Bedouins alike.

"When I visit my tribes, I sit at the head of the tent with other guests around me. Members of the tribe stand in front, dancing their traditional dances and singing. When my name is mentioned in a song, they shoot their rifles in the air as a salute. After I sit down, coffee is served. Then the chief of the tribe makes his traditional welcome speech, composing it as he goes along. Soon a poet appears and makes up poetry as he talks.

"Then comes dinner—usually a *mansaf* consisting of yellow rice and lamb cooked in large pots. Literally, mansaf means a big dish, and sometimes a score of lambs will be slaughtered. We recline on silken cushions in tents 50 yards long. No women are allowed, and no members of the tribe—even the chief—eat until all the guests are finished."

This is hospitality, Bedouin style. The pattern of their lives varies according to the size of the tribe. Some tribes consist of only a few families, or of a father, the families of his sons and his unmarried daughters. Tribes like the Beni Sakhr often have 2,000 to 3,000 inter-related families, all of whom owe family allegiance to the tribal *sheikh*, the ruling head of the family. In such a tribe there may be as many as a dozen sheikhs.

For the entertainment of guests there is camel racing, while the food is being prepared.

The meal is served buffet style, with neither plates nor cutlery. Desert protocol demands that all eat from the same dish, with the right hand. Before the meal and between courses, bowls of warm water and soap and towels are passed round so that each person has clean fingers for the repast.

King Hussein is never too busy to receive a Bedouin visitor.

CITY LIFE

In contrast to the life of the desert people, the city folk of Amman are on the whole a well educated crowd; cosmopolitan in approach, friendly to strangers and dressed in Western style. Balls and concerts are often held in Amman for the purpose of benefiting some public causes—and King Hussein may donate a car or some other expensive object as a drawing card to attract more participants. In this manner a new Fine Arts building has come into being in Amman.

The King himself is often seen in public in Amman. Passing alone in his jeep through the city some years ago, he noticed a street demonstration and flare-up. The Army had been sent for to maintain order, but Hussein drove into the disturbance, walked out of his jeep, strode in the midst of the fray and casually conversed with the angry crowd. In minutes all was peaceful and citizens were shaking hands not only with His Majesty but with each other. This is the spell of Hussein, reputed to be the most unafraid person in the Hashemite Kingdom.

A confectioner makes fresh sweets in the "souk" at Amman—he always offers his customers a taste before they make a purchase.

THE SOUK TRADERS

A different world exists in the bazaars, or *souks*, of Jordan. Peopled by shrewd but friendly merchants who own every kind of goods, the bazaars have a jovial air, yet serious business is carried on (with hourly tea and coffee breaks). A tourist is coddled—the customer has refreshments on the house, no matter whether he is local or foreign. In the jewel sections, one sees craftsmen ply their trade and wait on ladies with great gallantry. The *souks* have an Arabian Nights air, out of another era, seldom changing and extremely picturesque.

Women in traditional dress proceed cautiously over the mud along the banks of the Seil, a narrow drainage channel running through Amman. The Seil was being provided with a concrete cover when this photograph was taken in 1969.

These wary-looking Bedouin schoolboys are just getting used to settled life in a new village.

EDUCATION

The modernization taking place in Jordan requires a high standard of education. No longer does family and social status determine the future of aspiring youth. Jordan has not yet become a society where people of all backgrounds can advance on their merits alone— yet many leadership positions cannot be maintained without specialized education. For most Jordanians, education has become a status symbol and a true source of social prestige.

The expansion of educational opportunities at all levels has led to great changes. Many children from the poorest families have been able to become university graduates, doctors, scientists and engineers. This came to pass because of the system of free education at all levels—elementary, preparatory and secondary education—with scholarships offered to those who show promise. In the new life-style of Jordan, education has become top priority and schools are now found in the most remote stretches of the southern and eastern part of the country, desert areas included.

Education is compulsory for all children. Books are free and about 70 per cent of Jordan's children now go to the government schools.

Villagers who were traditionally against education for girls no longer object to the fact that their daughters have to sit in co-educational village schools in one classroom. This is due to the achievements of the government as well as the participation and new interest of parents who have come to realize the immense value of education as the best way to fulfilment.

Indeed, village fathers tell future grooms: "My daughter can do more than sew and cook. She is a scholar, she reads and writes and is an asset to you and your farm. With her education, no one can cheat you." This makes the young man take notice. He accepts less dowry and secretly attends night classes to improve his own status. Love and a well stocked farm are no longer sufficient. He has to match her in brain power before her father allows him to accept her hand in marriage.

The Ministry of Education not only runs the schools, it establishes the curriculum, and sets the state examinations throughout the system, which calls for 6 years of elementary and 3 years of secondary studies. Young Jordanians seeking higher education attend the University in Amman. The University started with but one faculty in 1962. Since then, five faculties have been added. These are the Faculties of

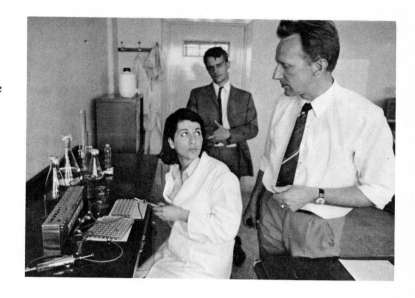

United Nations livestock experts work with a Jordanian woman laboratory assistant in examining samples of chicken blood.

Science, Economics and Commerce, Medicine and Islamic Law. From an original enrolment of 167 men and 18 young ladies, the student body had grown to 4,700 by mid-1974. New buildings are under construction for post-graduate study in social sciences, geology and antiquities, as well as a mosque and another library.

COLLEGE OF SHARIAH

This is the new faculty of Islamic Law. It is unusual, for no system exists to prepare clerics in Islam. A student must truly want to be a teacher, a preacher or a religious judge in Islam. Formerly young Jordanians had to go to Egypt and live and study at the Al Azhar University of Islamic studies in Cairo. The Government aimed to keep Jordanian youth at home, by creating the Shariah, where education and living expenses are given free. There are opportunities for immediate assignments upon completion of the 4-year course, which confers a bachelor's degree in religion. Some graduates become judges in Islamic courts of law, others will be speakers and preachers in the mosques.

OTHER SCHOOLS

Other educational facilities are the Banking Institute, the Television and Audio-Visual Apparatus Centre, and the School Health Divisions and Teacher Training Colleges. There are also private schools and missionary schools. Always crowded is the Agricultural Training Institute, where the students, many of whose forefathers were farmers who considered school-learning a waste of time, now absorb all the knowledge they can.

A large number of vocational schools including nursing and military institutes exist besides private and missionary schools. The impact of the 1967 war curtailed new projects that had commenced for children on the West Bank and in Jerusalem.

LIBRARIES

In Amman there are many libraries filled with books in Arabic, English and other languages. The American Embassy has a fine library open to the public, with current American magazines as well as books for pleasure or study. Other embassies have small libraries filled with literature in their own language.

CULTURE

Jordan's most famous poet is the late Mustafa Wahbah at-Tal, whose poetry ranks him among the most important Arab poets of the 20th century. Government efforts have been directed toward promoting the arts, under the guidance of the Ministry of Culture and Information. A fine art gallery is open every day in Amman and there is an archeological museum there, also. Due to strong Western influence, traditional Islamic art is not as abundant as in former years. However, there is a great deal of Islamic decoration in architectural design, though it is mixed with the artisans' desire for today's modernity.

FESTIVALS

In the big cities, as well as in the villages, weddings call for dances and a festival which lasts for days on end. There are special songs for all occasions—for births, funerals, weddings, circumcisions, sowing, planting, plowing and harvesting. The festivals for harvesting are traditional rituals. Jordanians would not harvest without them and all the family, along with relatives, take part. Many dances begin with the pounding of feet on the floor to mark the rhythm—this is called the *debkah*. The dance known as the Sahjeh is the one performed by the Bedouins, while the Circassians have their own sword dance. Like the gypsies, the Circassians create dances to match their mood. The government has formed a national Circassian troupe that goes from town to town and also appears on television, while their songs are played on the radio.

A girl in elaborate costume performs the "debkah," Jordan's most popular folk dance.

When the desert patrol comes to call upon the Sheikh of the local Bedouin tribe, it is a highly ritualized occasion. While sheep are killed and cooked, the guests are entertained with camel races. When the meat and rice are done, everyone is seated on layers of spread blankets under the tent, and the huge trays of meat and rice or "mansafs" are brought in, hot and highly seasoned.

FOOD

Jordanian cuisine is hearty and satisfying. Many Western-style restaurants have opened in recent years, featuring American and European specialities, but they also proudly feature Jordanian dishes. In Aqaba, fish dishes are popular—charcoal-broiled, highly seasoned —especially shrimp and lobster caught in the Red Sea. Jordanians enjoy *mansaf*, which is a dish of lamb, sweet peas and yellow-gold rice, cooked long and simmered well. Food is never undercooked in Jordan, but is always well done.

Dinner in a prosperous Jordanian home may begin with appetizers, such as small shish-kebabs, roasted sardines and tiny meat balls, accompanied by conversation. The meal itself starts with a spicy cup of soup, a combination of lamb broth and onions with green peppers. This may be followed by *mansaf* or by thick chick peas or quite often roast lamb. The dessert may be anything from a chocolate pudding, a very sweet coconut dish, or a flan, followed by fresh fruit and thick, dark, pungent Bedouin coffee, without which a meal is never complete.

The Jordanians enjoy beer—they toss down olives and nuts with it any time of the day. Jordanians delight in cold drinks. Small clay barrels hold home-made fruit concoctions, sold in stalls in every city and hamlet. These beverages are made from papaya, sugar cane, pineapple, oranges and lemons. Between the beer and the fruit drinks, one never goes thirsty in Jordan.

Acres of slums along the Seil in the heart of Amman have been cleared to make way for new construction. Here the Seil is in the process of being roofed over.

HEALTH AND WELFARE

In former times, health and welfare services were dispensed by private organizations. It was only in 1951 that a Ministry of Social Affairs was established in Jordan, which now supervises 350 social and charitable organizations, and administers welfare projects.

Infectious diseases have been brought under control and a national health insurance plan covering medical, dental and eye care is available at a very modest cost. Those who cannot afford it are treated free. Excellent hospitals and clinics exist in Amman and all the larger cities. The villages are supplied with rural medical services and visiting nurses.

The Ministry of Health has upgraded an old school of nursing into a college to train nurses. Instruction is in English, although the students must be Jordanian citizens between 17 and

The town of Jubeyha is one of many communities built in recent years in the Amman metropolitan area.

Not a swimming pool, this is a small reservoir in the middle of new housing at El Jafr.

25 years of age. They are offered free tuition and all maintenance, plus a comfortable stipend. After graduation, they work for the Ministry as visiting nurses. The Ministry of Defence has a similar institution whose graduates work in the hospitals of the Jordanian Army. There are also medical clinics in all the refugee camps.

The Social Ministry trains young men and women for family care, social work, child care and community and individual welfare. The social development of the country is furthered by the Jordan Institute of Social Work, where specialists are trained in research, general economics, social statistics and social surveys.

HOUSING

Housing in Jordan is still inadequate, even though new construction goes on without interruption. In the 1960's many families were found to be living in one room. Even today, most of the newer dwellings are available for people in the middle-income range.

The Housing Corporation, established in 1965, is trying to alleviate this problem, knowing that about 14,000 houses for the very low-income groups must be under construction each year. So far about 6,000 houses annually have been completed, a step in the right direction for the working class.

Not all of Jordan's reservoirs are new— north of Jerash are Roman pools built 20 centuries ago over springs, to provide water for the city.

The Palace of Culture is one of the main structures at Hussein Youth City.

HUSSEIN YOUTH CITY

King Hussein envisioned this vast complex when he proposed this city within a city as a meeting place for youth of all ages, hoping that eventually it will attract the Olympic Games to Amman. Located just outside Amman, Hussein Youth City today embraces activities such as exhibitions, concerts, lectures and all types of athletics. It was completed in 1972 after 8 years of intense and careful construction.

Built to exacting international standards, with the Jordanian government donating 94.3 acres (37.7 hectares) of land, the Youth City grew with the help of donations from the people. Schools, scouts and the general public raised money for its inception with the help of a committee appointed by the King. Construction was handled by Jordanian firms who used mostly fine Jordanian tiles, marble, cement and asphalt, following the plans of British architects.

The seating section holds 2,500 spectators. Green and red marble walls reflect the hues of the country's flag. The cultural building with theatre, press, radio and conference rooms is an impressive sight, while the football field has a carpet of grass and extensive illumination for night sports. The swimming pools meet Olympic standards, and there are even small ones for small children. Lunch spots range from grandiose to cafeterias. Surrounding this vast complex are 30,000 trees.

The massive ruins of the Temple of Jupiter at Baalbek, Lebanon, are seen against the snow-covered Anti-Lebanon range.

A

Lebanese schoolboys wearing smocks file into their classroom in Beirut.

The Ministry of Finance and Petroleum in Kuwait gleams, appropriately, like a great block of gold against the night sky.

B

The tall clock tower of Al-Sief Palace dominates Kuwait Harbour. The palace is the official residence of the Emir of Kuwait.

C

A mule driver rests his animals in the shade close to the façade of one of the colossal buildings carved from solid rock at Petra, Jordan.

D

Feluccas sail along a Nile canal in Egypt.

A guide explains inscriptions on a mighty pillar at the Temple of Karnak, Egypt.

E

Pilgrims from as far away as Morocco and Indonesia throng the courtyard of the Great Mosque at Mecca, Saudi Arabia. The black pavilion at the right houses the Holy Kaaba.

F

(Above) Oil revenues have brought modern highways and acres of greenery to Bahrain. (Below) Girls of northern Iraq engage in a traditional dance.

G

The International Airport at Doha, capital of Qatar, is a transport hub of the middle East.

The Arabian oryx was nearly exterminated by the mid-20th century. These, at the Al-Ain Zoo, Abu Dhabi, United Arab Emirates, are part of one of the few remaining herds.

H

With United Nations aid, the Baq'a Valley is being turned into irrigated fields like these.

5. ECONOMY

THE HASHEMITE Kingdom's chief natural resources are land and water, and therefore it is only natural that its major economic activity is agriculture and at least one third of the active population takes part in it. However, Jordanian agriculture in part is unstable because a large proportion of the total agricultural output comes from dry farming in areas which have numerous droughts. Special emphasis has been given in the past and in the present to irrigation schemes, soil and water projects which have raised quotas of drought-resistant crops in areas where irrigation is not possible.

AGRICULTURE

Steady improvement and increased cultivation have rewarded the Ministry of Agriculture's efforts. Annual fruit and vegetable production has risen from an average of 196,000 tons (176,400 tonnes) in the 1950's to above 550,000 tons (495,000 tonnes), with tomatoes and eggplants in the lead. Melons, cabbages, cucumbers and rice are the most popular food for Jordanians, and olives and nuts are also major crops. The country has attained self-sufficiency in most of its produce, and even exports large quantities to other countries.

MINING

Jordan's most important minerals are phosphates and limestone (for cement). Since the Dead Sea contains many dissolved minerals, the recovery of potash and magnesium is carried on. Clays, copper ore and silica are plentiful. Other minerals of commercial value to the land are manganese and oil shale.

Mother-of-pearl is found in large quantities in the Gulf of Aqaba, and is made up into beautiful necklaces and decorative religious objects. Marble abounds in Jordan and ranks high among its exports, along with the mother-

Jordan's economic development plans call for increased export of products derived from Jordanian minerals. Here a government exploration team searches for clay suitable for pottery manufacture.

of-pearl. The phosphate deposits contribute a great deal to the economy by their export. At least 6,000 persons are employed in the mining and quarrying fields.

FISHERIES

Current plans include adding to the fisheries in Aqaba and the factory for processing fish meal and other fish products. The once small fishing village by the side of the Red Sea is to be transformed into a hub of both business and tourism.

INDUSTRY

Industrial activity is diversified and has emerged as a rapidly growing force. Local materials are now being utilized to produce light consumer goods, such as canned fruits and vegetables, cigarettes, pure olive oil, vegetable fats, batteries, underwear, shirts and other light items of everyday use.

There are cement, paper and pharmaceutical factories, plus several marble works, employing thousands of Jordanians. Some of the many

foundries, the tannery and an enlarged phosphate plant have day and night shifts. Further full-time industrial activities include milling, oil pressing, bottling and brewing, tobacco products, footwear, metal production, furniture, glass printing and canning of Jordan's famous cashew nuts and Jordan almonds. Recently King Hussein opened a textile factory which operates on a 24-hour basis. The designs show a craftsmanship that is said to equal the textiles from New York, Paris and London.

HANDICRAFTS

The artisans of Jordan today use techniques that blend methods as old as the Bronze Age and as new as power-driven drills. Reflecting the long influence of Islam (which forbids representations of the human body), designs used in carving, metal work and embroidery are mainly plant, flower, animal and geometrical motifs. Reflecting Christian traditions, other designs portray crosses and images of saints. A popular theme is Saint George and the Dragon. Proverbs engraved in Arabic and

Built on Jebel Ashrafiyah, one of the 7 hills of Amman, this new mosque is adorned with the brilliant tiles for which Jordanian architecture is famous.

English in delicate lettering are usually part of the design.

The carved wood industry is flourishing—its products are purchased by tourists and local people. Most of the carvings are made from Jordan's own olive trees, with the strong grain showing as part of the figure and design. The artisans wait a whole year for the olive wood to dry and harden. The finished objects are polished off by hand rubbing with beeswax, varnish or plastic coating. Imported wood of other types is used to make furniture.

Metal work, such as costume jewelry with religious motifs very beautifully done, is largely silver. However, wrought iron furniture is used a lot, and goldsmiths can be seen sitting outside their shops and stalls in the bazaars working in the daylight, using techniques handed down from father to son. Their specialities are Crusader Crosses and Islamic symbols. Bronze work is also done to adorn churches and houses.

Mother-of-pearl is obtained in Aqaba, where refugees from Bethlehem make boxes, necklaces, prayer beads and countless fine objects which have achieved world fame. Embroidery too (done by young girls who learn it from their mothers) is much in demand by tourists in the form of tablecloths and other domestic items.

TOYS

Toys have become a new important industry. Extremely attractive are the painted and handmade dolls in regional costumes. Earthenware toys found in excavations have been copied by factories which now turn out large quantities. Toys are also made from raffia. Shopping and laundry baskets more handsome than those found in Europe or America are inexpensive in Jordan. Table mats and wastepaper baskets are produced by the thousands in local factories.

MOSAICS

Village dwellings and modern homes traditionally have some mosaic work on walls and floors, as well as mosaic objects of art. All kinds of trinkets are made in mosaic and some are formed into bracelets, earrings and brooches. Cloisonné enamel work is also done by native artisans.

CARPETS

Most carpets for local trade are made of sheepskin and are the kind which the Bedouins use to cover the ground in their tents. The Bedouin can wash his rug, as it is very strong, does not fade and lasts for years. Villagers make many rugs in bright wools. Goat and camel threads are used, tinted in many hues. In Kerak and Shaubak (hubs of rug making), the designs are more Western.

THE WORK FORCE

Early in the 20th century, Jordanian women did not go out to business or work. Even the domestics were men, since strict Moslems do not permit their wives to be seen by other men with the exception of relatives. Therefore, women could not go to work and mix with

JORDAN ◇ **195**

At Aqaba, conveyor belt installations can load phosphates at the rate of 500 tons (550 metric tons) an hour.

strange people. Jordan has since become far more modern and 20 per cent of workers are women in factories. In the cities, elegant young Jordanian women work as secretaries, in public relations jobs, in the television and radio stations and as clerks and saleswomen. Some of the leading families have boutiques run by their womenfolk. Many a lady, widowed or divorced, has surmounted her problems by opening a business dedicated to what she excels in.

The real work force, however, is the male population and the economically active workers number about 540,000. Many operate their own shops with the help of relatives.

TRADE AND FINANCE

Jordan has special laws designed to encourage and promote development by foreign investment, by offering tax exemptions and many facilities. The Industrial Development Corporation studies projects and prospective offerings. The Industrial Development Bank, a joint venture between private and public sectors, established in 1965, provides credit for industrial projects. By 1972, it had extended loans totalling 3,500,000 Jordanian dinars. The Jordanian currency, the dinar, is equal approximately to U.S.$3.11.

The Three Year Development Plan (1973-75) aims at expanding trade by opening up new markets. Jordan is one of the founding members of the Council for Arab Economic Unity and the Arab Common Market. Trade agreements have been made by the Council with many countries, including India, Yugoslavia and the Republic of China.

TRANSPORT

Private transport in Jordan consists of approximately 25,000 cars, trucks and motorcycles used by civilians. Above 85 per cent of inland freight is carried by road, 2 per cent by rail and 12 per cent by pipeline.

Jordan has a main, secondary and rural road network about 4,400 miles (7,050 km.) long— 80 per cent of it good hard-surfaced roads. This system, maintained by the Ministry of Public Works, links major cities and towns as well as nearby countries. Local authorities are responsible for road repair. Syria is linked to Jordan via the Amman to Jerash-ar-Ramtha Highway. The Gulf of Aqaba is easily reached from Amman by the Ma'an Highway, a fairly new road and the principal route to the sea. From the town of Ma'an, the desert highway links Jordan with Saudi Arabia. The Amman-Jerusalem road passing through Na-ur is a major tourist artery.

Into Jordan come major airlines from all parts of the world. The national airline,

Modern freighters from all over the world now berth at Aqaba, bringing much needed supplies to Jordan.

however, is ALIA, the Royal Jordanian Airline, named after Hussein's eldest daughter. ALIA's routes span almost all the Arab lands, and include London, African and European stops several times weekly.

Early in the 1960's, air transport became very active and the main airport in Amman and a small one in Jerusalem (built by Jordanians, now in Israeli hands) received all international carriers.

Jordan's Mediterranean sea trade before 1948 passed through Haifa. The Arab-Israeli clash of that era broke the link and Jordan's outlet became Beirut in friendly Lebanon. Expanding

economy enabled the Jordanians to develop Aqaba.

The Ministry of Transport spends an average of 4,000,000 dinars a year on new road construction and maintenance on arterial highways. Travellers from afar have been heard to remark that Jordan has fine roads.

COMMUNICATIONS

The Hashemite Broadcasting Service, established in 1964, is financially independent, though it is responsible to the Minister of Culture and Information. Broadcasts in Arabic play 20 hours a day and those in English are transmitted 4 hours each day.

Jordan did not begin its television services until 1968, though the plans had been brewing from 1964 when suggestions were made to the government at that time.

In 1972, Jordan opened its first satellite station which brings live news to Jordan's television.

Jordanian television is received in Israel, Syria, southern Lebanon and parts of Saudi

Until completion of the new port facilities at Aqaba, merchandise was unloaded from freighters onto lighters (small, flat boats) to be carried ashore.

JORDAN ◇ 197

Aqaba has been built up considerably from the way it looked 20 years ago.

Arabia. Channel 6 is specially directed to the West Bank and Channel 3 to the rest of the country. Over 2,500,000 Jordanians dwell on 10 per cent of the land in the six urban areas, where the concentration is perfect for television. At least 80 per cent of the population sees the broadcasts, which start in the late afternoon, while 75 per cent of the people own television sets. Since a lot of the womenfolk are still bound by ancient traditions and do not step out alone, this indoor entertainment has brightened their life.

The press is free in Jordan. Four daily newspapers are issued, the most prominent ones being the Ad-Dustur and Ar-Ra'i in Arabic. A weekly is published by the Armed Forces.

Numerous magazines, both monthly and quarterly, are published by government and non-governmental agencies. Some of the daily and weekly publications are issued under private control. A magazine in English called "Jordan" comes out every 3 months under the direction of the Ministry of Tourism.

TOURISM

Tourism is a great advantage to Jordan's economy. The loss of the West Bank—Jerusalem, Bethlehem, Nablus, Jericho and all the other historical and religious places—was a severe blow to Jordanian tourism. Jordan is now devoting all its efforts to restore tourism to what it once was.

The rapid growth of tourism during the late 1950's and early 1960's was astounding. All the hotels were full and new hotels of international repute were in the process of being built. Later these too prospered. Foreign visitors increased from 132,000 in 1960 to 617,000 in 1966 and the visitors brought strength to the economy, besides the foreign exchange so desperately needed. Money poured in, raising that sector's funds to 11,300,000 Jordanian dinars. After the

These tourists on camels, with their guides, have spent 3 days and nights following caravan trails first established by the Roman legions 1,900 years ago. They are heading for camp at Wadi Rumm, where a hot meal, a shower and a good bed await them.

1967 war, tourism fell off and in 1971 a mere trickle of tourists came to Jordan, cutting the revenues way down.

For many years now there are tourist police in all the principal spots where tourists go. They speak fluent English and several other European languages and are not only helpful, but extremely gracious in their manner to strangers. Each year when the Tourist Festival season starts, these police are doubled, so that a visitor does not lose his way easily.

The festivals are advertised extensively with huge inviting posters, depicting scenes from the Camel & Horse Festival in April, the Water Ski Festival, the Jordanian Theatre Festival (May and November), and the Roman Amphitheatre performances each summer, with both local and foreign groups performing.

Tourists pass by the old walls of Amman.

After lunch, school girls relax on the cool green grass of the school grounds.

Kuwait

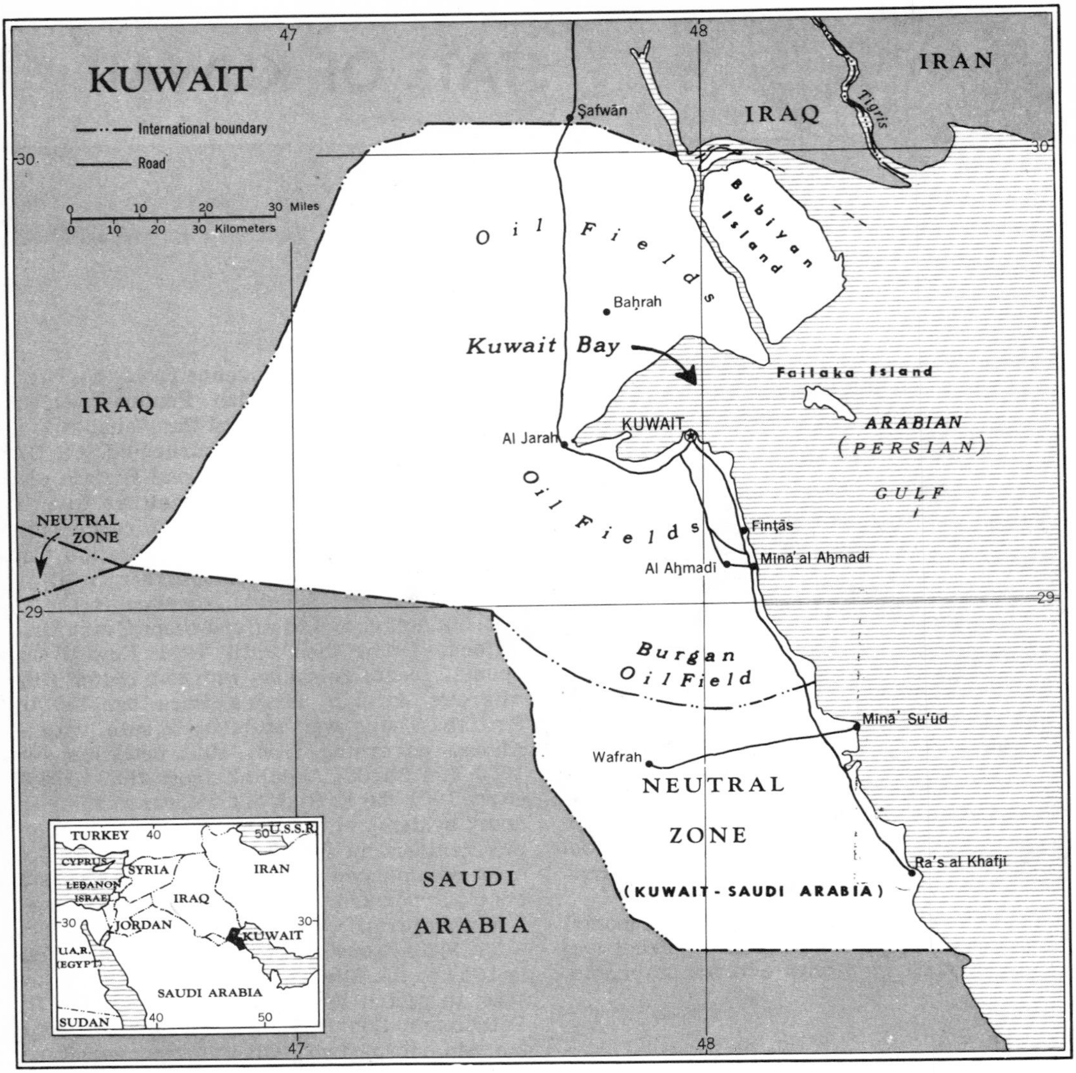
KUWAIT
International boundary
Road
0 10 20 30 Miles
0 10 20 30 Kilometers
IRAN
IRAQ
Tigris
Ṣafwān
Bubiyan Island
Oil Fields
Baḥrah
Kuwait Bay
Failaka Island
KUWAIT
Al Jarah
ARABIAN
(PERSIAN)
GULF
IRAQ
NEUTRAL ZONE
Oil Fields
Finṭās
Minā' al Aḥmadī
Al Aḥmadī
Burgan Oil Field
Minā' Su'ūd
Wafrah
NEUTRAL ZONE
(KUWAIT - SAUDI ARABIA)
Ra's al Khafji
SAUDI ARABIA
TURKEY
U.S.S.R.
CYPRUS
SYRIA
IRAN
LEBANON
ISRAEL
IRAQ
JORDAN
KUWAIT
U.A.R. (EGYPT)
SAUDI ARABIA
SUDAN

A few years earlier this was but a newly laid-out street with no trees at all.

INTRODUCTION

SURROUNDED BY THE sands of the desert and sitting on the world's largest proven oil reserves, Kuwait has embarked upon a new era of progress with a high standard of living, with wealth spread and shared among its citizens. And not only the citizens but thousands upon thousands of foreign residents—scientists, doctors, nurses, the engineers, professors, office staff members, oil crews, workers and tradesmen—enjoy a way of life superior to that in their own homelands.

In the years since oil was discovered, the transition to the bright, flourishing present from a past harassed by poverty, lack of water and tropical heat—has been likened to a miracle. This "miracle" was planned and carried out by

His Highness, the late Sheikh Ahmad Al-Jaber Al-Ahmad Al-Sabah who ruled Kuwait from 1921 to 1950. By granting a concession in 1934 to the Kuwait Oil Company, he laid the foundation of the oil industry. Such was the success of this venture that commerce, of which there was previously little, became a growing and prosperous factor in Kuwait life—resulting in the construction of the great port of Al-Ahmadi, inaugurated in 1946.

Further progress was carried on by His Highness, Sheikh Abdullah Al-Salim Al-Sabah, who became ruler in 1950 and poured the now flowing oil wealth into building up the country —with a share for every Kuwaiti and countless jobs for the hordes of workers who came from near and far. Schools, hospitals, houses, parks, gardens and gleaming ultra-modern government buildings sprang into being. Creative administration brought forth plans for the present and the future, manned by educated personnel and guided by sons of the Royal Household. In many areas the sands of the desert vanished to be replaced by shining expanses of stone and steel. Trees that thrive in warm, dry places were planted along the new city streets. Flower beds began to bloom, and local industry, bazaars, shops and supermarkets appeared as if a genie had rubbed his magic lamp and commanded them to arise. In the once sleepy fishing village that was Kuwait—where building dhows (Arab ships) and pearl diving were the main sources of income—the development which took place in the past two decades was indeed amazing.

Companies from abroad were invited to open offices in Kuwait and gleaming hotels rose up almost overnight to accommodate the influx of people. Poverty was ruled out, comfort took its place, and there were no longer any poor Kuwaitis. Each citizen had a suitable share in the nation's wealth. Special institutions with the most modern scientific equipment were built for the blind, the crippled and the aged. Not a single need for public welfare was overlooked. For children—hope of the future— Kuwait is a fairytale world.

Introductions in Kuwait start with an Arab greeting. The oil tycoon and his drillers from Texas hear the words "Ahlan Wasahlan" meaning "you are so welcome" upon arrival. An air of immediate friendship surrounds them. Then they discover fine air-conditioned quarters, swimming pools, excellent clubs, and modern shops where they can purchase luxuries of all kinds. They can listen to English-language radio and television broadcasts and swim in the sea every day.

The streets of Kuwait have become palm-lined boulevards, wide and spacious—lit at night with lamps of golden hue. People from abroad and citizens, all well-dressed, mingle and ride in cars of every make. Along with the new, the old still exists—picturesque fishermen still ply their trade, bazaars still have an Ali Baba Land look and the Kuwaitis themselves generally wear traditional flowing garb. All this is found in the "Never-Never Land" that has become a reality. All this—and no income, property or sales taxes.

Little Girl Guides of Kuwait pledge allegiance to their land.

Dusk falls on Kuwait Bay, making silhouettes of the dhows.

I. THE LAND

KUWAIT IS A LAND of the old and the new, with the best of both mingling. With an approximate area of 6,178 square miles, Kuwait is tucked into the north-west corner of the Arabian (Persian) Gulf. It is bordered on the west and north by Iraq and on the south by Saudi Arabia and the Neutral Zone, an area jointly administered by Kuwait and Saudi Arabia.

PHYSICAL GEOGRAPHY

The principal physical feature of the country (other than its fabulous oil deposits) is the deep indentation in the coastline which forms the Bay of Kuwait. The bay enables the capital city, called Kuwait City, and other places on this shoreline to attain a position of great maritime importance in the Middle East. About 25 miles south of the capital is the port town of Al-Ahmadi, located on a 400-foot-high ridge. This, and the hills in the interior break the flatness of the desert sand. Rivers and streams are non-existent, except for man-made streams in parks. A further feature are the islands of Kuwait—Failaka is the most important. The others are Bubiyan, Warba, Miskan-Kubbar, Karo, Um-Almaradem, Un-Alnamel and Oahah. The largest is Bubiyan, uninhabited because it is so low-lying.

The interior of Kuwait is all desert, with low ridges and hummocks rising to 900 feet above sea level. Strewn here and there are several

FLORA AND FAUNA

Between October and March, when a little rain falls, parts of the desert bloom, and grass and foilage become plentiful for sheep and goats to graze upon. Plants and flowers spring up; even truffles and mushrooms appear in April and May. Gazelles, foxes and jackals are found in Kuwait, but these are slowly disappearing. Migrant birds—swallows, wagtails, chiffchaffs, skylarks and wrens—are to be seen the year through.

Camels, goats and sheep are raised locally for meat and milk. Fish caught by the small fishing boats are used for family meals and also fed to animals.

Although forests are not possible in Kuwait, there are more than half a million trees which have been induced to grow and lend shade. The government actively supports private persons who try to grow more trees and other plants in their gardens and farms. Already the spreading branches of trees are reducing

oases, which in the spring, with only slight rainfall, become quite green, cool and refreshing.

This vast plant processes sea water into fresh water. Without it, Kuwait's new cities, gardens, and green fields would not have been possible.

More and more crops are being grown in ultra-modern hothouses.

severe climatic conditions in the streets during summer. With or without trees, Kuwait is a cool place to live in, for the country has more air conditioning for its size than any other in the world.

CLIMATE

The intense humidity experienced elsewhere in the Gulf area lasts only during the few weeks of August and September in Kuwait. From November to April, the climate is milder, with a pleasant coolness in the evening. July and August are the hottest months—maximum day temperatures range from 120 to 135 degrees. Occasional south-eastern winds bring the humidity down, and in January, considered the coolest month, the relative humidity ranges from 60 to 80 per cent. Sand and dust storms blow in summer, but winter is full of mild breezes, sunshine and agreeably warm days. The average annual rainfall is slight, varying from 3 to 6 inches.

The State of Kuwait has never ceased searching for fresh water. Though some brackish water was discovered in 1951, suitable for domestic and agricultural purposes, it was thought that none other would be available. Then, after extensive exploration, a great underground reservoir was discovered at Raudhatain. Recently an agreement was concluded with Iraq, according to which fresh water will be pumped through pipelines from there to Kuwait. The present water supplies come mainly from the Sea Water Distillation Plant, built in 1953 with a capacity of 7,000,000 gallons per day. The giant turbines of the distillation plant also produce enough electrical power to meet the needs of home and industry.

The dhow is a vessel used throughout Arab waterways. From Zanzibar to the far reaches of the Gulf and out to the open seas, the dhow sails with the wind, sturdy and dependable. The dhows of today are much the same as those made centuries ago.

Great tankers are berthed at the North Pier of Ahmadi Port.

THE SEA

The story of the land of Kuwait could not be written without mention of the sea. The sea for centuries has played an important part in its destiny, when heavy dhows plied nearby waters and astute Kuwaitis knew how to trade their offerings of produce, pearls, and sheep for fruits, silks, clothes and needed wares. Everything is now easily available in their oil-rich land, but the magic of the sea still exists along the 120 miles of coastline. The dhows plow their way as always and pass high-powered launches with decks covered with thick Oriental carpets. The passengers on the launch may be Kuwaitis and their guests—who look with rapture upon the dhow's teakwood deck—may be on their way to watch pearl divers pursuing their fascinating livelihood, or may just desire to see Kuwait's islands, inhabited or not.

One of the reasons which made the Kuwaitis turn to the sea was the fact that so little grew or could be done in their barren desert. The sea gave them food. The sea was their highway for travel. The sea made them mariners, shipbuilders and natural traders. The sea is still a treasure to them for it carries the oil from their pipelines to destinations far and wide. The sea brings them travellers and tourists from Asia, from the Western world and from other lands

on the Gulf. Its temperature remains warm at all times and never drops below the point of bathing comfort. The sea has aided in the development of the land, a development unparalleled in any other country.

FAILAKA ISLAND

Failaka Island forms part of the State of Kuwait and lies 20 miles east of the mainland, opposite the Bay of Kuwait, and is approximately 8 miles in length. In recent decades archeological excavations have revealed traces of an ancient settlement on Failaka. It is known that Greek ships used the island as a stop-over base. The existing extensive ruins of a city point to a larger population in ancient times than the few families living there in recent times would suggest. The modern people of the island live mainly in villages like Qurainiyah, where the principal occupation is fishing and boat-building. What happened to the original inhabitants of centuries ago is a mystery—since Failaka appears to have possessed excellent water, natural resources, and facilities for commerce. Theories range from attacks by pirates who may have wiped out the islanders, to epidemics.

The island today is a pleasure spot, visited by the Sheikhs in their yachts for a change of pace and even a holiday. Gazelles roam through

Excavations on Failaka Island off the mainland coast have revealed these ruins from the time of Alexander the Great. The island is being developed as a tourist resort, with modern beach facilities, cafés, restaurants and overnight accommodations.

it, placed there by rulers of other times. The island is farmed by the local villagers. Many visitors to Failaka are childless wives who wish to become fertile. According to the writings of H. P. R. Dickson (who grew up in Kuwait as the son of a British consul), the Shrine of Al-Khidr, a legendary saint, situated at the end of a small promontory, is the place these women go to on Wednesdays and Saturdays. The spirit of the saint, on his way to Mecca and back, stops off on those days, according to the legend. Miraculously the women become pregnant, and, as orthodox Sunni Muslims, believe it is all due to the beloved saint in whom they have faith. Though attempts were made by the Sheikhs to stop these pilgrimages, the belief in the saint is so strong that the population has risen to a very contented 3,000 souls and the island has become richer through the gifts of the women whose prayers for children have been answered.

Tourists, along with many Kuwaitis, cruise to Failaka just to lie on its sunny beaches. The islanders are extremely friendly. Dickson informs us that in physical type and customs, these natives of Failaka, though true Muslims, do not resemble the average Kuwaiti.

Among the curiosities of the island are ancient graves over 20 feet in length, considered as graves of giants who once resided in the ruined city. The fresh breezes of sun-washed Failaka, its calm and loveliness beneath a cloudless sky, are a far cry from such legends.

AL-AHMADI AND OTHER TOWNS

Al-Ahmadi, or simply Ahmadi, owes its charming British air to the large number of English engineers and their families residing among the city's 100,000 people. The Kuwait Oil Company has a Display Centre (situated near Ahmadi post office) in the heart of the town. The exhibits are impressive, showing the

Al-Sief Palace, isolated but a few years ago, is now surrounded by modern buildings and a thriving business district.

Students from the Law, Political Science, Economics and Business Adminstration Schools of Kuwait University visit Ahmadi's famous Display Centre and find out what makes Kuwait an economic and social wonder.

The "Nadi Al-Ahmadi" Club is run by the Kuwait Oil Company for Arab employees.

story of oil and what it did for the land. The central part of Ahmadi has its British and Kuwaiti clubs (similar to Western country clubs) flower-filled public squares, and quaint little lanes and pathways leading to shops and boutiques in the pattern of a maze. It resembles a prosperous, modest-sized metropolis in Florida.

The Kuwait Chamber of Commerce Building features traditional Arabic windows in an overall modern design.

The Al Salem Palace in Kuwait is surrounded by gardens and bordered by the sea. The openwork design of the V-shaped panels allows for currents of air which cool the external galleries, while the inside of the building is all air-conditioned. The Palace is used by the Emir for official receptions.

The other main towns of Kuwait are Al-Sabahieh, Fahaheel, Al-Jahra and Shueiba, quiet places inhabited by an older generation of Kuwaitis—who choose to remain in the atmosphere of the olden days, although they have radios and television and keep up with rest of Kuwait with their free telephone system.

KUWAIT CITY, THE CAPITAL

This capital city is different from all other capital cities, perhaps because of its newness and ultra-modern look. It sparkles with a Hollywood air. The streets are never empty and while the busy traders are serious, they have smiling and friendly faces.

Wide pavements bordered with trees surround the handsome government ministries, each one with its own huge parking lot. Clutter does not exist. The supermarkets rival those of the West. The shops and department stores glow, and restaurants pour forth music—often the latest popular records for which the demand is tremendous. Sleek, bright-hued motor cars glide almost silently in and around the streets. Serenity seems to be written on city walls and faces. The well dressed appearance of the inhabitants complements the background.

The effect of Kuwait on a traveller at the airport is powerful. When a tycoon arrives, he is overwhelmed by the delegation meeting him, including his associates and others in the same business. He is escorted to the VIP lounge while his documents are checked, and he enjoys refreshment amid an air of diplomatic elegance, as though he were a guest of the State. Then he is whisked away to either the Hilton or the Sheraton Hotel. The sumptuous Kuwait

The Kuwait Hilton stands on the shores of the Gulf at the eastern end of the city overlooking the sea. The hotel features all the luxuries, comforts and conveniences of a resort hotel, and its proximity to commercial and government offices makes it a convenient headquarters for both businessmen and tourists.

Hilton, next door to the American Embassy, is a castle by the sea, built on the shores of the Gulf, in the fashionable district of Bnaid Al-Ghar, only three miles from the business and shopping district of Fahed Al-Salim Street. From the windows of the traveller's plush, air-conditioned suite, the Bay of Kuwait stretches out before him. Before and after business hours (during which time his luncheon and dinner engagements will seem like banquets), he can enjoy a swim in the sea below, or choose the elegant hotel pool, a sauna bath or the health club for relaxation before the events of the evening.

At the Kuwait Sheraton, other luxurious amenities await, for each suite resembles a private apartment belonging to royalty. There are so many servants around, that the tycoon will feel like a prince of the Arabian Nights.

There are a number of other first-class hotels, including the Carlton and the Golden Beach, run by Lebanese. These hotels have lower rates, but the food and service are excellent.

In Kuwait, beautiful structures rise up

The Kuwait Sheraton was the first hotel of a Western chain built in Kuwait. Each room and suite is luxurious, and the essence of the décor is Oriental.

against the sharp blue of the sky. No two are alike, yet whether government building or department store, the design blends with the new look. The tall minarets of mosques gleam and form exotic contrast to the Christian churches. Touches of Oriental beauty adorn ministries.

The hospitals of Kuwait do not have the usual institutional look, but rather resemble great apartment houses studded with balconies. Inside each one, the most scientific and modern equipment that money can buy, is used for the survival of man, free of course to one and all. The doctors, surgeons and medical staffs have been gleaned from all over the world. The Al-Sabah Hospital, built in the time of the Emir Abdullah is a model institution with separate wings for maternity, physiotherapy, research and related needs.

The Al-Sabah Hospital has one of the largest maternity units in the Middle East.

Spaciousness is the keynote in Kuwait supermarkets. All shops are recessed and shaded from the tropical sun by wide porticos.

SUBURBS

The environs of Kuwait have blossomed in recent years with splendid suburbs—Al-Dasmah, Al-Shamiya, Shuwaikh, Kifan, Al-Fayha, Al-Quadisiyya, Al-Khalidiya, Al-Mansouriya, Aludailiya, Al-Sharqiya, Al-Gharbiya and Al-Shi'b. Two more have just been completed—Rawda and Haiqua. Each suburb is a small town in itself, with schools, social facilities, playing fields, parks and mosques. The architectural design of the suburbs is attractive, a combination of beauty and practicality.

This seal from the early Bronze Age (c. 2500 B.C.) is made of a stone called steatite, and is one of many such objects found on the island of Failaka.

2. THE HISTORY

OIL REVENUES have enabled Kuwait to restore certain archeological sites about which very little is known. Recent archeological excavations revealed an ancient settlement on the mainland, as well as several on the island of Failaka, near the mouth of Kuwait Bay. One site clearly shows that the island was an important port of call for commerce with India as far back as 5,000 years ago. Greek statuettes found on a second site indicate that Failaka was a calling point for Greek ships. A third site, Tall-Sa'ed, dates from the later Greek period, Alexander the Great's eastern expedition in 334 B.C. Alexander named the island, "Ikares," after a Greek isle in the Aegean Sea.

At other sites, yet to be fully explored, some buildings have been brought to light which were completely furnished in the manner of 2,500 B.C. Several of these are related to similar findings on Bahrain Island, farther south on the Gulf. A rare find has been more than 400 almost perfect cylindrical seals, different from the round seals commonly found in Iraq. Some archeologists maintain that Failaka Island could be a site of the Elamite culture mentioned often in the Sumerian inscriptions. A museum has been built on Failaka to house all the discoveries.

During the early Islamic period, the chief settlement was in Kazimah, a small peninsula

The Al-Jahra Gate is one of the few remains of the old fortifications of Kuwait.

at the head of Kuwait Bay, near the present town of Jahra. Because of the natural and the fertile surroundings, it became a trading station of repute, where pilgrims paused to rest from their travels and caravans stopped on their way to Mecca and other towns in the peninsula. Moslem armies were stationed there, making it a strategic point in the 7th century A.D.

Kazimah became famous in history as the scene of the "Battle of Chains," which was won by Arab armies led by Khalid Ibn Al-Walid, a renowned warrior, against the Persians in A.D. 636. The name of the battle refers to a tactic used by the Persians, who bound each other with chains to form a rope of flesh and steel—in order to prevent any one soldier from fleeing before the enemy. This was their undoing, for they were all killed. Kazimah was once frequently mentioned in Arab literature and praised for its green fields, abundant water for drinking and its blossoming plateaus. Today

it is part of an almost empty desert—where just a few old-time fishermen dwell with their families.

In the 16th century, European navigators first reached the Gulf. These were the Portuguese, and their influence lasted about 100 years, during which time they built forts along the coast. To the Portuguese mariners, the place was called "The Grave," while the Arabs called it Al-Qurain, meaning "The Little Horn."

Now preserved in London's British Museum is a map of the Gulf which lends understanding to the name of Kuwait. In shorter form it was called "Kut," which means "Fort." The famous Danish explorer, Niebuhr, discovered the location of Koueit (as it was then spelled) and in his account of it, he described Kuwait of 1765 as a most pleasing place, small, simple and inhabited by hard-working fisherfolk.

Modern Kuwait, which is slowly becoming

recognized throughout the world as a shining example of a welfare state, traces the origin of its present capital, known as Kuwait City, back two and a half centuries.

FOUNDING OF KUWAIT

In A.D. 1710 there was a terrible and continuous drought which caused the Al-Sabahs, who were the leaders of an Arab tribe, the Anaisas, to migrate from the Inner Nejd area of the Arabian Peninsula in search of a less difficult place to live. With them went the Al-Khalifah family of the Amarat tribe, and together they stopped at Qatar on the shores of the Gulf. Again there were droughts and monsoons and they left, hoping to find a more suitable climate elsewhere. At length they travelled in slow marches with their flocks and herds to a promontory, where there was fresh water, the present site of Kuwait, and remained there.

They found it a good place to stay, and decided to remain. The tribe mingled with the small population already there and engaged in trade and commerce. They became as one people, worked hard and prospered. No contact was as yet made with the outside world, though the explorer Niebuhr described Kuwait as a small town of 10,000 people with a fleet of 800 vessels whose livelihood was made by barter, fishing and pearling. The first Emir of Kuwait, Sabah the First, was elected in 1765.

Ten years later, in 1775, when the British-operated Persian Gulf-Aleppo Mail Service diverted its route from Basra, then under Persian occupation, to go through Kuwait, a friendship began with Britain. The Emir tried to obtain support from the British in order to maintain independence from the Turks and the many powerful Arabian tribes, including the Ibn Raschids and the Wahabis. Legend has it that among them reigned Sheikh Al-Nasser, who, hearing of the charms of Mariam, daughter of Sheikh Abdullah of Kuwait, desired to marry her. The Sheikh did not approve and sent word back that he could not allow his daughter to

Kuwait's own "Arch of Triumph" stands at the entrance of the university.

marry a person whose name and ancestry were unknown.

This was cause for invasion, but the Sheikh was prepared for this. He organized a large fleet of ships and Mariam enlisted the aid of her gallant cousin, Salim Ibn Mohammad Al-Sabah, whose strategy helped repulse the invaders. One dark night Salim gathered enough followers to man five huge dhows and discovered the hiding place of the enemy. They slew the sentries and were then able to drive off the warlike intruders.

THE TURKS

On several other occasions, Kuwait was forced to declare war against the then great Ottoman Empire and its allies—who tried to seize Kuwait and add it to their domain. The Turkish allies numbered among them the Ibn Raschid and the Al-Sa'doon tribes. However, royal relatives who lived in Saudi Arabia came to the aid of Kuwait. These were the Imam Abd Al-Rahman Al-Faysal Al-Saud, and his son, Abd Al-Aziz, who arrived after defeating the Ibn Raschids in battle. Together with Kuwait's Sheikh Mubarak, they occupied Riyadh, stronghold of the Ibn Raschids.

Thereafter Kuwait enjoyed its own way of life and its own sovereignty. Sheikh Mubarak was surnamed "The Great" because of his good deeds. In 1899 he had signed a treaty with Great Britain pledging himself and descendants neither to cede territory nor receive agents of foreign powers without British consent. In return, he was offered protection and support and Britain's good offices. After World War I, the Government of Britain declared its full recognition of Kuwait as a sovereign state under British protection.

THE PROTECTORATE

Kuwait held its head high, yet still endured invasions by outside raiders who were jealous of its stability, trade and commerce and wished to seize it for their own. The most famous battle took place in 1920 when Faisal Al-Duweesh, Sheikh of the Bani-Mutair tribe attacked the Kuwaiti town of Al-Jahra. The battle was a fierce one, but under the leadership of Sheikh Mabarak Al-Sabah—whose people rallied to his side—the battle was won. The Kuwaitis did not wish to have any more wars, and each person who could work, helped build a wall around the city of Kuwait, 5 miles in length and 14 feet in height. This was a fine

Modern Kuwait is proud of its youth. Here a crowd gathers to view the annual parade held by the Boy Scouts before departing for summer camp.

At Burgan oilfield, the world's largest, the drillers work in harmony as highly paid employees of oil concessionaires.

protection against further invasion and the wall remained until 1957. No further raids were attempted and Kuwait became a peaceful place.

DISCOVERY OF OIL

During the reign of His Highness, the late Sheikh Ahmad Al-Jaber Al-Ahmad Al-Sabah who ruled from 1921 to 1950, the foundation of the oil industry was laid. Early in 1938, oil was discovered, a concession having been granted four years earlier to the Kuwait Oil Company, whose ownership was shared equally by the British Petroleum Company and the American Gulf Oil Corporation. The efforts of all parties concerned made the discovery possible.

Kuwait took its place on the map of the world with assurance and the population grew rapidly to fill the needs of the new industry. Most important of all, the new wealth started to change the face of Kuwait, as the oil revenue provided the government with capital to build a complete new environment for its citizens.

No production of great volume took place until after World War II. Then output rose sky-high and little Kuwait became the third largest oil producer in the Middle East, sur-passed in the world only by the United States, the Soviet Union, Saudi Arabia, Venezuela and Iran.

END OF THE PROTECTORATE

A notable historic event took place in 1961 when the British abolished their own court system, which took care of the cases and problems of the foreign residents of Kuwait. The Kuwait Government then began the exercise of legal jurisdiction, based on new laws of Kuwaiti design, over all persons in the State. And on June 19, 1961, the Emirate of Kuwait became fully independent by virtue of an exchange of notes with the United Kingdom. Kuwait had come a long, long way since the arduous days of 1710. The friendship between the Kuwaitis and the British is stronger than ever—without enforced bonds. Kuwait with its immense oil wealth holds out its hands to Britain diplomatically and socially, on equal terms.

The post-war period in Kuwait's history is associated with commercial prosperity, affluence and crowned with the construction, in 1946, of Mina Al-Ahmadi, the port which sends Kuwait's vast oil shipments throughout the

The proudest day in the modern history of Kuwait occurred when the country became a member of the United Nations. Seen on that day at the United Nations in New York is Sheikh Sabah Al-Ahmad Al-Jaber Al-Sabah (in Arab robes).

world. Succeeding Sheikh Ahmad after his death in 1950, His Highness Sheikh Abdullah Al-Salim Al-Sabah became the the new Emir, and the young State began to take on an international role by becoming a member of the Arab League and by joining other important international organizations. Perhaps one can say that Kuwait's proudest day was when it became a member of the United Nations on May 14, 1963.

Ahmadi Port glitters brightly at night.

His Highness, the Emir of Kuwait, Sheikh Jaber Al-Ahmad Al-Jaber Al-Sabah ascended the throne in 1978.

His Highness the late Emir of Kuwait, Sheikh Sabah Al-Salim Al-Sabah, is remembered as a friend to his people.

3. THE GOVERNMENT

KUWAIT IS an independent state with a democratic form of government of the type known as a constitutional monarchy, where the rule lies with the people as the source of all powers, and where there is complete separation of those powers into three branches—executive, legislative and judicial.

EXECUTIVE AND LEGISLATIVE

The chief executive, or head of state, is the Emir, who governs through a cabinet. The head of the cabinet, or Prime Minister, is appointed by the Emir. The Prime Minister and all cabinet ministers are jointly responsible to the Emir, as far as general policy is concerned. There are 50 seats in the National Assembly occupied by representatives who are chosen in general elections every four years. The Assembly is in session at least 8 months of each year and is convened by the Emir any time in October. Each minister is responsible to the Assembly on all policies pertaining to his ministry.

JUDICIARY

The judicial system in Kuwait is essentially based on Islamic law (Shariah), although it was reorganized in 1959, when courts of law were established and modern codes adopted to fit in with the necessities and realities of society today. There are two degrees of courts in Kuwait. The first is the Court of First Instance, which has jurisdiction over matters involving personal status, civil and commercial, as well as criminal cases. The second is the Court of Appeals, which is divided into two chambers— one dealing with appeals relating to personal status and civil cases, and the other dealing with appeals in commercial and criminal cases.

THE CONSTITUTION

The Constitution affirms that Kuwait is an independent and sovereign Arab state and the Kuwaiti people are an integral part of the Arab "Nation." It also guarantees equal opportunities to all citizens. Ownership, capital

and work form the basic constituents of the social structure of the State as well as of the national wealth. Freedom of the individual is guaranteed, as are freedom of religion, freedom of the press, and freedom to form societies or trade unions.

DEVELOPMENT PLANNING

The wise policy utilized by Kuwait's rulers, using the vast resources of the land for the advantage of all classes of society have resulted in the fact that Kuwaitis can boast of the highest per capita income in the world! This achievement was made possible by painstaking effort and planning, commenced in 1952 when the Development Board was formed to prepare a scheme covering every aspect of social and economic activity. Electricity and water were given top priority, as no other plan would have been feasible without them. The power plant, started in 1954 with a capacity of 30,000 kilowatts, now has a capacity of 560,000 kilowatts. By the end of 1973, the capacity had increased to 1,096,000 kilowatts. The water distillation plant, which had an output of 1,000,000 gallons a day in 1953 has now reached over 32,000,000 gallons daily. By 1973, the output had reached 52,000,000 gallons a day. More achievements of the plan include 920 kilometers of hard-surfaced highways (which were once desert sands), 90 per cent of which are spacious two-way roads and boulevards.

On holidays, the façade of the Municipal Building in Kuwait is lit up like a Christmas tree, as are all public buildings.

The modern structure housing the Ministry of Guidance and Information is in the heart of Kuwait.

There are now 5,000 excellent housing units for low-income groups, plus scores of modern clinics and hospitals, and vast new market-places for various professions and trades, the Kuwait Port is being enlarged, 580 kilometres of rain-water drainage pipes are under construction; work is almost completed on the vast new sewage system for the capital city of Kuwait.

The Research Station, which conducts research on plants of the arid zones, has made green places where not a blade of grass ever grew. And perhaps one of the most forward-looking projects calls for the construction of a third airport. The construction of the second International field is well under way—with a 3,400-metre runway, 45 metres wide, suitable for landing giant modern jets. When completed in the very near future, Kuwait will have a key position on the world's air routes.

THE FLAG AND SEAL

The flag of Kuwait and the seal of Kuwait emphasize the country's life, past, present and future. The flag flying proudly above all is a horizontal rectangle, twice as long as its height. It is divided into green, white and red horizontal stripes with a black trapezoid against the staff, equal in length to the breadth of the flag. The flag is based on a well-known Arab poem in which green shows the fertility of the land,

white stands for great achievements, red symbolizes chivalry and swordsmanship, and black is for bravery in war.

The official seal tells its own story. The base of it represents the flag. The falcon above it stands for the ancient sport of game-hunting. The sailing ship illustrates dhow-building which made the Kuwaitis prosperous seafarers in the past two centuries. The inscription on top gives the official name of Kuwait in Arabic.

EDUCATIONAL POLICY

Fundamental education is considered of great importance. The aim is to raise the standards of the people, especially those living in outlying villages who need more knowledge of hygiene, public health, arts and crafts and basic reading and writing. Vocational guidance is offered to raise the technical qualifications of the unskilled worker. Extraordinary attention is paid to the girls of Kuwait. Separate institutes exist where the young girl receives training in domestic science, maternity and child care. The new Girls' Training Institute provides young women with knowledge in modern sociology, home economics and secretarial work, so that they may fit in—well equipped to take full advantage of the countless opportunities that Kuwait's expanding economy offers them in various fields.

At the inauguration of Kuwait University, on November 27, 1966, the Emir greets the new and eager students.

More schools and colleges are being constructed and the dreamed-of Kuwait University is now a reality. From the moment its doors were opened officially on November 17, 1966, by His Highness, The Emir of Kuwait, in the presence of ministers of education and rectors from universities all over the world, it has become the pride and joy of the entire state. The coat of arms of the univeristy represents the desert and the sea—symbolizing the State, together with a verse from the Holy Koran: "My Lord, increase in me knowledge." And within this spiritual message lies the meaning of the university. Among its pathways and "halls of ivy" are the men's college, the main library, a theatre, a concert hall and a gymnasium. The College for Women, Business Administration College and Law College have since been inaugurated, and the Arts and Science Faculties are now full of eager students.

The academic life of Kuwait is truly enriched. The youth of Kuwait today are served as are princes of royal families. Learning is a continuous process and the Kuwaitis believe in advancing frontiers without limitations of age, status or nationality. Since oil has brought fabulous wealth to Kuwait, it has also brought the wisdom of the ages in its stride. No one needs to beg admittance to its schools—no one needs to knock—the doors are always open.

A visiting dignitary, the Prime Minister of Somalia in East Africa (in white hat, upper right), listens to a lecture in progress at Kuwait University.

The Emir welcomes a young woman leader of the Algerian independence movement.

FOREIGN POLICY

Kuwait is more than anxious to find a settlement for the conflict between the Arab States and Israel, but insists that the first matter to settle is the disposition of the displaced Palestine Arab people. This is the essence of the conflict and continuing strife, in the Kuwaiti view, between the Arabs and the Israelis.

Kuwait's point of view is expressed in these words, spoken by His Excellency, Sheikh Sabah Al-Ahmad Al-Jaber Al-Sabah, Kuwait's Minister of Foreign Affairs, at the 24th Session of the General Assembly in the United Nations on October 7, 1969:

"The experience of the past 21 years, and in particular the past year, shows that forgetting or ignoring the existence of the Palestinian people cannot serve to simplify the Middle East crisis or facilitate its settlement, but in fact, renders it more intricate and its settlement more remote. People do not vanish just because others prefer to forget that they exist; nor are their rights lost simply because they are forcibly deprived of them for some time."

During the Arab-Israeli War of 1973, Kuwait, along with other non-combatant Arab states, declared an embargo on oil exports to the United States. This was intended to protest United States support of Israel.

Kuwaitis in traditional costume gaze upon the Umm Al-Aish Earth Station for Satellite Tele-communications. The people of Kuwait have moved from a pastoral life into the space age in one generation!

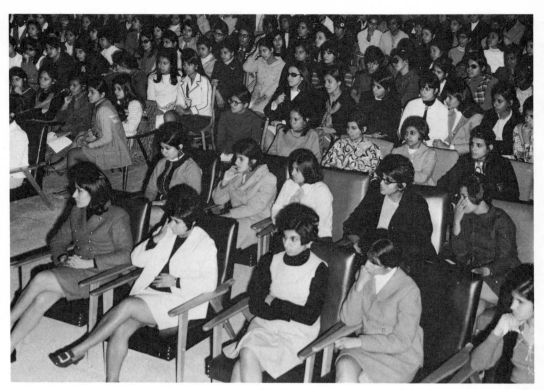

A lecture at the Kuwait Women's Club is attended by some of Kuwait's modern young ladies.

4. THE PEOPLE

KUWAIT, THE MODERN STATE, is unique in countless ways, but the most unusual fact concerning its nearly 1,100,000 people is that more than half of them are not Kuwaitis. Economic growth in any country is dependent upon manpower. The Kuwaiti citizens realized the need for people experienced in science, technology, medicine, engineering and the thousand and one skills required to master and harness the gushing oil and its allied industries. They also believe in human rights. So, numerous foreigners of many nationalities came to aid in the growth of the suddenly wealthy state, and were offered equal rights.

After years of struggles and hopes, when oil was discovered, the Kuwaitis had a leader to model themselves on—the Emir Abdullah, who lived to be 70 years and whose way of life never changed, though his income of $500,000 a day made him perhaps the world's richest man. His diet remained a simple one. He lived on grilled meat, fruit, and curdled milk seasoned with mint. He did not drink alcohol or smoke and was extremely generous to the poor. When he chose, he could make the city tremble, yet he had a sympathetic heart. Under his rule, Kuwait became banker to the Arab world. He shared his increased wealth with

These Kuwait University students clearly enjoy their studies.

every Kuwaiti citizen. When he passed away in November, 1964, he became a legend and his work and efforts were carried on by his half-brother, Sheikh Sabah Al-Salem Al-Sabah, Crown Prince since 1962, who was sworn in as Constitutional Ruler on November 27, 1965.

As first citizen of Kuwait, the present Emir brought great experience to his rôle as ruler, for he was formerly the Prime Minister of his country. He belongs to the conservative group in the Kuwait royal family, which seeks good relations with all Arab countries. Today he is admired as a youthful, democratic ruler who will pause to greet his tailor should he cross his path.

YOUNG PEOPLE

The younger generation of Kuwait, born since the oil wealth began, are a special breed of youth attuned to a background of security

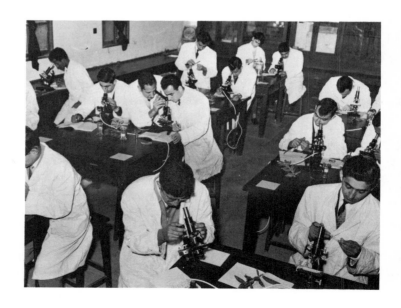

Classes in chemistry in Kuwaiti Technical Institutes have foreign as well as local students— who one day will return to their homelands to practice their profession, and tell the story of Kuwait.

Children in a kindergarten library look at books in both Arabic and English.

and plenty. Both sexes take advantage of the great opportunities awaiting them, and appreciate and accept the bountiful plans made on their behalf. They are smiling, friendly young people, alert to the world today. Those who travel abroad (and many of them do) master languages, study up on scientific data and become more than just rich men's sons and daughters. They are true ambassadors of Kuwait, eager to tell people everywhere what their land is like.

Each plane returning from Europe brings home young Kuwaitis who have made friendships with youths of other countries and often are bringing them home for a visit. They may bring back a country boy from distant farmlands, a scholar's son or the daughter of a tradesman as guest. The young visitors will come to know Kuwait and feel at home, and return to their own lands to tell of the Kuwaiti hospitality, understanding and wholesome way of life.

Visitors during their stay can sample a very special way of living, where nature's gifts and man's technology are combined to make life better for everyone. In an atmosphere of peace and calm, they may partake of foods unknown to them and enjoy the quality of simple meals cooked in part over pungent wood fires, as the Arabs have done for thousands of years. They often visit schools of very high standards, and see hospitals finer than any in the world, where medical care in all its phases is free to one and all. They may browse through libraries designed for the young, or designed for the old. They may hold in their hands precious literature from the days of Haroon Al Raschid, written on parchment. Museums where history is recorded will be on their itinerary. They may tour manufacturing plants, all new, where commodities are made by the most up-to-date machinery. They can watch oil, the golden liquid, pour through shining steel into tanks ready for shipment to all parts of the earth. They

Members of the tennis team receive instruction at Kuwait University.

see business run by private interests, unhampered by government control, and find other enterprises sustained by the helping arms of the State.

RECREATION

The huge playing fields and the miles of warm sandy beaches are open to all for heathful recreation. The less active may rest and relax in the man-made parks and gardens hewn out of desert soil. The old people of Kuwait who often did not have these opportunities in their youth whisper to the grandchildren sitting on their knees, telling them how things were in their own childhood. Old prejudices have fallen away and the thinking fits in with the clean air-conditioned environment. The people

Spacious, modern swimming pools provide escape from the blazing heat.

The Arabian Nights come to life in a theatrical production presented by students of Kuwait University.

Basketball is a popular sport with girls at Kuwait University.

Future musicians of Kuwait rehearse with their own orchestra.

still adhere to the maxim of their beloved Prophet, Mohammed, who urged his people to simplify their lives. "The tyranny of too many possessions," he said, was "as a millstone around one's neck. Rich clothing and elaborate dwellings . . . and too much luxury are but hindrances to man. An elevated soul requires no adornment. A person is elevated with strength and energy, whose life is not cluttered with possessions."

Young men line up for a bicycle race.

From infancy through kindergarten, the very young Kuwaitis are watched with tender care but also with discipline, so that they may take their place in a world where space ships may be as natural as today's jets. In this land, no efforts are spared to inspire the young with the works of renowned writers and philosophers. Homer and Aristotle are among the authors likely to be found on the bookshelves of a Kuwaiti home. When questions are asked by the children, there is always an answer and good books printed in Arabic for reference. The young Kuwaiti today is not stuffed with education, but he knows his subjects well.

FAMILY LIFE

Family life in Kuwait is happy. One for all and all for one rules the day. Together the family enjoys the quality of laughter, and shares tears and feelings of sorrow. Joy and success are always marked by a celebration. Watch any plane arrive in Kuwait's new airport—it looks like a carnival. The family and even more distant relatives and crowds of friends come to welcome home a young person who has had a successful stay abroad.

CLOTHING

At home, youthful Kuwaitis wear Western dress, but on very special occasions such as Independence Day, they proudly dress in exquisitely made flowing Arab robes, edged in pure gold threads, wearing the traditional head-

Kindergarten children play round the fountain in the gardens. They have real ducks to feed!

In a domestic science class, students are busy preparing lunch.

dress. The finest linen under-garments are used, the finest in woollens and silks. As for uniforms of officials and the military, they are modelled on the English fashion. Tiny Kuwaiti boys look as though they have stepped out of the pages of Ali Baba, complete with a miniature headdress to match.

The wives, mothers and daughters of Kuwaitis, who are always accompanied by their menfolk, wear the burka, a black cape which completely covers them. However, underneath they are wearing the latest modes, made by good Indian and Pakistani tailors, or purchased abroad. Often the dresses of the ladies are bordered with family jewels. A Kuwaiti student working for her degree in chemistry or medicine dresses as smartly as her foreign sister, when she puts aside her spotless white work-uniform.

The shops are full of beautiful clothes of the best quality. In the bazaars, locally made merchandise is often more enticing than imported goods. The Kuwaitis use their own ideas in design—and one needs only to look at the New York and London newspapers (flown in daily to Kuwait) to read advertisements of Western women's wear with such expressions as "Harem Pants," or "Caftan," both borrowed from Arab styles. Western women delight in copying Oriental modes, while Kuwaiti women of higher birth delight in the simplicity of the basic Western clothes.

WOMEN

The Kuwaiti women travel these days, from the Minister's to the tradesman's wife, all in search of things which they do not have in Kuwait. They spend summers in the cool mountains of Lebanon, their fellow Arab state. However, the Kuwaiti woman shops in Kuwait, where she enjoys the opportunity to see Western modes in an informal setting. In old days the Kuwaiti woman led a limited life, as in other Arab countries, but life has changed within the past 25 years for her in all spheres.

Modern young women study ballet at Kuwait University.

In many ways she has gained equality with men. Years ago, she was merely the homemaker who took care of the children and her education was not considered important, but that attitude in Kuwait has long since vanished. Kuwaiti men realize that learning and an understanding of life is an important factor towards progress, and that culture and knowledge is the only way for women to take their place and have social standing with dignity in today's world.

Emancipation for women began in 1937 with broadened education for them and now it is a flood tide, leading to the highest opportunities. Many women occasionally wear the burka

The Dean of the Girls College at Kuwait University presents trophies to students who have excelled in sports.

Young Kuwaiti girl athletes demonstrate physical fitness.

because they know that secretly their parents like it, but they are not looked down upon for appearing in complete Western attire. Many young women can, in fact, be seen wearing the very latest fashions from Europe.

Contrary to popular belief, Kuwaiti gentlemen may address foreign ladies. At the October, 1969 debate in the United Nations, the Chairman of Kuwait's Delegation, Sheikh Sabah Al-Ahmad Al-Jaber-al-Sabah (who was also Minister of Foreign Affairs) addressed Miss Angie Brooks, President of the 24th session of the Assembly, saying he congratulated her on the emancipation of women in Africa (her country is Liberia) and praised her direction of the proceedings.

The young girls of Kuwait are equally at home in the world of art. Apart from those who have made design, painting and decoration their career, there are many talented young women in the Institutes of Special Education (which are devoted to the physically and mentally retarded), who are natural-born

artists and show a high degree of skill in spite of their disability. This speaks volumes for the care and interest shown by Kuwaiti administrators.

MEN OF ACHIEVEMENT

One Kuwaiti of noble lineage is Mr. Faisal Soud Al-Fuleij, chairman of the government-owned Kuwait Airways. The accent is on youth in Kuwait, so although he has been in office above five years, he is still in his thirties. He has done much to promote his country's airline ever since he took over the running of it.

There are several talented Kuwait citizens who excel in the art world. Among them, the most noted is Ahmad Zakariya Al-Ansari who studied in schools and universities abroad and returned to Kuwait to work as an architectural assistant in the Department of Education from 1956 to 1958. He then went to Italy to further improve himself in the knowledge of art while learning Italian. By 1959 he was back in his own land and worked until 1962 as an archi-

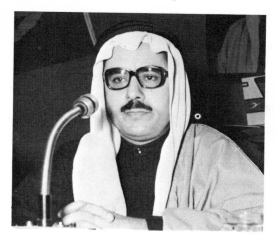

place of his birth. He portrays Kuwait in a human light, covering all nature, from butterflies to moonlight, and his "Mother and Child" themes are of expressive simplicity. Much of his work is on permanent exhibition at the Kuwait Museum.

VILLAGE LIFE

In the outlying villages of Kuwait, old traditions are held sacred. A village chief may own a fine large grocery, built in front of his own rambling stone house, for it is the custom to have one's business together with one's dwelling. Yet no matter how humble the villager, a television set, and the very latest model at that, may be seen in his home. When there are many children, there is always more than one radio, and the youngsters carry small

tectural designer for the Department of Education, later moving to the Ministry of Public Works. His paintings and design, both realistic and modern, show his love for the

Workers' houses in South Ahmadi are clean and comfortable.

Kuwaitis entertain at home with true Arab cordiality and formality.

A Kuwaiti bride and groom can look forward to a happy life in their advanced and prosperous country.

transistors with them even to the marketplace. They cannot bear to miss out on the news of the day and the latest music. Literacy having invaded Kuwait along with its wealth, books in Arabic and English are found in all homes. The most popular book, of course, is the Koran (The Mohammedan Holy Scripture), as important to a Kuwaiti as is a Bible in the Western world.

HOSPITALITY

Hospitality is as much a part of the land as are the desert sands. One cannot visit a Kuwait home without being expected to partake of refreshments. This happens in the shops, too, whether owned by a Kuwaiti or a foreigner— the latter having acquired the habit through living in Kuwait. During fittings at the tailors,

A reception for a visiting Iraq delegation features cakes, fruit, and non-alcoholic beverages.

who are usually Pakistanis and sometimes Indians, the cheerful proprietor expects his customers to have an ice-cold fruit drink. Fresh fruit drinks are very popular in the hot land of Kuwait. This gesture is also customary in the airline offices and government bureaus throughout the land.

Elderly patriarchs, resplendent in tribal Arab dress, are employed by the government especially to serve Bedouin coffee and tea in dainty china cups (or small gold-rimmed glasses imported from Czechoslovakia) to all people who come, regardless of the nature of their visit. In the last few years, an individual

The Emir of Kuwait lights the cigarette of a visitor in his office. Courtesy is an important part of Arab life.

In a kindergarten, very young children are led in prayer by their teacher.

can of fruit juice is offered to those who do not wish coffee or tea.

It is the practice in Kuwait to visit one or another of the various ministries with a request or a problem to be solved. Applicants line the waiting rooms or the inside offices. Prominent people are always taken directly to the Minister's private office, usually a luxurious, spacious chamber. When the Minister appears, they rise and stand in the same manner one does as a king approaches. The request or problem will be handled if it can by the secretaries in the ministry. If not, the visitor may wait and see the Minister or be given an appointment for a later time. The ordinary man with

his problem is content to sit in the waiting hall, since he can chat with other people as he waits his turn and can enjoy a refreshing drink of fruit juice, courtesy of the Minister.

The Al-Hilaly Mosque in Kuwait is approached by a spacious pathway. Five times a day, devout Kuwaitis pause from their duties and go to the mosque to pray. There are many mosques in Kuwait City and its environs, so that no Muslim need go far to practice his faith.

These employees' houses built by the Kuwait Oil Company have a mosque for the use of their occupants.

RELIGION AND LANGUAGE

Freedom of religion is guaranteed by the Constitution.

The majority of the Kuwaitis, almost the entire population, are Muslims. There is, however, a non-Muslim Indian group, some Christian Arabs, and a great many Europeans of Protestant and Catholic faiths. Besides 10 mosques, there are two Catholic churches and two Protestant ones, besides an Orthodox church. The spoken languages are Arabic and English, the latter having become the second basic language taught in public schools.

CITY LIFE

Stadiums at the Kuwait University and the high schools can compare with any in the West. So many things, so many buildings are large in Kuwait, that as valuable as space has become, it is still less valuable than spaciousness. No structure is allowed to crowd another out. Views, fresh air, breadth and width are equally

The feeling in Kuwait is that one is never too old to learn—these men are learning to write in English.

Each of these simple but comfortable homes, built for people with limited incomes, has its own courtyard—offering a degree of privacy highly valued in Mohammedan life.

as important to the land as buildings. The supermarkets are big, and the space in front of them for cars rivals that of famous cities elsewhere. Four-lane drives make highways a delight for the motorist and even the bazaars are opened out to allow more space for people.

Nevertheless, one feels the spell of the Orient in Kuwait markets. Arab traders remain true to their background, offering wit to passers-by with or without sales. A picturesque sight in these places is the Arab coffee-seller strolling along, selling hot coffee from his brass or stainless-steel portable pots and stove.

The old white-walled mud homes of the past have vanished, replaced by all that is new. Inside, most of them have gardens for privacy and for the children to play in. A Kuwait home without a garden is unthinkable. Some have courtyards and all have flowers and a bush or two.

At night the people of Kuwait crowd the cinemas. Television is less expensive, but films rank high in the entertainment field and there are many motion picture houses, one more sumptuous that the next. Music is popular in the restaurants and in the hotels, large and

small; record players provide lilting Arab songs for breakfast, lunch or dinner.

When His Highness, the Emir, holds a fête for a special occasion, such as the visit of a foreign dignitary, all the Kuwaitis living near, and some living not so near, line the roadway for at least half a mile to watch arrivals. It is a great pastime.

Rows of young trees, new buildings under construction, lines of parked cars—these are three of Kuwait's typical sights.

One of Kuwait's handsome parks is surrounded by an industrial and commercial area.

A common sight and one that seemed incongruous to the English, American, European and Asian resident a few years back, was that of the Arab father shopping in the supermarket, and furthermore in a supermarket even bigger and more splendid than any in the United States. Fancy soups, juices, soaps of world television fame, baby foods, frozen viands of every kind, and American and British periodicals—all are available, along with American and British cigarettes.

Today in Kuwait, a young Arab mother will be looking at prices, keeping an eye on a baby at the same time, accompanied by her mother

Kuwait has many smart shops and department stores.

The television studios in Kuwait are manned by highly trained Arab technicians.

and aunt, choosing this and choosing that, filling up her cart with the choicest of things, including the best chocolates, the best cosmetics (from which leading companies make a fortune here) picking up finally, the Arab-published newspaper in English—if the guest for dinner that night happens to be European. Then she pulls out a 10-dinar note to pay for it all, while the delivery boy wheels it out to the family car.

CULTURAL INTERESTS

Culture in Kuwait is at an all-time high. A number of public libraries, overflowing with books in English and Arabic, pamphlets and periodicals, contribute to the cultural life. The Kuwait Museum exhibits objects and writings from the period of Alexander the Great, *c.* 325 B.C. and ancient Babylonia, *c.* 1000 B.C. Animal

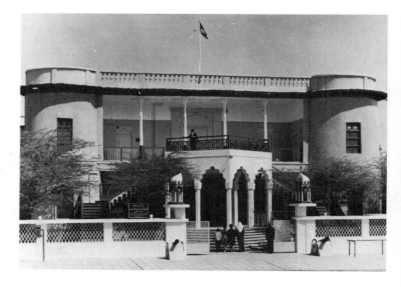

The Kuwait Museum houses a wide range of collections in the fields of art, history and natural science.

New buildings at Kuwait University are connected by covered galleries, to ward off the hot sun.

and plant life can be seen in the Museum and records from the beginning of Kuwait's history are found there, too. The television presents special films of educational value. Music, played on all instruments, may be either Arabic or classical Western. For children, culture is offered on television with special shows, dances, stories and poetry.

EDUCATION

Education is free to one and all—whether a person is Kuwaiti or foreigner. More than 198,000 students of all ages attend Kuwait's 392 public schools with free transportation, free lunches, free medical care. For the old people who did not have time or funds to

Girl guides pretend to be injured, during a lesson in first aid.

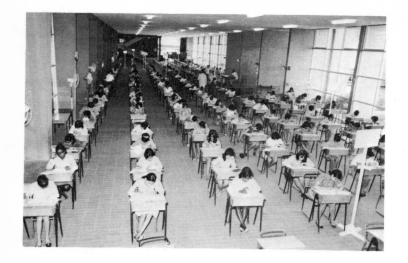

In airy, spacious classrooms, the students of Kuwait prepare for examinations.

Chickens are used for demonstration in this biology class.

Technical students are served well-balanced meals in the college dining hall.

Secondary school boys conduct experiments in a marine biology class. Fisheries have always been important in the life of Kuwait and may become more so. One of these students may contribute one day to increasing his nation's food supply through scientific control of animal and plant life in the sea.

study, there are schools attuned to their needs. Tuition is also free at the Kuwait University for 4,400 students.

Annual exhibitions of arts and crafts show the talent of Kuwaiti people. Music festivals for the blind are held for the enrichment of all.

To see the Kuwaitis at lectures or in their great auditorium or in the gymnasium, where the girl students dress like ballerinas, is to see a dream realized from oil benefits. Culture in Kuwait is important.

The immense expenditure on education

Future mathematicians and architects of Kuwait study with diligence in high school.

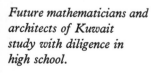

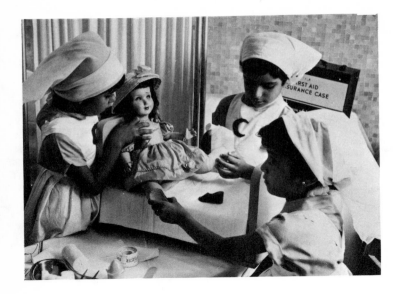

Kuwaiti children love playing nurse to "dolly" and enjoy dressing up for the part. In this way they learn first aid.

represents one of the government's most important and basic investments, and the nationwide awakening covers all spheres of life in Kuwait. Education fits the ancient adage of the Prophet Mohammed who said: "Seek knowledge even if you have to go to China to find it . . ." and Arab children of all ages are learning and receiving skills and knowledge in the most enlightened form, absolutely free from kindergarten through college.

Oil-rich Kuwait is using its overflowing profits not just for the promotion of commerce and public welfare but for the happiness of its children by literally putting scholastic opportunities in their path, with incentives aimed to please a childish heart.

Nursery schools for the junior set have spacious rooms decorated from story books. Shallow swimming pools are geographically arranged so that small youngsters can wade

This music class is very special—the students are all blind!

A block-building session is in progress at a nursery school. The girls love it as much as the boys.

Hearing aids are supplied to students and graduate students so they do not miss a word during a lecture.

from the "Gulf" to "Suez" or any port in the hemisphere. Each child has his own desk with his name painted on it. Luncheons, fine school clothes and medical attention are included in the curriculum.

From the age of 10 years, Kuwaiti children are taught English along with Arabic. At this age the pupil's aptitudes are determined to start him or her on the kind of academic career, with the co-operation of parents and teachers, he or she is most suited for.

Handicapped children attend special institutes, many as residents. Others, who do not adjust to being separated from their parents, are brought each morning in Ministry of Education cars and returned each afternoon after a pleasant day of lessons, rest, training and play. Many students are sent abroad for specialized subjects.

The Kuwait ruling heads are proud, intensely so, of their new modern life.

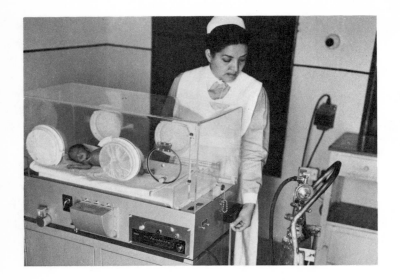

In a Kuwait hospital incubator, this premature baby stands a better chance to survive than most such infants in other lands.

The Kuwait Oil Company maintains this modern private hospital for its employees.

Future instructors of the nation exercise at the teacher's college in Kuwait.

Foreign dignitaries visit the indoor swimming pool at Kuwait University.

Young girls in traditional dress applaud a performance.

A few miles from Al Sabahiya is Kuwait National Petroleum Company's new refinery. Designed, engineered, and constructed by Fluor, it is the world's first all-hydrogen refinery and contains the largest hydrogen plant ever built. The refinery produces high quality petrochemical naphtha, gasoline, kerosenes, automotive and marine diesel oils, fuel oil, and sulphur.

5. THE ECONOMY

KUWAIT PLAYS A rôle in the world economy far greater than its size and population would indicate. This small arid country ranks as the 7th largest producer of oil on earth. Its proven reserves of crude oil, including the half share in the Neutral Zone are currently estimated at 16.5 per cent of the total world reserves. The cost of oil production in Kuwait is probably the lowest in the world . . . about 5.4 cents per barrel. Oil accounts for 92 per cent of government revenues in Kuwait and for 96 per cent of commodity exports.

KUWAIT'S OIL INDUSTRY

Five firms make up the oil sector in Kuwait, four of them foreign concessionaires. The Kuwait Oil Company is owned 50-50 by British Petroleum Company and Gulf Oil Corporation (U.S.A.). The American Independent Oil Company (AMINOIL) operates in the Neutral Zone in co-operation with the Getty Oil Company. The Arabian Oil Company (AOC), a Japanese company in which the governments of Kuwait and Saudi Arabia have

This drilling crew from the Getty Oil Company are at work in the Neutral Zone, an area administered by Kuwait and Saudi Arabia, who share equally in the profits.

an equal interest, operates in the Neutral Zone. The Kuwait Shell Petroleum Company operates in the Arabian Gulf, outside the 6-mile territorial limit. The Kuwait National Petroleum Company (KNPC) is a Kuwait national concern with 60 per cent government participation. KNPC markets the products of Kuwait Oil, Aminol and Getty, as well as its own. It has a new all-hydrogen refinery with a capacity of 95,000 barrels daily, situated in Kuwait proper. During 1968, the KNPC and the Spanish state-sponsored group known as HISPANOL, formed a concern jointly, the Kuwait-Spanish Petroleum Company (KSPC). KSPC has an international bunkering business and an aviation fueling company and is building its way into a worldwide marketing organization.

KUWAIT'S INDUSTRIALIZATION

Established and profitable, adding to the country's economy, is the Kuwait Fertilizer Company, producing annually 100,000 metric tons of ammonia, 65,000 tons of sulphuric acid, a still larger amount of ammonium sulphate and urea. The Kuwait Flour Company is expanding rapidly and now operates a modern automatic bakery, macaroni and noodle factory.

In 1972 the huge Kuwait Cement Company was inaugurated.

Other industries of note are the Kuwait National Industries Company, having a 40 per cent share in Kuwait's Metal Pipes Company, a 75 per cent share in the Asbestos Company and a 30 per cent share in the thriving Kuwait Cement Company with plans underway for a storage battery plant and a chemical detergent plant. The Kuwait Industrial Development Committee has authorized the establishment of 100 new industries, including cement, dry cells, batteries, electric cables, plastic tubes, garments and woollen blankets.

Customs duties are but 4 per cent on all imports. No personal income tax on foreigners or citizens is levied.

The spotless work clothes of this Kuwaiti oil driller and the freshly painted equipment gleam in the desert sun.

This sand lime factory is one of Kuwait's new industrial projects.

IMPORTS AND EXPORTS

Kuwait, besides its oil, exports fish, shrimps, books and publications, truffles, goat and lamb skins, oyster shells, wool, goat hair and animal hides. Last but not least are the pearls of Kuwait, and Oriental carpets.

AGRICULTURE AND FISHING

In spite of tropical heat and dry desert land, with only 3 per cent of it considered worth cultivating for farm produce, the Kuwaiti government has nevertheless started an experimental farm which produces eggs, milk and poultry and also carries on research in hydroponic or soilless farming (growing of plants in chemical solutions).

One of Kuwait's oldest industries is fish. The Gulf has a plentiful supply of fish and fishing has now progressed into a business with profits. Four major companies export the delectable big shrimps (frozen) to Europe and the United States in 118 vessels. A boat-building scheme is underway to enlarge this further and a seafood packing plant has been constructed at Shuaiba.

The famous Arab dhows which Kuwaitis have built for centuries are not the same as the export vessels. They are still built, lovingly constructed by hand, popular as ever, and grace every dockside and sea view in Kuwait. Long before the modern age, the sturdy Kuwaitis were traders whose dhows were as

Imports and exports come and go on the dockside in Kuwait—shipping goes on 24 hours a day.

The Kuwait Agricultural Experimental Station includes this hydroponics house, where plants are grown without soil in special solutions of plant nutrients in water. Plants so grown can be planted much closer together than is possible in the field, and thus many more plants can be grown in a given space.

important to them for traversing sea lanes as the automobile is to the average man. The dhows were their homes and many of them would not dream of living ashore.

Pearl-fishing for the pink pearls of Kuwait is a personal source of income to dhow captains, and each one has his own divers searching for pearls. Kuwait craftsmen are artists in fashion-

This chemical fertilizer factory is helping to make the Kuwait desert bloom.

These shiny new trucks are for public service projects.

ing Oriental jewelry, embedded with Kuwaiti pearls, some of them as tiny as the smallest seed, but very beautiful and silky to the touch. Every Kuwait woman from infancy up always has rings and bracelets made with Kuwaiti pearls. Foreigners, of course, snap them up. Their lustre, a gentle one, never loses its soft gleam.

Kuwait is proud of its own fleet of oil tankers, such as this one at Ahmadi Port.

At the control tower in Kuwait Port, a Kuwaiti pilot scans the horizon for approaching ships.

COMMERCE

Every street corner in Kuwait has a bank. There are foreign banks and Kuwaiti banks, and they are always crowded. A Chamber of Commerce and Industry exists as well as a large number of insurance companies belonging to Kuwaiti, British, Lebanese, Indian, and American concerns. The Kuwait monetary unit is the dinar, which is subdivided into 1,000 fils. Recently the metric system replaced the British weights and measures as legal standard.

FOREIGN COMMITMENTS

Kuwait has a special fund for Arab economic development. Extending aid to sister Arab countries has long been cherished by Kuwait's rulers as a means of sealing bonds of Arab friendship. The fund commenced in 1962 and its loans have helped finance irrigation, land reclamation, grain silos, railways, factories and other projects in Algeria, Jordan, Lebanon, Morocco, Sudan, Tunisia, Egypt and Yemen.

Since Kuwait depends almost entirely on imports for its foodstuffs and most manufactured products, it imported more from the United States than from any other land. The United States supports Kuwait's independence and is extremely interested in the security of free-world petroleum sources in Kuwait. The United States Consulate in Kuwait has been elevated to embassy status.

Kuwait's Long Range Plan (1967–73) involved spending heavily on further productive sectors, such as supply and communications systems, housing and public buildings.

As a member of the Arab League and of a number of United Nations technical organiz-

Shuwaikh Port is well equipped with cranes for loading and unloading cargo.

This airy structure is the Kuwait National Petroleum Company Building.

ations, including the International Bank for Reconstruction and Development and the International Monetary Fund, Kuwait was accepted into membership in the United Nations, though the Soviets blocked it in July, 1961.

PRESS AND COMMUNICATIONS

The Government Press, equipped with modern printing facilities, publishes books and periodicals, directories, pamphlets, laws and decrees. Freedom of the press is guaranteed and private sectors publish two English dailies, the *Kuwait Times* and the *Daily News*, five Arabic dailies, seven weeklies and one monthly Arab magazine. The government issues a weekly official gazette, Al-Kuwait Al-Yom, meaning "Kuwait Today." Very popular is the monthly, *Al-Araby*, similar to the *Reader's Digest*, which circulates in all the Arab countries as well as Kuwait, and which deals with cultural, scientific and literary subjects.

The Ministry of Guidance & Information issues a weekly called *Majallat Al-Kuwait*. The top English, American and European daily newspapers arrive by air each morning as well as those from Lebanon, India, Egypt and other countries. The Government Press employs above 600 technicians and workers, using 70 large modern presses and all facilities for photos, offset printing, engraving and binding. In addition there are many private printing presses operating in Kuwait.

Communications include 68,000 telephones, an automatic telephone service, all operated as a free public facility. Modern tele-communications facilities connect Kuwait with the rest of the world. The first local broadcasting station opened in 1951 and was small, run on a very limited scale. It grew and grew with intensive expansion, including short-wave transmitters clearly audible to listeners in America. Major medium-wave broadcasting already functions. Outside broadcasting has been available since 1962. About 210,000 radio sets are used in the homes of Kuwait. There are 8 radio stations.

Television went into operation in November, 1961, as a 525-line, 100-watt (American) transmission, later shifted to the European norm of 625 lines. Two 2,000-watt transmitters were installed for this purpose on the northern

Among the numerous publications of Kuwait are two daily morning newspapers in English, several newspapers in Arabic, and a number of weekly and monthly magazines.

frontiers. Improvement of programming and continued development of the station is the chief concern of the Ministry of Guidance and Information. Latest survey reveals that about 180,000 television sets are in use by Kuwaiti citizens. There were 7 stations in 1980.

KUWAIT AIRWAYS

Kuwait for the business traveller or tourist is a place of superlatives. The long shoreline is an ideal recreation ground for those who love water sports, fishing, sailing or sunning. People arriving daily on Kuwait's National Airline are offered pamphlets aboard describing all that Kuwait has to offer. Their routes reach London in the west and Bombay in the east and include Frankfurt, Paris, Geneva, Rome, Athens, Cairo,

Amman, Aden, Karachi, Teheran, Beirut and Damascus. From Kuwait one may also fly to such nearer points as Dhahran, Aden, Doha, Bahrain, Abadan, Dubai, Sharjah, and Abu Dhabi.

The preview for passengers begins with the traditional Arab greeting of welcome. Besides, fine meals and refreshments, newspapers, writing paper and many practical odds and ends are offered with smiles. This airline, which began as a shareholding company in 1954, serving just the Middle East has now come into its own. In 1965, the Kuwait Government passed a law defining Kuwait Airway's Corporation as a public one with full autonomy. Its Board of Directors are appointed by the Ministry of Finance, who in turn appoint the Chairman and Managing Director from among

Kuwait Airways employs a fleet of Boeings and Tridents. Pictured here is a Boeing.

themselves. This Board assisted by Management draws the economic policy with long-term plans for expansion.

The Kuwait Airways Corporation (known as KAC) has a jet fleet of Boeing 707–320 C's and Tridents. Progress has been so great that the corporation has been able to open a training school (1967) for cabin staff, crew members and engineers. Catering for the flights is done in a new model kitchen. Last year, flights to London were increased to five weekly services non-stop. The IBM World Trade Corporation now supplies electronic data equipment for use in KAC's Personnel, Accounts and Stores Departments.

KAC Chairman Faisal Al-Fulaij has expressed the philosophy of his company and his country in the following words:

"May God help us in carrying out the great task laid on our shoulders—in the service of Kuwait, our dear Arab homeland—and the entire world."

A vendor of "kaak," a kind of sweetened bread, sets up his tripod stand on the beach at Beirut.

Lebanon

LEBANON

Major road
Other road
Rail

0   5   10   15   Miles
0   5   10   15   Kilometers

MEDITERRANEAN

SEA

34°
00'

33°
30'

SYRIA

36°00'   36°30'

Hamidiyah

An Nahr al Kabir

Halbā

El Mīnā
Tripoli
Zaghartā
Al Harmal

Amyūn
Besharre

Al Batrūn

Jbail
(Byblos)
Nahr Ibrāhīm

Ghazir
Baalbek

Jounieh

BEIRUT
Al Judaydah
Zahlé
Riyāq

B'abdā

'Ālayh
Zabdānī

Beit-ed-din
Nahr al Bārūk

Sidon
Dūmā
Baradd

DAMASCUS

Jazzīn

Rāshayyā
Qatanā

Marj
l'Uyūn
Mt. Hermon
Nahr al Hāsbānī

Tyre
Nahr al Litāni
Nahr al A'waj

Bint Jubayl
ISRAEL
*Demilitarized
Zone*
Al Qunayṭirah

BUHĀYRAT
HIMS

34°
30'

Plain of Bekaa

Orontes

Lebanon Range

Anti-Lebanon

Ante Lebanon Range

S Y R I A

34°
00'

33°
30'

BOUNDARY REPRESENTATION IS
NOT NECESSARILY AUTHORITATIVE

*Demilitarized
Zone*
35°30'   36°00'   36°30'

INTRODUCTION

LEBANON, A REPUBLIC since 1923, has been one of the most important regions of the Middle East since Biblical days. As the homeland of the Phoenicians, the country was a crossroads before the time of Christ and it has been a meeting place of civilizations ever since. It has been a port of call and a place of refuge where different beliefs, languages and liturgies have confronted one another.

Lebanon, the only Arab nation that is half Christian and half Moslem, combines European and Oriental influences; a maritime nation since ancient times, it now seeks to improve its agriculture and develop its industry. Lebanon, land of rocks, cedar trees and locusts, laced throughout with archaeological grandeur, looks down from its mountains to the sea. As the international crossroads of the Middle East, it links the great cities of the earth to Beirut, its capital, with easy access by air. London is but four hours away, New York, a scant eight, while Paris, Frankfurt, Rome, Stockholm and Copenhagen are all reached in three to four hours.

In Lebanon's five provinces, Beirut, North Lebanon, South Lebanon, Bekaa and Mount Lebanon, there are towns known and beloved by archaeologists of both hemispheres. Among them are Trablos, Jbail, Beirut, Saida and Sur, whose familiar ancient names are still used more often than not—Tripoli, Byblos, Berytus, Sidon and Tyre, all of which were great cities in Phoenician times.

Various races of people later invaded and conquered Lebanon—the Chaldeans, Assyrians, Persians, Egyptians, Hittites, Greeks, Romans, Byzantines, Arabs, Franks and Turks, all of whose cultures left some trace. The Arabs left the greatest mark, although the impact of the Crusades was great—citadels were built then that are still used and traditions of that period are still upheld. The Crusaders came chiefly from France, Germany, Italy and the Low Countries, but all these fair-skinned invaders were called "Franks" by the Arabs.

In modern times an Armenian influx, due to Turkish persecution, added an important element to Lebanese life. Ties with France and with European culture were renewed in the years between World Wars I and II, when France held a mandate over Lebanon. The descendants of all these people, whose knowledge, talents, blood and common interest mingled, form the present population of Lebanon.

The Great Mosque at Tripoli dates mainly from the Mameluke period, but incorporates parts of the older Christian cathedral of St. Mary of the Tower. The minaret at the left, which is Italian in style, is believed to be the bell-tower of the cathedral.

Like a scene from the voyages of Sinbad, an underground river flows through this vast grotto in the Caves of Jeita.

The main grove of surviving cedars is at Besharre. Known as "Cedars of the Lord," these average 100 feet in height, and the circumference of some of them is from 40 to 50 feet.

I. THE LAND

LEBANON, "LAND OF CEDARS," situated at the eastern end of the Mediterranean, occupies an area of 4,015 miles—somewhat smaller than Connecticut or Northern Ireland. Actually it is only a tiny strip on the map of the world, bounded on the north and east by Syria and on the south by Israel. The strip is 156 miles long but only 31 miles wide. Djebel Libnan, its Arab name, means "White-as-Milk Mountain." Two ranges traverse it, lying parallel to the sea, separated from one another by the high plains of the Bekaa. Set geographically between three continents, Europe, Africa and Asia, with all of its length on the beautiful coast, it is a true Mediterranean country. Charles Corm, a renowned Lebanese poet has said: "Never in the memory of mankind has so small a land so vast a destiny."

Much of Lebanon's natural beauty is easily accessible—almost any city or village can be reached from the capital, Beirut, within an hour or two. Beirut itself is just about in the heart of the country, a lively, cosmopolitan city with an ancient history and a modern outlook.

SURFACE FEATURES

The coastline from Tripoli in the north to Beirut is rocky and often steep. South of Beirut are sandy stretches, especially in the vicinity of Tyre.

The peak of Sannine, visible from Beirut, is covered with snow for much of the year.

The first mountain range, the Lebanon, from which the country takes its name, rises sharply from the coastal plain, and follows the shoreline from the Syrian border in the north to the mouth of the Litani River in the south, attaining its greatest height (11,024 feet) in the peak of Al-Qurnat-al-Sawda. The Bekaa plain, a plateau 70 miles long by 15 miles wide, lies between the coastal range and the inland range or Anti-Lebanon. The Anti-Lebanon, unlike the Lebanon range, which is entirely within the Lebanese Republic, is partly in Syria. Its highest peak is Mt. Hermon (9,232 feet) of Biblical fame, which lies on the border with Syria, near the point where both countries front on Israel.

Terraced hillsides rise above the beautiful Bay of Jounieh, on the coast a few miles north of Beirut.

Near Besharre is the beautiful valley and gorge of Qadisha, whose villages on the edge of precipices figure in the works of Gibran.

Between the snow-capped ridges of the Lebanon and Anti-Lebanon ranges, the intensely cultivated plain of the Bekaa has served as a granary since ancient times.

RIVERS

The River Litani (the ancient Leontes), which flows into the sea just north of Tyre, is wholly within Lebanon and drains the southern part of the Bekaa. The Hasbani, which is one of the sources of the international Jordan River, rises within Lebanon. The Nahr-el-Assi (the ancient Orontes River) rises in the northern part of the Bekaa and flows northward into Syria.

THE CAVES OF JEITA

The Dog River (Nahr-el-Kelb) which supplies Beirut with its cascades of bountiful pure water, leads to a magic spot—the Grotto and Caves of Jeita, discovered accidentally by a hunter named Thompson in 1837. Stumbling onto the entrance and hearing distant rumbles within, he fired a shot from his gun. The echoes that resulted made him realize that there were vast chambers and a foaming river inside. Thompson was not believed when he

The Pigeon's Grotto is a rock formation in the cliffs at Beirut. Water-skiers gain an additional thrill from the sport by dashing under its natural arch.

From the Cave of Adonis, in the side of a precipice in the mountains east of Byblos, the Adonis River or Nahr Ibrahim, gushes forth. Legend associates the cave with the handsome youth loved by Aphrodite, in Greek myth.

told of his findings, and no exploration was made until 1873, when two engineers from the Government Water Supply Department decided to follow the course of the Dog River.

Equipping themselves with life-rafts held up by inflated goat skins, they started out, eventually reaching the entrance of a different underground cave with narrow and low-vaulted spaces. Their amazement knew no bounds as they entered a high-roofed hall (still travelling on their raft) and beheld fantastic icicle draperies hanging in various shapes. They saw other strange and beautiful arrays of stalactites as well as ice formations of unusual form on the river banks. The engineers, Maxwell and Bliss, continued their exploration into this natural wonderland, hidden from the world for so long. Hours later, after learning the secret of the river's source, they emerged to tell of their unearthing of the caves.

Later the Caves and Grottos of Jeita were visited by speleologists (cave experts), who went along with Bliss and Maxwell to verify the findings, and excitement waxed high when the discovery was made public. Not until recent years were sightseers admitted. Since then, Jeita ranks high as a Lebanese attraction—just 12 miles from Beirut on a winding coast road.

PORTS

The Port of Beirut, sheltered by a breakwater, is today one of the best equipped in the eastern Mediterranean. Its two basins, capable of berthing 10 large vessels, were joined in 1969 by a third basin costing 40,000,000 Lebanese pounds (about $13,000 U.S. at that time), which will now double the facilities.

The ports of Tripoli and Sidon have special importance, as the former is the Mediterranean terminus of the pipeline from the Kirkuk oilfield in Iraq, and the latter of the pipeline from the Saudi Arabian fields.

The Beirut International Airport at Khalde (a few miles from the city's heart) is modern in the extreme, possessing technical installations comparable with the most up-to-date jet airports in the world. Every day there are more than 100 take-offs and landings which is double the amount of 1965, while the total number of passengers visiting Lebanon has tripled since then. The airport has become an important and essential junction of routes linking the East and the West.

NATURAL RESOURCES

Lebanon's greatest natural resource is its geographical location near the junction of three continents, as a result of which the country has become a major point of transshipment and the commercial hub of the Middle East. The great number of tourist attractions and excellent climate, winter and summer, must also be counted among the nation's assets.

Mineral resources are not great—iron was mined until recently, but the veins are now depleted. Lignite (brown coal) is mined to some extent, and gypsum is abundant. A great potential source of energy exists in the country's swift-flowing rivers, notably the Litani, which are being developed for irrigation and hydro-electric power systems.

The gleaming white city of Beirut rises abruptly from the rocky Mediterranean coast.

In spring, melting snows of the mountains cause even tiny brooks to overflow, permitting these boys of the Bekaa to fish in what appears to be a flooded field.

CLIMATE

The climate of Lebanon is Mediterranean, similar to that of southern California or the French Riviera. There are four equal seasons: winter, spring, summer and autumn, with 300 sunny days a year. During certain months, one can swim in the sea and just half an hour later ski at an altitude of 4,900 feet. The climate is temperate all year through. In summer, the temperature seldom exceeds 90 degrees at sea level, or 68 degrees in the mountains, where cool breezes always blow. Between June and October, the beaches are golden and dry, and it rarely rains. The average winter temperature on the coast is 56 degrees, and rainfall is more plentiful then. Most of the rain falls on the coastal mountain range, the Anti-Lebanon being somewhat arid.

In winter heavy snow mantles the boughs of the cedars.

An unusual, close-up view of one of the beautiful Cedars of Besharre. Growing to an average height of 100 feet, some cedars have a circumference of as much as 40 to 50 feet.

FLORA AND FAUNA

The road from Tripoli leads to some of the few remaining cedars, through the village of Amium. On the way lies a small summer resort, Hasrun, overhanging the Valley of Qadisha. Besharre, where the poet Kahlil Gibran was born and brought home for burial, is in a beautiful setting—the Cedars of Besharre are one of the last traces of the gigantic cedar forests which covered Lebanon in Biblical days. King Solomon built his Palace from the wood of the Cedars of Lebanon. They cluster on a hilltop, forming a magic mantle of green, snow-covered in the winter, beneath cloudless blue skies. Some of the trees are over 1,000 years old. The cedar is the national emblem and is portrayed on the Lebanese flag. Near the cedars are ski runs and hotels, used both summer and winter for holidays. A 7,550-foot ski-lift has been constructed by the Government Tourist office, making the area a first-class winter sports area. In summer the pure air, gushing waterfalls and green valleys attract many visitors.

In the intensively cultivated coastal region, wild plants, which are not numerous, include poppies, tamarisks, anemones and buckthorn. In the highlands are stands of oak, fir, cypress and pine, in addition to the famous cedars. On the high Bekaa plain, which is nearly treeless, various wild herbs are found—mostly of the daisy and pea families.

Of large wild animals, bears and deer are sometimes found in the mountains; smaller species include polecats, hedgehogs and hares as well as squirrels and other rodents. A curious mammal of this part of the world is the hyrax, or cony, which is about the size of a house cat and resembles a rodent superficially—but is actually a hoofed creature whose nearest relatives, according to zoologists, are the elephants!

In the marshes, flamingoes can be observed, along with pelicans, ducks and herons, while the higher ground supports many smaller birds, such as cuckoos and woodpeckers; falcons, kites and other birds of prey are also to be encountered in the mountains. Insects, especially locusts, are common; and eels, bass and mullet are among the fish found in lakes and rivers.

In spring the Lebanese mountains are covered with many wild flowers. These flowers are one of the numerous varieties of the large daisy family.

Beirut is a unique blend of the timeless and the ultra-modern.

The business district of Beirut is one of the liveliest in the Middle East.

CITIES

BEIRUT

Rising like an amphitheatre on the hilly shore, against the background of the Lebanon mountain range, the capital city enjoys an ideal climate. Its 1,000,000 citizens have one of the highest standards of living in the Middle East; their city is a charming blend of old and new, of European and Arabic influences, of brisk commercial activity and relaxation. Their homes and businesses are minutes away from splendid beaches, half an hour from cool, green mountains.

Beirut has been a trading city since 1500 B.C., when it figured as one of the chief ports of Phoenicia. Conquered by Alexander the Great, it passed to the dynasty of the Seleucids, descendants of one of Alexander's generals. In 140 B.C., the city was destroyed by fire, and for over a century its name disappeared from history.

The Avenue de Paris in Beirut is a tranquil tree-lined promenade, overlooking the sea.

Cypresses and palm trees impart a typically Mediterranean quality to the many parks and private gardens of Beirut.

Well-known to world travellers, the striking Phoenicia-Inter-Continental Hotel overlooks St. George's Bay in Beirut.

New office and shopping facilities, such as the Starco Urban Centre, are changing the face of Beirut.

The Place des Canons, called the "Burj" by the Lebanese, lies in the heart of Beirut's business district. Beirut streets have both French and Arabic names.

The Goldsmiths' Market in Beirut is world-famous for the exquisite workmanship of the jewels in its many tiny shops.

Occupied by the Romans under Pompey in 64 B.C., the city was rebuilt and once more rose to prominence. Emperor Caesar Augustus appointed his son-in-law, Marcus Vespasianus Agrippa, as governor. The port was reconstructed and trade increased, but the jewel in Beirut's crown was its school of law which outshone the schools of Constantinople, Athens and Rome. The fame and beauty of Beirut spread far and wide and inspired the poet Nonos of Panopolis to call it "Goddess of the Sea."

Two earthquakes in A.D. 502 and 551 accompanied by a huge tidal wave destroyed much of the city. Then, in A.D. 560 a fire completed its destruction. What remained was, during the Arab conquest, occupied by Omar Ibn el-Khattab in 635. Rebuilt once more, Beirut was captured by the Crusaders and became a dependency of the Crown of Jerusalem in 1110. The Franks held it until 1187, and one of their governors, Baron Foulques de Guignes, built the large Church of St. John, later changed into the Great Mosque, the only surviving monument of that era. Conquerors came and went until the 15th century when the port was again reconditioned and ships once more began to anchor in Beirut waters.

The Lebanese Emir Fakreddin El-Maani made the city his capital between 1590 to 1634. He was responsible for pacts with Europe, for the establishment of consular agencies, and he restored the pine forests in the suburbs. After his death Beirut declined, but later regained its prosperity when the Ottomans acknowledged the city's supremacy over other ports on the coast. When French intervention in 1860 resulted in Lebanon's gaining self-rule within the Ottoman Empire, the city became the true capital of Lebanon and from that time developed in all fields.

The Place des Martyrs is the central square of Beirut, and in the middle of the square is a statue commemorating those who died fighting for their country.

A short distance from the rocky promontory of Beirut are excellent sandy beaches, where the city's residents can enjoy surf bathing.

TRIPOLI

With 200,000 inhabitants, Tripoli is the second city of Lebanon. Capital of the Phoenician Federation after 700 B.C., the city maintained its prominence under the Seleucids, Romans and Byzantines. The Arabs took it in A.D. 638, but it was reoccupied by the Byzantines from 685 to 705. In 1109, it fell to the Crusaders under Raymond, Count of Toulouse, after a long siege, but it later passed back into Moslem hands.

Modern Tripoli consists of two parts—the port district of El Mina, on a small peninsula; and the city proper, which is two miles inland, and is in turn divided into two districts separated by the Nahr Abu Ali, a stream that enters the sea east of El Mina. The great Frankish castle of St. Giles looms above the many picturesque small streets that wander off from the Place du Tell, the hub of the city.

Tripoli is important as a seaport and rail terminus, and since completion of the petroleum pipeline from Iraq, has added oil refining to its economic activity.

The minaret of a mosque rises above a narrow street in Tripoli.

The Sea Castle, a ruined fortification built by the Crusaders in 1227–28, still stands in the port of Sidon.

SIDON

Sidon (still called Saida by old residents) is a small city of 22,000, but is like a large fishing village in many respects, and its name in fact means "fishing." Christ preached a sermon here on one of his journeys. The Castle of the Sea, built by Crusaders in 1228, guards the entrance to its port. The ruins of the Castle of St. Louis, and the burial grounds with their catacombs and mosques are revered relics of Sidon's impressive past.

At Sidon fishing boats are beached against a background of minarets and towers.

Ancient Sidon, a leading city of the Phoenicians and often mentioned in the Bible, is today a small, bustling seaport.

Today Sidon is prosperous, due in part to its importance as the administrative hub of south Lebanon and as a shipping headquarters for the oil industry. From Saudi Arabia, petroleum arrives via the Trans-Arabian Oil Pipeline direct to Sidon where it is loaded on tankers and sent to refineries in Europe.

The old and new mingle in Sidon. The townspeople are lively and yet a serenity of spirit prevails in this progressive small city, where the past is always present. A few years ago in Sidon, workmen digging a foundation discovered an ancient tomb containing a female skeleton covered in precious jewels. For use on her voyage to the after-life, a bronze mirror, mascara and other beauty aids lay beside her, as well as a pure gold statue of Venus. Archaeologists tell us that she must have been a royal personage, so perfect is the quality of her jewels. From time to time, such finds remind the people of Sidon of their city's ancient grandeur.

Ruins of an aqueduct from the 2nd century A.D. *are among the antiquities of Tyre.*

TYRE

Tyre (12,000), built on a small rocky coastal promontory, which in ancient times was an island, is today a small, quiet city shaded by palm trees against the background of the sea. Its castles and cemeteries tell of its periods of greatness and bear witness to the skill of its artisans. Recent excavations have brought to light remarkable remains of a city paved with mosaics, and restoration of these is in progress.

It was Tyre's own King Hiram who supplied the 80,000 woodcutters, masons and brass-workers who built Solomon's palace and whose chief architect is remembered today for his skill and brilliance. And it was Europa, the daughter of a King of Tyre (in Greek myth) with whom Zeus fell in love—and fled to Europe with her and named that continent after his stolen princess. Although Tyre today is a minor port, the people of the town still bear a proud air, for are they not descendants of the Tyrians of old!

OTHER TOWNS

Beit-ed-Din, a charming mountain town a few miles inland from Beirut, is noted for its splendid Palace of the Emir Bechir, a show-place whose gardens bloom with white roses for much of the year.

Byblos, which claims to be the oldest town in the world (a claim made also by Damascus in Syria), boasts tombs, temples and ramparts from Phoenician days, although most of the town dates from the Middle Ages—a huge Crusader castle still stands there. Located on the coast 20 miles north of Beirut, Byblos today is little more than a large village. Yet it was at one time the commercial and religious capital of Phoenicia.

The palace at Beit-ed-Din, built at the beginning of the 19th century by the Emir Bechir II (1788–1840), is considered a gem of 19th century Lebanese architecture. The palace is now used as the summer residence of Lebanese presidents.

The richness of traditional Islamic design embellishes a chamber in the Palace at Beit-ed-Din.

Egyptian records show a brisk trade with Byblos as early as 2800 B.C. Byblos was a source of papyrus, the reedlike plant from which the Egyptians made a sort of paper, and in time the city gave its name to history—for the Greek word for book, "biblos," from which is derived our word "Bible," is none other than the name of the city itself.

Arcaded galleries look down upon a serene pool in a courtyard of the Palace at Beit-ed-Din.

At Byblos, the visitor can inspect this royal sarcophagus, carved from basalt, over 3,000 years ago.

Zahlé, with 33,000 people, is Lebanon's third largest city. About 50 miles from Beirut, on the slopes of the Anti-Lebanon, this flourishing resort and market city is known for its flowers, vineyards and cascading mountain streams.

Archaeologists say that this grave at Byblos dates from sometime between 2,000 and 3,000 B.C. The practice of burying the dead in grain jars has no exact parallel anywhere else on earth.

The massive grandeur of Baalbek draws a steady stream of visitors, both Lebanese and foreign.

This sculpture from Baalbek represents the Greek sun god, Helios, from whom Baalbek derived its former name of Heliopolis.

Wheat, poppies and twining vines—symbolic of Bacchus—are delicately sculptured in this detail from a doorway in the Temple of Bacchus at Baalbek.

Floodlights illuminate the stately columns of the Temple of Bacchus at Baalbek.

BAALBEK

Among Lebanon's many splendid architectural remains, Baalbek is remarkable. This small town in the foothills of the Anti-Lebanon, was a famous city in Roman times, when it was known in Greek as Heliopolis—"City of the Sun." It is generally believed that it takes its name from Baal, a Phoenician deity, and that the city was a religious seat before the Seleucid dynasty changed its name to Heliopolis. The vast ruins include an Acropolis (hilltop temple) and an early Christian basilica, imposing temples to Bacchus and Jupiter, and numerous lesser buildings.

The Court of the Altar in Baalbek was richly decorated on three sides with colonnades, of which only a few columns remain.

2. HISTORY

LEBANON, WHILE TODAY a young and modern republic, nevertheless is steeped in 5,000 years of history, for its territory corresponds closely to that of ancient Phoenicia. Its origin is practically lost in time; however, in the dawn of the first recorded events (around 3000 B.C.) a branch of the Canaanites of the Bible occupied what is now Lebanon. They were called Phoenicians by the Greeks and later the term Phoenicians became synonymous with Canaanite. About 1500 B.C. the main cities of Phoenician civilization were Byblos, Sidon and Tyre, each important in the maritime and commercial activities of that world of long ago.

Tyre was considered the greatest Phoenician city-state—its seamen ventured forth to establish the first business empire known to mankind, founding Carthage in the 9th century B.C. and reaching the Straits of Gibraltar some 200 years after, carrying on a continuous trade in marble, glass, bronze, highly prized cedarwood and silks and brocades, valued beyond gold in that era. It was the Phoenicians who are credited with devising the first alphabet of 22 consonants from which most ancient and modern scripts were derived.

THE PHOENICIANS' INFLUENCE

Historians are unanimous in their recognition of the influence of the Phoenicians in spreading civilization throughout the ancient world. Yet there never was a Phoenician state in the true sense of the word, because of jealous rivalry among the independent Phoenician cities, some of which surpassed others in fame and prosperity. Not one of them was strong enough to subdue the others and achieve unity in order to form a great state, although at different periods they formed federations.

In the barbarian countries they invaded, they occupied islands which were easy to defend and established markets to which merchants of the world flocked. They colonized part of Cyprus, Rhodes and the Aegean Islands, and worked the mines of Thrace before crossing the Black Sea (then the terror of sailors). They founded Tarshish, a great commercial colony, on the coast of Spain. The historian Herodotus tells that after reaching Greece, Italy and Malta, navigating at night by the polar star, the Phoenicians were the first people to sail around Africa. Starting from the Gulf of Aqaba they returned to Egypt, passing by the pillars of Hercules (the ancient name for the Straits of Gibraltar).

For a long time, beginning about 1500 B.C., the Phoenician city-states were under Egyptian rule, except for a period of Hittite domination. The Hittites, an Indo-European people living in what is now Turkey, extended their power southward into Syria, but were eventually overthrown and Egypt re-established its influence in Phoenicia.

In the Archaeological Museum in Beirut are sculptures from all the periods of Lebanon's long history. This relief of a ship (3rd century B.C.) was unearthed at Sidon.

Phoenicia extended as far north as the town of Ruad (ancient Aradus) in Syria, and was bounded on the south by Mount Carmel (now in Israel), on the east by the mountain chain of Lebanon and on the west by the Mediterranean. The high ranges which separated the Phoenician cities from the plains of the interior, and the Mediterranean sea at their feet, were the two factors which determined their maritime destiny. The ports of Byblos, Aradus, Sidon and Tyre ensured for themselves a dominating place in Asian trade. Sidon and Tyre were the most flourishing ports and acquired supremacy over the other towns along the coast.

Phoenician sailors were navigators with intellectual powers and adventurous spirits. They explored the Mediterranean, east, west, north and south and brought to European shores the inventions of their civilization. They were pioneers in naval warfare besides merchant sailing and directed their efforts toward the conquest of North Africa and Spain.

At Beit Mery, near Beirut, are many Roman and Byzantine remains, such as this mosaic dating from about A.D. 500.

The great Temple of Jupiter at Baalbek was destroyed in a series of earthquakes. Seen here are some of the surviving Corinthian columns of the peristyle, or colonnade, that formerly surrounded the temple.

The Macedonians under Alexander the Great overthrew Persia, and Alexander was welcomed by all the Phoenician cities except Tyre, which he eventually took after a 7-month siege. After Alexander's death, Phoenicia was the object of a struggle between the rulers of Egypt, the Ptolemies, and those of Syria, the Seleucids, until its conquest by the Romans in the 1st century B.C.

THE ROMAN EMPIRE

The Roman and Byzantine period lasted seven centuries and was the most prosperous; Lebanon became heavily populated, an important part of the Roman world. During this era Tyre was the metropolis of Phoenicia, Baalbek was endowed with its majestic temples, and later Christianity appeared and flourished.

THE MIDDLE AGES

During the Arab and Frankish periods, the former extending from A.D. 636 to 1085, trading in seaports lessened to the point of standstill. From 1095 to 1291, two centuries elapsed in a struggle between the Frankish and Moslem

Towards the 9th century B.C. Egypt fell into a decline, during which time Phoenicia enjoyed a period of great independence. Soon, however, the Assyrians became mighty, sought an opening on the Mediterranean and subdued the Phoenicians. By the 6th century B.C., the Chaldean Empire, with Babylon as its capital, held sway over Phoenicia. Then, from 538 to 333 B.C., the Phoenician states were under Persian rule.

This Greco-Roman sarcophagus in the Beirut Archaeological Museum depicts an episode in the life of Orestes.

A detail from a mosaic pavement of the 5th century A.D., formed at Jnah, south of Beirut, depicts a variety of birds and beasts.

elements, mainly the Seljuk Turks and their successors. A new phase in Lebanese history came with the Egyptian Mameluke domination (1281–1516) when the Lebanese were kept in confinement within their hills. The old maritime cities of Phoenicia were occupied by rulers who collected duties without earning them, leaving the people to rule themselves, giving privileges to some and ignoring the rest. In this era, the Syriac language began to disappear and Arabic began to be spoken.

THE OTTOMANS

Syria was conquered by the Turkish Sultan Selim I (1512–1520), who put an end to the Mamelukes of Egypt. Selim did not attempt the conquest of Lebanon, but was able to exact

The great Crusader castle (left foreground) looms over the modern buildings of Tripoli.

tributes from the Lebanese Emirs (princely rulers). The native dynasty of the Maans, and later the Shehabs, sought to obtain greater autonomy for Lebanon and even total independence, hoping to unify all areas within the natural boundaries of Lebanon.

EMIR FAKREDDIN

The story is still told around hearthsides of the noble Emir Fakreddin who resisted Turkish rule and made history by building Lebanon into a land of strength and justice. From his palace at Deir-el-Kamar, he dispensed wisdom in spite of jealous enemies posing as friends. Fakreddin fell in love with a young and beautiful girl called Itr Allayl (meaning "Perfume of the Night") who, on behalf of the citizenry, presented him with a golden sword, while singing of her devotion. The romance of the Emir and Itr Allayl is still a popular subject of Lebanese legend and folklore.

Fakreddin ruled from 1590 until 1635. Although a Druse (see next page), he protected Christian interests, introduced European influences and even imported architects, engineers and other experts from Italy. In 1613 the Turkish army moved against the Emir and he went into five years of exile in Italy. After his return he succeeded in holding off the Turks, extending his power from Aleppo in Syria to the Egyptian border. The Turks at length succeeded in defeating him and carried him in chains to Istanbul where they executed him.

Though the Emir met a cruel end, his sacrifice was not in vain. He was never forgotten by his countrymen and the land for which he gave his life endures. In the Palace at Deir-el-Kamar his spirit lingers still, and in the legends of his countrymen.

BECHIR II

Of the successors of Fakreddin, the most distinguished was Bechir II (1788–1840), who temporarily succeeded in ousting Ottoman rule and placing his country under the protection of Egypt. During the period of Egyptian in-

Deir-el-Kamar, once the capital of the Emir Fakreddin, is a small town built around a central square, or "midan," a corner of which is seen here.

The 14th-century mosque of Taynal in Tripoli incorporates part of an earlier Carmelite church.

fluence, Bechir sought ties with the West. It was at this time that the American missions were established at Beirut and other places. However, in 1840 the Ottomans drove the Egyptians out and once more established a precarious control over Lebanon.

RELIGIONS

Internal strife had been developing between two of Lebanon's many religious groups—the Maronites and the Druses. The Maronites, a Christian sect, had been isolated from the main body of their co-believers, until in 1736 they became affiliated with the Roman Catholic Church, whereupon France declared unofficially that it would protect their interests. The weak Turkish government encouraged a heretical Moslem sect, the Druses, to oppose the Maronites as tools of a Christian European power.

During the period from 1840 until 1860, Maronites and Druses both rebelled against the government and also engaged in hostilities with one another. In 1860, angered by further European interference, the true Moslems joined the Druses in a drive against the Maronites, which resulted in a series of massacres of Christians of all sects. A French army invaded Lebanon and occupied it. In 1864 the Turks were induced to appoint a Christian governor-general for Lebanon and to grant the country a considerable degree of home rule.

The new régime was guaranteed by the European powers. Poverty was reduced, though many of the struggling citizens emigrated to new worlds and to Africa. The Turkish domination lasted until the occupation of Lebanon by the victorious Allies in 1918, at the end of World War I, and the country was occupied by France. Lebanon and Syria were later established as autonomous republics under French mandate. Lebanon, from 1918 to 1942, thanks to the new régime enjoyed a new way of life. The French mandate did not meet the wishes of the Lebanese for full independence, but had

The Church of St. John the Baptist at Byblos dates from the days when the old city was a Crusaders' stronghold.

Lebanese Christians throng to the shrine of the Virgin of Harissa, especially in May, the month of Mary. About 15 miles north of Beirut and over 1,500 feet above sea level, this colossal statue contains a chapel in its conical base.

THE PRESENT

Before assuming office, after being elected President in 1964, Charles Helou took the oath of fidelity before Parliament to the Lebanese nation and to the Constitution, in the following terms: "I swear by Almighty God to observe the Constitution and Laws of the Lebanese People and to maintain the independence of Lebanon and its territorial integrity."

Formerly the Minister of Education, President Helou (a Maronite) commenced his term peacefully, despite fears of possible violence resulting from pressures to re-elect his predecessor, and strove to uphold Lebanon's

certain benefits—with the encouragement of agriculture and industry, and the preservation of security, prosperity was restored. New schools were built and good roads and highways connecting the main points along the coast came into existence.

WORLD WAR II AND AFTER

In July, 1941, Allied forces took Lebanon from the control of the Nazi-supported Vichy French government. The Free French government, based in London, declared Lebanon fully independent. In 1943, the Lebanese elected their own government.

When the country was officially recognized by the United Nations in 1945, the Republic of Lebanon had come into its own. Strong ties with other Arab countries have been cemented while Lebanon maintained friendship with other nations. The history of Lebanon has been relatively stable since independence. One exception occurred in 1958, when rebel groups whose aim was to make Lebanon a closer participant in the Arab League were put down with the aid of United States intervention.

In 1958 an attempt was made to overthrow the Lebanese government. At the request of President Camille Chamoun, United States Marines were sent into the country to help maintain order, but were withdrawn in the same year. These departing "leathernecks" are receiving a last-minute offer from a local rug vendor.

democratic processes. President Helou had numerous crises to face. In September, 1966, when the nation's renowned Intra-Bank closed because of huge sums drawn out by other Arab states, he authorized the closing of all banks in Lebanon within 24 hours for a short period, to restore stability and maintain the confidence of the public. In June, 1967, he had to face the sudden Middle East War with Israel, in which Lebanon was not actively engaged, but which still has repercussions on all fronts. Discord in his Parliament often upset normal routines and he had, on occasion, to call forth deputies at midnight or dawn and sit with them in conference until agreement ruled.

Although situated in the heart of the Middle East trouble zone, Lebanon had been able to maintain a certain detachment in pursuing its own national aims, until 1968, when Israeli commandos destroyed a number of planes at Beirut Airport. Israel alleged that the attack was in retaliation for Lebanese involvement in the sabotaging of an Israeli airliner in Athens.

In 1969, the growing activity of Palestinian Arab guerrillas on Lebanese soil led to open clashes between them and the Lebanese army, and in the fall of 1969, the Lebanese cabinet resigned.

In 1970, Suleiman Franjieh was elected President, and faced an increasingly tense situation. Pressure from the other Arab states was mounting, and Israel had sent guerrilla forces across the Lebanese border again.

In 1973, there were an estimated 150,000 Palestinian refugees in Lebanon. The Lebanese have attempted to keep a tight control over them, not always with success. The continued activity of Palestinian terrorists and commandos, notably at the 1972 Olympics in Munich, led to stepped-up Israeli reprisals across the Lebanese border during 1972 and 1973.

In 1973, an Israeli commando raid against Palestinian terrorists in Beirut sparked a brief war in Beirut between guerrillas and the Lebanese army. Following the Arab-Israeli War of 1973, in which Lebanon did not participate, Israeli reprisals and Palestinian terrorism continued. In March, 1975, the Christian and Moslem communities came into open conflict, presumably about the Palestinians, but in reality because of longstanding Moslem dissatisfaction with Christian dominance.

By 1976, a full-scale civil war was in progress and much of Beirut was damaged or destroyed in the ensuing 15 months of battle. Syria sent in troops to occupy large areas of Lebanon, to maintain order. The civil war ended in 1977, thanks to a cease-fire arranged by the Arab League, and Lebanon slowly began to get back to normal. President Franjieh was replaced by another Christian, Elias Sarkis. In March, 1978, Israeli forces occupied a strip of southern Lebanon adjoining Israeli territory. United Nations troops were sent in to police the area and Israel withdrew. Israeli-backed Christians in southern Lebanon proclaimed a "Free Lebanese State" in 1979.

3. THE GOVERNMENT

LEBANON IS GOVERNED by the President, who is Head of the State, and is elected by Parliament for a term of 6 years. The members of Parliament are elected directly by the people. The Cabinet is appointed by the President of the Republic and is responsible to the Parliament. Only after an interval of 6 years may a President be re-elected. No person shall be eligible for this office unless he fulfills the conditions of eligibility to the satisfaction of the Chamber of Deputies.

EXECUTIVE POWER

It is traditional for all Presidents in Lebanon to be Christian, while the Cabinet is traditionally headed by a Prime Minister who is a Moslem of the Sunnite sect. The five provinces of the land are administered directly by the central government. The President's executive powers are numerous. He may promulgate laws after they have been adopted by the Parliament. He supervises their execution and issues regulations to enforce them, but he may not modify or set aside their provisions. The President can negotiate and ratify treaties, which he may bring before the Parliament. He appoints and dismisses ministers and presides over national ceremonies. He maintains freedom of speech and the press.

Riyadh Solh Square in Beirut commemorates the first Lebanese Prime Minister to hold office after independence.

LEGISLATIVE POWER

The Parliament consists of a single house, the Chamber of Deputies, comprising 99 members, elected for a term of 4 years. Membership is apportioned among the religious communities, the Maronites claiming the greatest number, followed in descending order by the Sunnite, Shi'ite (Moslem), Greek Orthodox, Druse, Greek Catholic, Armenian Orthodox and Armenian Catholic communities.

CONSTITUTIONAL RIGHTS

With so many separate communities within its boundaries, Lebanon stresses civil and political rights in its Constitution. Personal freedom, free enterprise, and equal employment opportunities are all guaranteed. Religious freedom is assured, and each religious community may maintain its own schools, provided they conform to the educational standards set by the state, and do not give instruction that is damaging to other creeds.

FOREIGN AFFAIRS

Lebanon's foreign policy is a broad one, encouraging free enterprise. No distinction is made between national and foreign capital or workers. Taxation is extremely moderate and ideal conditions are offered to foreign investors. As a member of both the United Nations and the Arab League, Lebanon aims to preserve its independent identity, to be on friendly terms with Arab countries and to serve as a bridge between the West and the Middle East.

Beirut is the headquarters of regional activities of the United Nations—such as the Relief and Works Agency, which is responsible for the care of Arab refugees. The United States, which contributes approximately $23,000,000 a year to this cause, has always had traditional close ties with Lebanon and has assisted in the preservation of Lebanon's independence, integrity and the promotion of its economic development.

While a member of the Arab League, Lebanon has never been an active participant in the League's front against Israel. When Israel struck back against the Arab states in 1967, it is noteworthy that Lebanon was the only nearby nation not invaded. The more recent Israeli action in sabotaging the Beirut airport and the stepped-up guerrilla activity near the Israeli border brought Lebanon closer to the Middle East conflict. Yet, when Arab-Israeli warfare was resumed in 1973, the leaders of Lebanon again managed to avoid open conflict with Israel.

Batroun, where these cheerful boys live, is on the coast 35 miles north of Beirut, and is one of the most picturesque villages in Lebanon. Its houses are built of "ramleh," a stone found in abundance near the coast, and its people, mainly fishermen and craftsmen, are also famous for the manufacture of lemonade.

4. THE PEOPLE

A VARIETY OF GROUPS make up the 3,300,000 population of the Republic of Lebanon. Just about 50 per cent of the people are Christians, most of whom are of the Maronite sect, while the other half are of the Islamic faith.

The Lebanese people are mainly descendants of the Phoenicians, Greeks, Byzantines, Crusaders and Arabs who, at different periods, dominated the country. The national language is Arabic, although French is to be seen on signs and heard on every street. Many Lebanese are fair, though almost all of them have the dark eyes of the Orient.

Racial equality is natural among these folk of

mixed descent and the shade of a man's skin is immaterial. The standard of living is high for the Middle East, especially in Beirut, where banking, commerce, shipping, industry and the pursuit of entertainment are part of daily life. Country life is tranquil and old-fashioned.

POSITION OF WOMEN

Young secretaries arrive at their respective offices, dressed in the latest fashions of the West. While nearby Arab lands seldom allow young women to work in offices, in Lebanon very high positions in radio, television, medicine and science (to note just a few) are held by

This young woman is wearing the conical "tant-our," a headdress worn by noble Lebanese ladies as late as the end of the 19th-century, and which resembles the graceful headdresses worn by European ladies in the 14th and 15th centuries.

COUNTRY LIFE

In the coastal villages and mountain hamlets, the village folk of Lebanon often own a plot of ground and grow their own food; daughters go to school to learn to read and write. When that is accomplished, they are often hired out to more affluent city families. The monthly stipend which a girl earns goes to her parents. This has been the custom for a long, long time and is an advantage for over-large village families with too many mouths to feed.

The farmer's children are a happy lot. Week-ends they stand on country routes where city cars fly by, headed for the cooler air of the hills, acting as astute salesmen all, with their baskets piled high, laden with delicious fruits, crisp green lettuces with loam still on the roots and all kinds of vegetables. They wait to pour the purchases in a bag for the city people who are pleased to buy just-picked produce at half of city prices. The fishermen too, stand by the side of the road with their catch, for which

daughters of families who, two decades ago, would have been shocked by a young woman working. The influence of the French in the early part of the 20th century had a great deal to do with this. French ideas, French culture and traditions and the practical methods of the French had a great effect in obtaining more freedom for Lebanese womanhood.

Where once the veil existed, it has now vanished forever. When occasionally women appear on city streets covered from head to foot in black *burqas*, revealing only their eyes, they are generally visitors from Saudi Arabia, Yemen or Kuwait who have come up with their oil-rich menfolk to shop and see the sights. In Lebanese villages, some totally Moslem, others totally Christian, it is seldom that one sees a lady in a *burqa*. Women in Lebanon enjoy the liberty of Western women.

This sturdy stone house is typical of villages in the mountains.

This farmhouse of the Bekaa features a "liwan," a room open to the outside through a large arch.

they find a ready market—in fact, the demand is often greater than the supply. A refreshing aspect of these transactions is the wit and charm of the vendors.

THE HEADMAN

The farmers lead a clan-like existence; in strictly farming communities there is always a headman, much like a tribal chief, to whom other farmers and villagers go in times of stress and need. Although the headman and the villager may belong to different sects, problems are pondered over with a personal approach, and solved. A large variety of Christian sects exist in Lebanon, including the Maronites, who are affiliated with Rome, and the Greek Orthodox and the Armenians. The Moslems include Sunnites and Shi'ites and the heretical Moslem sect known as the Druses.

A number of Bedouin—nomadic Arabs from the desert—are found in the Bekaa plain. Living in tents, they raise camels and sheep, and sometimes work as farm hands at harvest time. They are gradually shifting from their age-old nomadic life to a more settled existence.

Houses in the Bekaa plain are usually built of washed earth, since building stone is scarce in that region. The ladder leads to the flat mud roof of the house, which often needs repairs, as the summer heat causes it to dry and crack.

A Bedouin relaxes at the entrance to his tent.

While her little boy waits patiently on the back of a donkey, a village woman chats with a friend.

Wearing traditional desert costume, this Bedouin reflects the good-natured, hospitable aspects of the Lebanese.

RURAL DRESS

The apparel of villagers is charming and old-fashioned: the women wear loose ankle-length dresses tied round the waist with a cord, while men wear balloon-like trousers and loose shirts, much in the manner of the ancient Orient. Everyday clothes are gay cottons. For festive occasions, clothes are made of silks and shiny satins, with lots of braid for trimming. The girls and women generally wear head-scarves, often beautifully embroidered. These same ensembles are always worn when national folk plays are performed.

A kaak vendor passes a pair of gypsy entertainers on the beach. The girl dances to the music of her partner's "buzuk," a sort of two-stringed mandolin.

This man of the Bekaa plain sports a striking headdress.

The Place des Canons is the Times Square or Piccadilly Circus of Beirut, ablaze at night with neon signs and the lights of cafés, theatres and discothèques.

CITY LIFE

The life of Beirut is vivid and varied. The souks (markets) hold glitter that is rare. The food, flower and vegetable vendors have stalls piled high with many-hued products. On every street corner there are carrot-juice stands and the freshly squeezed, vitamin-rich liquid costs very little. In restaurants as lavish as in France, Oriental and European foods are served.

In the coffee houses, men spend their leisure time smoking the hookah pipe, while many a profitable transaction takes place also, for business is often carried on there. All business in

In the ordinary cafés of Beirut, which are patronized mostly by men, tea and coffee are served. Men come here to relax, to talk, to play cards or chess or dominoes (as these two men are doing), or to read their newspapers and to smoke the water pipe, or hookah.

Modern apartment houses rise above a street in Beirut.

Beirut is sealed with several cups of pungent Arab coffee, whether in the great banking establishments or on a café terrace.

Night in Beirut is a different world of its own, with cabarets, theatres and hotels offering entertainment to residents and visitors alike. The hotels range from plush castles on the sea along the Avenue de Paris to most inexpensive ones on Hamra Street. Flower stands are everywhere and flower pots on every rooftop, along with chickens, pecking for food in the city's heart. Beirut is fashionable, sophisticated, modern—but with a difference. East and West rub shoulders with aplomb and a homey friendliness exists, which makes the visitor feel he belongs. Sports and horse-racing are daily events. The world of Beirut is endless in its scope and variety.

FOOD

The food of Lebanon is noted for its richness and succulent variety—travellers come to Lebanon to eat as well as to do business. *Mezzé*, the native spread, is a gigantic selection of hot and cold hors d'oeuvres, ranging from piquant and spicy small salads to bean dishes (mashed and mixed with pure olive oil); zesty tiny meat balls with nuts; shrimps and sea-food

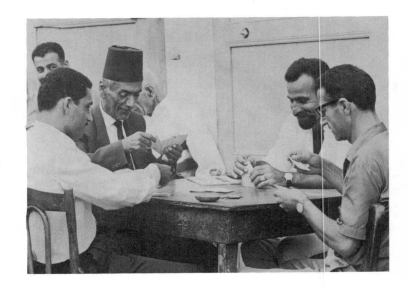

The fez, a hat style popularized by the Turks, is still to be seen on an occasional Lebanese, as on this man playing cards in a café.

This is not Lebanese smörgåsbord, but the famous "mezzé," a multitude of exciting dishes, each served on individual plates. Among the dishes seen on this table are stuffed vine leaves, shish-kebab, fried frog's legs, and "hommos" (a puree of chick peas with sesame oil), sea food, almonds, pistachios and liver.

tidbits that melt in the mouth; delicate, rolled, juicy vine leaves stuffed with rice and meat; sausage rolls in crisp hot pastry; these are but a few of the 49 dishes placed on the table, and taken as a complete meal. This is accompanied by *arak*, an alcoholic liquid which looks like plain water and turns milky white when mixed with water, which is the way it is taken.

Shish-kebab is a popular Oriental dish of skewered lamb cubes, green peppers, spices and onions. Arab bread—the round, hot, flat discs of wheat—supplements an Arab meal. Meals start with appetizers such as mashed chick peas in sesame oil, eggplant salad and *tabboule* (chopped tomatoes, scallions, parsley and wheat germ), plus stuffed grape leaves. Entrées, Middle East style, stress lamb, cooked in various ways, always served with rice. Desserts are rich: *baklava*, a flaky pastry, is filled with

chopped almonds and honey. Lebanese people prefer everything fresh and have not yet adopted frozen foods.

A quick lunch may be a slice of hot ground meat rolled with peppers and condiments in a thick piece of *khobez*, the Arab bread. Chicken is more than popular and the barbecued kind, ready to eat, sells like hotcakes in towns and villages. Local wines, which are excellent, go very well with all Lebanese dishes, and the drinking water is very pure.

HOSPITALITY AND HOME LIFE

An inherent part of Lebanese life is hospitality, bred through the centuries in homes both humble and rich. Visitors, whether strangers or not, are received into the warm intimacy of a Lebanese living room. Seated on the divan, they are immediately served a tiny cup of aromatic coffee, strong and freshly made, accompanied by Eastern sweets. Village homes,

This man takes a cooling drink of water from a "bre," a porous brown earthenware jug. These jugs are a common sight standing atop the pumps of service stations and in other public places, so that thirsty passersby may drink.

two storeys high and made of stone, are severe in lines but softened by a trellis for flowering vines and grapes. Wealthier homes show strong Italian and French influence, with tall windows and French doors of glass.

The tailor, the butcher, the baker and even a servant, when called upon, may be dining at the moment of call. Without hesitation, the guest, unexpected though he may be, is asked to join the table. To refuse is considered an insult and some slight drink or morsel is generally accepted. Because Lebanon has been primarily an agricultural land rather than an industrial one, thousands of Lebanese nationals have emigrated to all parts of the world, bringing with them the spirit of progress, energy, new ideas and the will to get ahead.

It is estimated that there are 1,500,000 people of Lebanese blood in other countries, mostly in the United States, Argentina and Brazil. Emigrants often return with hard-earned wealth to shower upon families and relatives (whom they have supported through their immigrant years). The ties are strong and many return to stay and to build a home and business, not possible in their early struggles.

MEN OF ACHIEVEMENT

Among famous Lebanese the most widely known is Kahlil Gibran, who wrote *The Prophet* (ranking second only to the Bible in total sales). Though his life ended in the New World, he was brought back to rest forever in the Valley of Besharre—where a museum dedicated to his life and work was built in his memory. Among the contemporary poets and writers of fame, there are Charles Corm, George Shehade and Fargallah Hayek. Dr. Michel Debakey, the famous heart specialist, and Danny Thomas, the television and film star, are Americans of Lebanese origin.

EDUCATION

In Lebanon today the literacy rate is 86 per cent, the highest in the Arab world. Schools exist in every mountain village and hamlet, as well as schools in the cities for foreigners who wish to learn Arabic. Of three main universities (there are 8 altogether), the American University of Beirut, founded in 1866, is perhaps the best known. It houses four faculties: arts and sciences, with 22 departments; medical sciences, including schools of medicine, pharmacy, nursing and public health; engineering; and agricultural sciences. Many noted leaders today owe their success to having been educated and trained at the American University.

Saint Joseph's University, founded by the Jesuit Fathers in 1875, has a law school, engineering and medical school, a special institute dedicated to Oriental studies, and a library containing 12,000 rare books.

Heavy snow lies upon the little town of Besharre, birthplace of the poet Kahlil Gibran.

A modern mosque adjoins the buildings of the College for Women at Beirut.

The Lebanese University stresses law, political sciences, art and statistics among regular courses. The statutes of this college have been handed down from the ancient Roman School of Law of Beirut, a background of which its students are proud. Attached to the university is the Sursock Museum, a treasury of sculpture, rare manuscripts and Oriental pieces of art.

Each mosque and church in Lebanon is not only a place of worship, but also of education, where classes are held for children who study the Koran or the Bible. Education is Lebanon's strongest line of fortification. (The country's armed forces number only 12,000 men.)

A touching sight takes place every October when school terms begin. Just by the Place des Canons in Beirut, in a small market place, children of all ages from lower-income families gather with their parents. They are there to buy school books, used but clean, at a fraction of original cost. From a café balcony, one may watch a scene of bargaining that would do credit to a film—hundreds of students swapping and selling books, those they have finished with and those they wish to purchase.

Armenian high school students, who are native-born Lebanese citizens, go to a school specially attuned to their background. While they study Arabic in school, Armenian is the language spoken in their homes.

School children of Beirut are taken by bus to Sidon and sketch with enthusiasm on the grounds of Sidon's castle by the sea—a good way for the youth of Lebanon to study their ancient history.

While receiving technical aid from other countries, Lebanon also provides aid. These Saudi Arabian students studying to become laboratory technicians are getting help in a chemistry experiment from a Lebanese professor in Beirut.

The painting class is enjoyed by children in this village school for boys only. In the strict Arab tradition, boys and girls study in separate institutions.

With snowy mountain slopes within easy reach, these young Lebanese have been skiing since childhood. The sun is bright and they do not have to be rich to enjoy it. It is a truly popular sport.

YOUTH HOSTELS

Lebanese Youth Hostels were commenced years before tourists came—when thousands of foreign young men and women discovered the country's forests, hills and river banks on hikes and camping trips. Their enthusiasm was so great, that it led to the creation of a Youth Reception Headquarters under the country's own National Council of Tourism—with headquarters in Beirut. Any Youth Hosteller from Lebanon or abroad may register and join in week-end trips to archaeological sites where lectures are given by professors on related subjects.

A special project called "Vacation Work Camps" is in full effect. Young people come in groups by arrangement, select a leader from among themselves and spend two weeks or more, assisting on farms, picking fruit, erecting farm buildings, aiding in geology exploration and other activities of benefit to the countryside. In return they are housed and fed free, and enjoy sight-seeing tours on off days so that it is not all work and no play.

MUSIC AND DRAMA

Music is heard everywhere and music classes flourish—a majority of Lebanese children start music lessons in kindergarten. At the age of 5, they perform at the school's concerts. Folk art is popular and many theatres are dedicated exclusively to traditional drama, consisting of romantic plays and dancing, in which all the magic of Arabian Nights comes to life in a

A young teacher and some members of her class enjoy the Mediterranean sunshine from the balcony of their classrooms. Balconies are a common feature of Lebanese schools.

From July to September every year, an International Festival holds forth at Baalbek. Lebanese and foreign companies present music, drama and ballet (seen here).

Lebanon looks East and West—at Baalbek, Lebanese performers play "Hamlet" against the background of majestic ruins.

Traditional Lebanese musical instruments include (foreground) the "nai," or Oriental flute and the "daff," a small, tambourine-like drum; the string instruments are the "buzuk" (left), reclining against the "kanun", or zither, and the "ud," (right) a very ancient instrument whose strings are plucked with a sharpened eagle feather.

passionate, breathtaking manner. Private enterprises and government tourist offices organize troupes of folk dancers and send them abroad to show other countries the song, dance and drama of Lebanon.

At Baalbek, folklore presentations are given, as well as the annual International Festival, an event which music lovers from around the world attend. This Festival was organized with

the idea of using the temple sites as a natural background—and the first Festival in 1956 was a great success, including French and English drama productions as well as symphonic music. The Festival annually presents ballet companies, philharmonic orchestras and leading stars of the stage. Among the guest performers, have been Margot Fontcyn, Rudolf Nureyev, the Bristol Old Vic players and countless other noted artists. The Baalbek Festival constitutes one of the world's most esteemed annual cultural events and tickets are sold out months ahead.

The Lebanese Casino, on the Bay of Jounieh, includes an ultra-modern theatre. Here a concert is in progress.

FESTIVALS

Aside from the Baalbek Festival, there are many others—festivals are part of Lebanese life and many are held throughout the year. Among them are: the Vineyard Festival held each September at Zahlé; the Arab Horse Gymkhana held in October, at Ablah in the Bekaa; the International Cinema Festival held in Beirut, late in October; the Festival of the Olive Trees at Koura, held early in November; and the Sea Festival and Boat Parade in Sidon, in spring.

Most of the year, Lebanon has special events: winter sports in December; the Christmas celebration and Mass and the lighting of the big Christmas tree in Beirut; the International Skiing Week at the Cedars in March; and in spring the Easter celebration.

ARTS AND CRAFTS

The arts and crafts of Lebanon are carried on by village artisans who were taught at their father's knee. Between planting the small crops for the family's food, each village boy learns the art of hammering brass; creating leather camel-seats, handbags and boxes in rare design; or making pottery in every form and in bright shades. Lebanese excel in the goldsmith's art and throughout the Bab-Idris section of Beirut one can see jewellers at work on intricate, exotic patterns. Every town has its special craft: Sidon, for example, is famed for

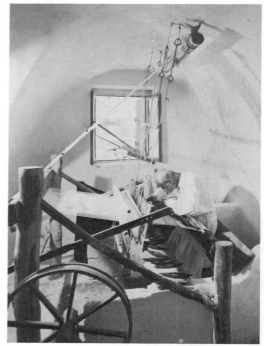

Lebanon has its own tradition of hand weaving— the same kind of loom has been used for generations.

the delicate workmanship of its bone-handled Jezzine cutlery. Throughout Lebanon, art exhibitions are held by young painters who study exclusively in art schools. Some specialize in painting the natural beauty of the local landscape, others follow the surrealistic trend.

At the weekly market held at Souk el-Khan, near Marjayoun in South Lebanon, a potter shows a customer his line of jars and vases.

Wicker chairs, seats, baskets and other useful and decorative objects—are crafted chiefly in South Lebanon and in the coastal strip from Beirut and Tripoli. This young man is framed by the products of his skill.

Kalamoun, a village near Tripoli, is celebrated for its delicately engraved copper work. This coffee pot and tray are good examples of local craftsmanship. ⟶

In the Tailors' Market in Tripoli, master tailors follow the craft handed down to them through many generations. ⟵

The art of glass-blowing is believed to have originated in Phoneicia in the 1st century B.C. Today the craft is carried on mainly in and near Tripoli.

A tanker lies off Sidon, waiting to be loaded with oil from the Arabian desert.

5. THE ECONOMY

THE ECONOMY IN LEBANON, since the dawn of history, has always been based on more than merely extracting the fruits of soil and sea: trade has been a primary activity.

TAPLINE

A great economic resource in Lebanon is the Trans-Arabian Pipe Line Company with headquarters at Sidon. "Tapline," its name in brief, is a modern trade route of steel running across the Arabian Peninsula—across northern Saudi Arabia, Jordan, Syria and Lebanon. The crude oil transported via Tapline from the oil fields of Saudi Arabia to the Eastern Mediterranean

moves nearly 900 miles overland. Otherwise an oil tanker would have to make a sea voyage between the same two points that would be ten times as far, round trip. This tremendous short cut has brought economic gain and intense new development to the countries through which it passes.

The company's marine terminal, south of Sidon, has four deep-water berths offshore. Tankers of all sizes, flying flags from around the world, take on cargoes of crude oil for the final stage of transportation to Western European and South American markets. Completed in 1950, the terminal in the ancient

A close-up of the pipes at the Sidon terminus of the Saudi Arabian pipeline dramatizes the modern side of this age-old city.

Phoenician city of Sidon has infused new life, new prospects and pride into the community. There are 330 different types of jobs held by employees, each one trained to do his part.

The Tapline is a small world by itself, with excellent housing, schools, clinics and other facilities. Tapline directs its over-all operation from its main offices in Beirut.

In Sidon a unique method was devised to install 36-inch submarine pipeline. This 6,650-foot length of pipe, welded into one piece, was towed to sea from the shore and slowly submerged by filling it progressively with naphtha, then sea water.

INDUSTRY

Lebanon is expanding its facilities for industrial production. It now possesses abundant electric power, produced by hydro-electric installations; easier and faster communications provided by a well-kept highway system and enlarged modern seaports and airport, plus a growing body of skilled workers. To increase the working force, a well equipped technical school has been established at Dikwaneh in which all trades are taught. To increase industrial expansion, the State has exempted from taxation all enterprises contributing to the country's development. Long- and medium-term credit facilities are offered to encourage industrial progress by the Development Bank.

A new and thriving industry is the manufacturing and processing of noodles. The textile industry ranks high in importance, with products ranging from raw thread to finished silks and woollens. Clothing is now mass-produced and the shoes and handbags of modern design are of very high quality. Over 1,000 furniture factories flourish throughout this small land and many more are springing up. The Lebanese have a feeling for design and their leather, wood and paper products are in demand.

Chocolate is a speciality, most of it made in Tripoli, and exported, either as a sweet or in biscuits, put up in attractive tins. Many United States soft drink companies have huge plants in Lebanon. These plants have thousands of Lebanese employees and because of the warm Mediterranean climate, the volume of business is great. The bottles are also manufactured locally.

Stone-masonry and brick-making are also up-and-coming industries, as are plastic and rubber products.

Soap-making is a major industry in Tripoli. This serene structure is not a cloister, but a former Turkish army barracks converted into a warehouse for soap.

This handsome hotel, the Al-Bustan, in the hills of Beit-Meri, was built in memory of Emil Bustani, the Lebanese industrialist and financier, who built a commercial empire throughout the Middle East and Asia, and aided greatly in developing Lebanon's economy.

TOURISM

Tourism in Lebanon was one of the happiest sources of profitable activity—since the hospitality of which the Lebanese are proud fits them admirably for this line of work. The fascination of the country and the special kind of friendliness that the Lebanese have for visitors are overwhelming. The Middle East War of June, 1967, dampened the enthusiasm of some travellers, but not for long, and the National Council of Tourism worked day and night planning new tourist facilities and improving existing ones, until the 1976 Civil War put such plans in abeyance.

At Byblos, fishermen inspect their traps. Fishing is an important economic activity on the Lebanese coast, and has been since Phoenician times, when Tyre and Sidon shipped purple dye, obtained from the shell of the local Murex mollusk, all over the Mediterranean.

The Bank of Lebanon is housed in this gleaming new building.

EXPORTS

Among the exports are live animals, fish, spices, leaf and manufactured tobacco, raw cotton, wool and animal hair, textile fabrics, floor coverings, chemicals, miscellaneous manufactured goods and last, but not least, precious stones, gold, art works and antiques. A great proportion of these exports are sent to the United States. Lebanon imports from the United States a huge amount of crude materials, machinery and transport equipment, iron and steel, tools, ships and boats, food products, unmilled wheat, rice, oils, fats, tobacco, beverages, general fuels and construction tools. These imports aid in the upbuilding of the many new plants and factories outside Beirut.

FINANCE

The banking system is noted for its flexibility. The Lebanese are natural money-makers. Their instincts for good business run in countless directions. Bank managers appear to have psychic powers, often cashing personal checks for strangers on presentation of a passport alone. The check almost always is good and the stranger later returns with his business to that bank manager.

Human interest, seldom expected in financial circles, is a fact in Lebanon's banks. Shortly after the Intra-Bank failed, the poorest among its depositors were paid off by the Lebanese Government, which assumed responsibility for the crash. Such losses can no longer occur, for a Development Bank has opened, designed to provide industrial and touristic institutions with help on long-range terms at low interest rates. This will strengthen the private sector and encourage more individual initiative. The Government's policy is to leave the field open to free enterprise. Their establishment of the Central Bank, some two years ago, has provided Lebanon with monetary independence, which assures full government backing to all commercial banks in financial transactions.

TAXATION

Income tax is light on both individuals and corporations. The greater part of government revenue comes from indirect levies. Lebanese residents enjoy one of the lowest income tax rates in the world. A family man, after deductions for children, education, medical and other numerous personal expenses, has to pay only 2 per cent on an income of 4,800 lire (the Lebanese unit of currency, 3.16 lire equalling $1.00). If he earns 8,000 lire, the family man pay only 3 per cent tax, with 10 per cent being the largest amount, taken above an income of 48,000 lire. This makes for firm economy and happy citizens.

COMMERCE

Commercial activity is high in this land of 88 banks, where exchange controls do not exist and foreign businessmen may remit whatever monies they wish to their homeland. The transfer of profits is free. Repatriation of capital is unlimited and foreign investors welcome the fact that in Lebanon their patents and trademarks have protection.

Lebanon has a first-class network of highways. Here the coast road from Tripoli to Beirut passes through the town of Jounieh.

Sheikh Najib Alamuddin, chairman of Middle East Airlines and descendant of a noble family, epitomizes the new leaders of Lebanon, schooled in the cultures of both East and the West.

These aviation students are using demonstration equipment in the Civil Aviation Safety Centre in Beirut.

AVIATION

A vital part of the Lebanese economy is air transport. In Beirut's Khalde Airport, the words, "Welcome to Lebanon" are blazoned on the walls. In the great halls of this almost new international airport, offices of world-wide aviation companies stand side by side with Middle East Airlines, Lebanon's own national carrier. Middle East has an up-to-date fleet of Boeings for its far-flung operations. The airline's network serves 36 countries in Europe, North Africa, Asia and flies throughout the Middle East.

WORKING CONDITIONS

Because the population is highly literate, skills are plentiful and tri-lingual workers and technicians are common. The average secretary in Beirut, male or female speaks Arabic, French and English and employee turnover is low. Maximum hours are 48 per week with overtime pay for more. The right to form trade unions is guaranteed by law.

The government is conducting a soil survey and irrigation project to increase farm output. These workers are planting an experimental crop.

The symbol of Middle East Airlines—a stylized version of the national emblem, the cedar of Lebanon— adorns the tail of each of these planes at Beirut's Khalde Airport.

A Chinese poultry expert from the United Nations confers with the owner of a modern chicken farm.

Modern, scientifically controlled farms, such as this, help make Lebanon a leader in poultry farming in the Middle East.

The Lebanese are carrying out an extensive scheme to replace the country's denuded forests. Here forestry experts inspect seedlings.

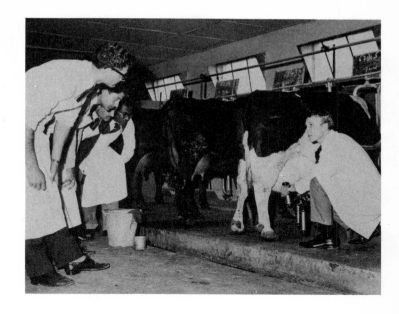

A Danish dairy expert demonstrates modern milking methods to Lebanese technicians at the Agricultural Station at Tarbol.

AGRICULTURE

On the great plain of the Bekaa, one of the foremost sources of Lebanon's past income was agriculture. Today, while yet a flourishing force, it counts for only 13 per cent of the economy, exactly equal to tourism as a source of national revenue. Yet agriculture continues to be one of Lebanon's principal activities, occupying half of the total population, and farm products are the major items. Despite its small area, Lebanon has a wide variety of landscape and cultivation.

More than one-fifth of cultivated land is given over to subtropical and temperate fruits. Apples head the list of fruits exported. Grapes are rampant in their growth and small country householders have vines rambling over wall and trellis. Olives and tobacco are next in value,

Under the Lebanese reforestation scheme, new access roads to timber lands are being built.

Age-old farming methods survive in rural Lebanon. This boy is threshing grain by driving over it in his sledge.

Sheep-farming is a main activity in Lebanon, since more mutton is eaten here than any other meat.

At Enfe, on the coast, windmills (seen through the blades of another mill) pump sea water into shallow enclosures, where it evaporates, leaving salt deposits.

followed by vegetables and cereals. Lebanon is sixth among the Mediterranean citrus-producing countries, with a production of 200,000 tons, half of this amount being exported, mainly to Arab countries, and to Eastern Europe.

Due to the range of climate, terrain and altitude, summer and winter fruits and vegetables are always available. Lebanon's agriculture is at present undergoing a renewal, known as the Verdure Plan, whose objectives are the conservation and improvement of the soil, the planting of trees to combat erosion, the provision of implements to small farmers, the training of qualified personnel and the placing at farmers' disposal of the financial resources required to develop their land.

The Government is also taking part in the financing of a navigation company, which transports Lebanese fruits in refrigerated ships. And to improve the balance of trade, an agreement is in effect between the Administration of the Verdure Plan and the U.N.'s Food and Agricultural Organization (F.A.O.) to survey new markets for further exports.

A village girl displays a huge sunflower head. The government is encouraging sunflower cultivation in depressed areas near Baalbek, whose people formerly gained their livelihood growing Indian hemp (cannabis), a crop that is now officially banned.

Dusk falls as this farmer of the Bekaa plain rides home on a bullock-driven sledge.

Traditionally Islamic in design, this structure is dwarfed by the fortifications of Muscat.

Oman

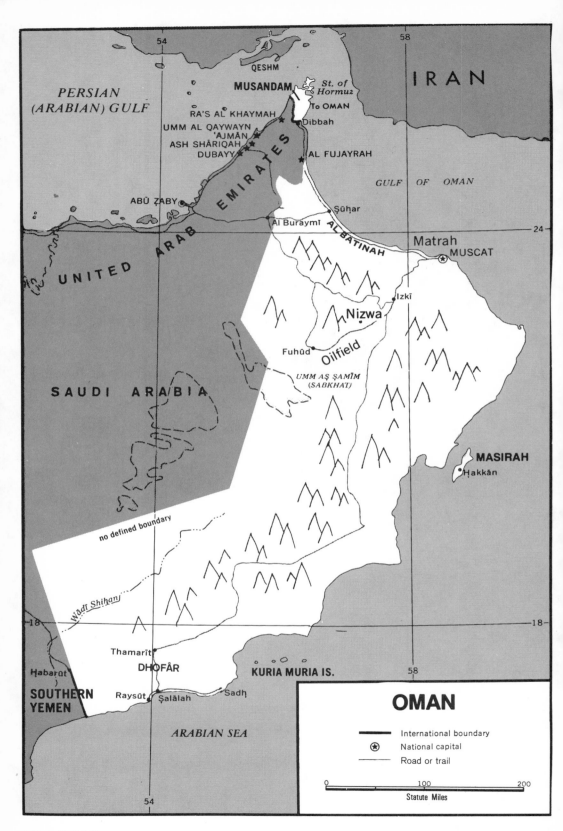

PERSIAN
(ARABIAN) GULF

QESHM

MUSANDAM

St. of
Hormuz

To OMAN

IRAN

RA'S AL KHAYMAH

Dibbah

UMM AL QAYWAYN
'AJMĀN
ASH SHĀRIQAH
DUBAYY

AL FUJAYRAH

GULF   OF   OMAN

ABŪ ZABY

UNITED   ARAB   EMIRATES

Al Buraymī

Şūḩar

AL BAṬINAH

Matrah
MUSCAT

24

SAUDI   ARABIA

Nizwa

Izkī

Fuḩūd
Oilfield

UMM AṢ ṢAMĪM
(SABKHAT)

MASIRAH

Ḩakkān

no defined boundary

Wādī Shiḩan

18

Thamarīt

DHOFÂR

KURIA MURIA IS.

58

Ḩabarūt

SOUTHERN
YEMEN

Raysūt
Şalālah

Sadḩ

ARABIAN SEA

OMAN

——— International boundary

⊛ National capital

——— Road or trail

0   100   200

Statute Miles

The rains have come and the bed of the Wadi Fanja is covered with running water, as women in traditional costume hasten to fill their vessels.

I. THE LAND

THE SULTANATE OF OMAN, occupying the southwest corner of the Arabian Peninsula, has land boundaries on the west with the United Arab Emirates, Saudi Arabia and the People's Democratic Republic of Yemen (Southern Yemen). The sultanate is bounded on the north by the Gulf of Oman, separating it from Iran, and on the east by the Arabian Sea. The boundary with Saudi Arabia is undefined, since it cuts through the Rub al-Khali, or Empty Quarter, a vast sea of sand, and the boundary with Southern Yemen is in dispute.

It is therefore difficult to give an exact figure for the area of Oman. According to the source, the figure may vary from 82,000 to 120,000 square miles (213,200 sq km to 312,000 sq km). For purposes of comparison, it could be said that Oman is more or less the size of Great Britain or of Nevada.

Also part of Oman is the small peninsula of Musandam on the Strait of Hormuz between the Gulf of Oman and the Persian Gulf. Musandam is separated from the rest of Oman by part of the United Arab Emirates.

New housing rises above the rocky hills of Oman.

TOPOGRAPHY

Oman is largely mountainous, with granite and limestone ridges rising to nearly 10,000 feet (3,000 metres) at the highest peak, Jabal Shams. Many of the valleys between the ranges are fertile and some have adequate water sources. Cutting through the mountains to the coast are *wadis*, or dry valleys that turn to stream beds whenever there is rain. The wadis have long been the only access routes to the interior.

The coastal strip is largely dry and barren except for a fertile stretch on the Gulf of Oman called Al Batinah. Off the Arabian Sea coast are the Kuria Muria Islands, five barren islets that formerly belonged to Southern Yemen, and the larger island of Masirah.

CLIMATE

The climate varies from region to region. The coast is hot and humid, while the interior is hot and dry, and a few places in the mountains have a year-round temperate climate.

Rainfall is slight and irregular except for the southern districts where heavy monsoon rains fall in the summer. Much of the land under cultivation is irrigated by a system of underground conduits which carry water from springs in the mountains, a method known as *falaj*.

ANIMALS, PLANTS AND MINERALS

Among hoofed mammals, the *wal*, a kind of ibex, is found in the mountains. Other mammals include hyenas, foxes, hares, wildcats, and a hyrax called the *wahr*. Among the birds are bustards, quails, partridges, sand grouse, doves and falcons.

Date palms, tamarisks and acacias are found throughout the land, along with the jujube, and junipers grow in the higher places. On the coastal plain around Salalah there are coconut palms, which are found nowhere else in Arabia.

Oil was discovered in Oman in 1964, and is now the country's greatest resource, although it is not present in abundance as it is in some other Arab states. Large quantities of natural gas exist and recent surveys have established the presence of copper—in fact, copper mines dating from 2000 B.C. were found—as well as asbestos, iron, nickel, coal, chrome and manganese. These all remain to be exploited.

CITIES

Oman has no large cities. The largest town is Matrah, on the coast, a short distance from Muscat, the capital, also on the coast. Matrah has 20,000 people and Muscat 7,000. Other towns are Salalah and Nizwa, each with 10,000 people.

Fort Mirani is one of the old defences of Muscat.

2. HISTORY

ARCHEOLOGICAL explorations in Oman are of recent date, since the country was a sort of forbidden kingdom until 1970. Diggings and finds made so far show evidence of civilized life dating as far back as 3000 B.C. The affinities of this ancient culture seem to be with both Mesopotamia and the Indus Valley civilization of India.

The first recorded Arabs to enter Oman came from Yemen in A.D. 120, some 500 years before the advent of Islam.

ISLAM

Oman became completely Moslem during the lifetime of Mohammed, founder of Islam, in the 7th century A.D. During the Middle Ages, Oman became a leading sea power, sending ships on voyages all over the coast of Africa and to the Far East. The period between the 7th and 15th centuries is known as the Golden Age of Oman, when Omani seamen introduced Islam into many faraway places.

In the 15th century, the Portuguese appeared off the coast of Oman and, by 1507, they had conquered the coastal area, which they held until 1649, when the Omanis finally drove them out. Zanzibar was annexed by Oman in 1652, and Mombasa in Kenya in 1697.

A GREAT MARITIME POWER

After the expulsion of the Portuguese, Oman once more became a leading maritime power—in fact, the dominant one in the western Indian Ocean. Omani settlements and colonies were established on the coasts of East Africa, Persia and Baluchistan (part of Pakistan).

The Omani ascendancy reached its peak under Sultan Said ibn Sultan, whose reign lasted from 1807 until 1856. In 1840, this sultan even sent emissaries to the United States. A

The Citadel dominates Nizwa, one of the leading towns of the interior.

number of European countries opened consulates in Muscat.

After the death of Said, Oman declined, having lost its East African possessions, when the Omani realm was divided between two claimants to the throne. After this event, a period of internal dissension, armed rebellion and poverty ensued.

THE BRITISH

The British never established a protectorate over Oman as they did over other Arabian states, but from the late 18th century their influence in Oman was so considerable that for a while in the 19th century, the sultanate was a virtual dependency of British India.

SULTAN SAID IBN TAIMUR

The father of the present sultan, Said ibn Taimur, was a despot who ascended the throne in 1932. He promptly banned singing (except for military chants), dancing, drinking and smoking. He closed the cinemas, forbade art exhibits, and forced all women to go veiled. Foreign influences were discouraged and foreigners kept out, except for some British officers and American missionaries. The sultan discouraged education, since he thought schools were hatcheries for dangerous ideas. During his reign Oman sank to the level of one of the world's most backward states.

SULTAN QABUS

In 1970, Sultan Said ibn Taimur was deposed in a lightning coup and banished to England, where he died in 1972. His English-educated son, Qabus, became sultan—and Oman began to move belatedly into the modern world. Qabus, whose father had once imprisoned him for four years, was determined to bring about in Oman the changes that had taken place elsewhere in the Gulf.

Crown Prince Hassan of Jordan greets Sultan Qabus during a state visit. King Hussein of Jordan is in the middle.

Students engage in exercises under the auspices of Sultan Qabus.

3. GOVERNMENT

OMAN IS an absolute monarchy, without a constitution, a legislature or legal political parties. The judicial system is at present wholly based on the *sharia,* or Islamic law. In parts of the interior, tribal law alone is in force—indeed, it has been said that there are denizens of the interior who have never heard of either the present sultan or his predecessor. A new legal system including secular, that is, non-religious, courts is being organized.

The country is divided administratively into districts called *wilayats,* ruled by governors called *walis.*

Sultan Qabus has abolished most of his father's restrictive laws, and has launched a major development plan to improve health and education and develop industry and natural resources. Since no such plan existed before 1970, the progress achieved in such a short time is considerable, although still far from the desired goals.

OPPOSITION

Insurgency has been a problem for the new Sultan, especially in the southern district of Dhofar, where a revolt has been in progress since 1964, with Southern Yemeni help since 1967. The insurgents belong to an illegal group called the Popular Front for the Liberation of Oman and the Arab Gulf (PFLOAG). This Communist-aided group seeks to overthrow all traditional régimes among the Arab states of the Gulf.

Tribesmen of the interior are of the classic Arabian type that surged out of the desert in the 7th century A.D. and conquered much of the known world.

4. THE PEOPLE

THE POPULATION of Oman is about 1,000,000 and is basically a mixture of North and South Arabian stocks. Along the coast there is a heavy Negro strain, including whole villages of blacks, a reminder of the infamous slave trade in which Oman engaged in the past. There are also numerous Pakistanis, Iranians and Indians. Among the native Omanis are many of Baluchi origin, whose ancestors came after Oman colonized the Baluchi coast of Iran and Pakistan.

In the coastal areas a visitor may hear such Indo-European languages as Urdu, English, Farsi and Baluchi, but elsewhere only Arabic is spoken.

RELIGION

Oman has a distinctive religious background —it has been dominated for years by the Ibadite sect of Islam. Ibadites differ from both Sunni and Shiite Moslems, who constitute the two main sects, in several respects. The main difference concerns the spiritual successors of Mohammed. The Shiites say that only descendants of Mohammed's daughter Fatima and her husband Ali can be termed *imam* or spiritual leader. The Sunnites call the spiritual leader *caliph* and aver that he must be a member of the same tribe as Mohammed. The Ibadites claim that any Moslem with the right qualities can be named imam. Out of the world's 500,000,000 Moslems, only 500,000 are Ibadites, and most of these are in Oman.

The Ibadites came into being in Iraq, but following persecution by the Sunnites, they fled to the beautiful barren mountains and green highland valleys of Oman to escape their enemies. In Oman, the Ibadite imamate continued as an institution into the 20th century. At times there was open hostility between the imam, Oman's religious leader, with his headquarters in the interior, and the sultan, its political leader, with his seat in Muscat. In

Sultan Qabus (left) in field attire visits a new school. Over 75 per cent of Omanis were illiterate at the time he assumed the throne—a percentage that is steadily decreasing thanks to the new impetus in education given by the Sultan.

Omani Boy Scouts now have modern equipment such as the "bullhorn" being used by the boy between the two drummers.

Omanis from the countryside pour into Muscat to celebrate the national holiday, November 18.

The new 300-bed hospital at Salalah on the southwest coast is one of the most modern in the world.

The Minister of Education (left) tells newsmen at a press conference about new developments in Oman's fast-growing educational system.

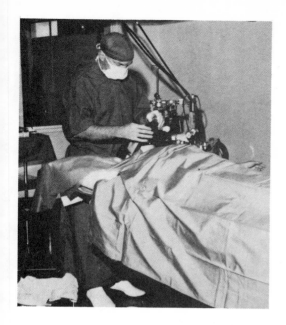

Medical care in Oman is now provided free by the state.

Sultan Qabus came to power he changed the name to Oman alone to symbolize the end of strife and the beginning of unity.

WAY OF LIFE

Omanis are undergoing an unprecedented change in the circumstances in which they live. Construction of new housing, hospitals, schools, factories, highways, and ports has become a ceaseless activity. Matrah, small though it is, is now the scene of traffic jams, with long back-ups of motor cars and other vehicles. Women, however, are still largely unaffected by change and the principle of equality of the sexes exists largely on paper.

1959, the last imam went into exile in Saudi Arabia. The country was long known as Muscat and Oman, reflecting the division between coast and hinterland—Oman being the interior highland and Muscat the coastal sultanate. When

Oman is trying to shift from the Middle Ages to the modern world in one short decade. The Sultan's aim is to put the quality of life in Oman on a par with that of Kuwait, Bahrain, Qatar and the United Arab Emirates.

The new air-conditioned hospital in Salalah was designed by West German specialists, and has the latest laboratory and treatment equipment.

The new deepwater port outside Matrah is named Mina Qabus, after the Sultan.

5. THE ECONOMY

AGRICULTURE WAS the basis of the Omani economy until the development of the country's petroleum resources. Until then, industry was purely on the level of handicrafts and the chief exports were dates and limes grown in the Batinah district.

Dates and limes are grown in a continuous strip of land irrigated by wells along the Batinah coast. Here the coastal villagers are both farmers and fishermen. In the interior, wheat and dates are leading crops, and on the high plateau near Jabal Sham, such cooler-climate fruits as apricots, walnuts, peaches and grapes are grown. Elsewhere, coconuts, tobacco, bananas, oranges, mangoes, melons, papayas, forage crops, and vegetables are grown, along with sugar cane and rice.

COMMERCE AND INDUSTRY

Apart from oil, the principal exports are limes, fish and dates—yet these three items amount to only one per cent of the value of exports, while oil amounts to 99 per cent. The

Omani metalcrafting is typified by this coffee pot presented to the United Nations by the Sultan.

In the span of a few years Omanis have been trained to operate the Sultanate's new telecommunications system.

Muscat on the coast and Nizwa in the interior are now connected by this modern highway.

chief imports are machinery, clothing, food-stuffs, and manufactured goods.

Omani industry, apart from petroleum extraction and processing, is in its infancy. Fishing and date-drying, two traditional industries, are scheduled for modernization and expansion. Oman's economic planners, looking to the day when their country's oil resources will be depleted, expect modernized agriculture and fisheries, along with diversified light industry, to be the future basis of the economy.

The 1970's have seen the construction of new highways—there were only 5 miles of paved roads in 1971—a new international airport, and a new deepwater port, Mina Qabus, near Matrah. In 1970, there was one post office in the entire country, at Muscat—today there is a modern postal and telecommunications system and a radio station. New housing, hotels, hospitals, schools and sewerage and water supply systems are under construction.

In September, 1972, the Permanent Representative of Oman to the United Nations (left) signs an agreement for the United Nations to provide technical assistance to Oman.

Exquisite filigree work in the traditional Islamic style adorns a doorway of the Qatar National Museum.

Qatar

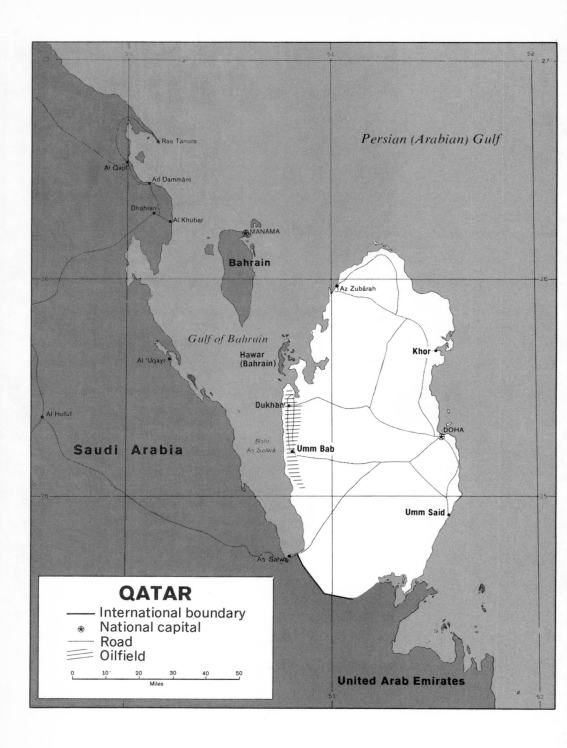

Persian (Arabian) Gulf

Ras Tanura

Al Qaṭif

Ad Dammām

Dhahran

Al Khubar

⊛ MANAMA

Bahrain

Az Zubārah

Gulf of Bahrain

Hawar
(Bahrain)

Khor

Al 'Uqayr

Al Hufūf

Dukhan

DOHA ⊛

Saudi Arabia

Bahr
As Salwā

Umm Bab

Saudi Arabia

Umm Said

Aṣ Salwá

United Arab Emirates

QATAR
—— International boundary
⊛ National capital
——— Road
▦ Oilfield

0   10   20   30   40   50
Miles

Old forts stud the coast of the Qatar Peninsula, reminders of the struggles that took place in the Gulf in the past.

I. THE LAND

THE STATE OF QATAR occupies a roughly oval peninsula jutting northwards into the Persian (Arabian) Gulf from the mainland of Saudi Arabia. The peninsula, which is about 100 miles (260 km) wide, is separated from the coast of Saudi Arabia by the Gulf of Bahrain. On the south, Qatar is bounded by Saudi Arabia and the United Arab Emirates. With an area of 4,247 square miles (11,042 sq km), Qatar is about half the size of Wales or somewhat more than half the size of Massachusetts.

TOPOGRAPHY

Most of the peninsula consists of a low plateau about 250 feet (75 metres) above sea level, which rises rather abruptly from the shore. The terrain is mostly flat, with occasional ridges of limestone, and the soil is generally barren, composed of gravel or sand. The land slopes very gradually from west to east.

Surface features characteristic of Qatar are *duhlans*, or crevices formed by rainwater collecting in cracks in the ground. The water eroded the underlying limestone and created underground caverns, which in turn led to the cracking of the surface and the formation of holes that collect water. Other features are the *riyadhs* (gardens), which are pools where rainwater has collected, and the *wadis,* dry valleys where water flows only after rainfall.

The coast of Qatar has many brackish pools and salt marshes, and a number of small islands, the largest of which, Hawar, along with its adjacent islets, belongs to Bahrain.

CLIMATE

The climate is of the desert type, with a long, very hot summer, and a mild, often warm winter. There is little rainfall, but high humidity, especially in summer. The cause of the humidity is the evaporation of sea water during extreme periods of heat. The temperature in summer averages 90°F (32°C) and may reach 120°F (49°C). The winter average is 61°F (16°C), but the temperature can drop to 41°F (5°C).

Looking like cheesecakes, huge oil storage tanks are now a common feature of Qatar's once empty landscape.

The winds in Qatar come chiefly from the north and the southeast. The north wind helps to cool the weather in summer and also brings rain. The southeast wind, which blows in from the deserts of the Arabian peninsula, is hot and dry in summer, but sometimes brings rain in winter.

The port facilities at Umm Said are used chiefly for loading oil on ships.

A broad esplanade (upper right) lines the bay at Doha. At middle right is the Clock Tower, a city landmark.

The graceful Guest Palace in Doha is reserved for visiting dignitaries.

FLORA AND FAUNA

The land is largely arid, sustaining relatively few plants and animals. However, water development schemes have converted sizeable areas to agriculture in recent years. Native wild plants include palms, acacias and other thorny small trees and shrubs and the lotus tree, or jujube, which produces a small, yellow, edible fruit.

Numerous species of birds—among them flamingos, cormorants, ospreys, swallows, larks, curlews, bustards and hoopoes—are found along with jerboas (jumping rats), lizards, rabbits and gazelles. Qatar is the home of a herd of Arabian oryxes, an antelope that has become largely extinct throughout the rest of the Arabian Peninsula.

NATURAL RESOURCES

Qatar has only one important natural resource—petroleum, which has become the basis of modernization and economic development in this small and otherwise poorly endowed country.

CITIES

The largest city, and the capital, of Qatar is Doha, situated on a bay midway along the east

Doha's Grand Mosque, whose minaret dominates the city skyline, is illuminated at night.

The new Gulf Hotel overlooks the port at Doha.

coast of the country. Before oil was struck, Doha was a small, impoverished village. Today it is a city of 100,000, with paved streets, electricity, modern buildings, a modern port and an international airport.

Other important towns are Umm Said, also on the east coast, an important petroleum town and the country's second seaport, and Dakhan, on the west coast and also important in the oil industry.

The Ras Abu Abbud overpass (flyover) outside Doha, is part of Qatar's new highway system.

The Emir of Qatar meets with the Sultan of Oman (left).

2. HISTORY

DANISH ARCHEOLOGISTS digging in Qatar in the 1950's and 1960's discovered Stone and Iron Age fragments indicating human habitation as far back as 4000 B.C. The early history of Qatar is largely unknown until the advent of Islam, however.

ISLAM

Qatar accepted Islam at the same time as Bahrain—in A.D. 628, just six years after the Hegira. One of the early commanders of the Arab armies that swept into Persia was a native of Qatar—Qatari bin al-Fajaa, who is remem-

Stone Age artifacts from Qatar's remote past can be seen at the National Museum.

Sheikh Hamad bin Abdullah al-Thani, who died in 1949, was the father of Emir Khalifa, the present Emir.

bered as a poet as well as a soldier. Qatar was ruled by various successor states of the Arab Empire, until A.D. 1076, when it fell to the al-Ayuni dynasty from Bahrain. Various Arab dynasties ruled the country in the succeeding centuries.

In the 16th century, the Portuguese appeared off the coast of Qatar, and later the Dutch, French and English, whose struggles for control of the spice trades with India and the silk trade with Persia spilled over the shores of the Persian Gulf. During this period Qatar was torn with civil strife as local sheikhs fought for its control. The Khalifa dynasty of Bahrain claimed dominion over Qatar and exacted tribute from Qatari chiefs until 1868, when British intervention ended the Bahraini claims.

THE BRITISH

The British did not stay, however, and in 1872, Turkey occupied Qatar. The Turks maintained a flimsy control over Qatar until just before World War I, when Turkey signed an agreement with Britain, relinquishing its claim to Qatar. The British recognized Sheikh Abdullah ibn Jasim al-Thani as Ruler of Qatar, and, in 1916, after the withdrawal of the Turks, an Anglo-Qatari treaty was signed, establishing a British protectorate over Qatar.

Qatar remained under British protection until 1968, when the British government announced its intention to withdraw all British forces east of Suez by 1971. Qatar entered into negotiations with Bahrain and the seven Trucial Sheikhdoms to form a union. When these negotiations became unproductive, Bahrain chose independence by itself in August, 1971, and Qatar followed suit on September 3, 1971. In the same month, Qatar joined the United Nations and the Arab League as a fully sovereign state.

In September, 1972, the Foreign Minister of Qatar (middle) signs an agreement for Qatari participation in the United Nations Development Program.

3. GOVERNMENT

QATAR IS a hereditary monarchy whose Head of State bears the title of Emir and who must belong to the al-Thani family. While not yet a constitutional monarchy, Qatar, under the guidance of the Emir, is clearly evolving in that direction.

The present Emir, Sheikh Khalifa bin Hamad al-Thani, assumed power in 1972, following a bloodless coup in which he deposed his cousin, Emir Ahmad bin Ali ben Abdullah al-Thani. Emir Khalifa, who was both Crown Prince and Prime Minister at the time, took over the throne with the backing of the al-Thani family and the armed forces, in order, it was implied, to speed up social and economic progress in the country.

As Prime Minister, he had in fact been the moving force in the government for a dozen years prior to the coup.

The Emir of Qatar (returning a salute) reviews a military parade. The Emir is Supreme Commander of Qatar's Armed Forces. The Qatari flag flies at the left.

Although Qatar as yet has no formal constitution, it has a "Basic Law" that is almost the same as one. The Basic Law, proclaimed in 1970, includes a bill of rights and provides for a Council of Ministers and an Advisory Council.

The Council of Ministers, or Cabinet, the chief executive body, is appointed by the Emir, and functions as a law-making body. The Council of Ministers is the agency that administers and carries out the progressive social and economic policies that are transforming Qatar from a wasteland into a modern industrial society.

The Advisory Council comprises 20 members appointed for 6 years. The main purpose of the Council is to review and draft legislation initiated by the Council of Ministers before such legislation is submitted to the Emir to be ratified and proclaimed by him. It also serves as an advisory body on social, cultural, political and economic affairs.

The judges in Qatar are independent of any authority other than the law of the land and are expected to dispense justice impartially, without interference from anyone. For purposes of administration the courts are under the Ministry of Justice.

The Qatar Monetary Agency is a government office that controls monetary and lending policy in Qatar.

This new primary school is one of 87 that have been completed since 1956. Although many older Qataris are illiterate, the younger generation has access to some of the most modern educational facilities in the Middle East.

4. THE PEOPLE

QATAR HAS THE smallest population of any Arab state, not only in the Middle East, but in North Africa as well. Furthermore, less than half of its 180,000 people are native Qataris. Iranians, Pakistanis, and other non-Arab foreigners make up over one third of the population. Arabs from other countries constitute the remainder. The presence of so many foreigners in Qatar poses a problem. Qatari citizenship is not easy to acquire, even for Arabs. If and when parliamentary government comes to Qatar, the presence of so many disenfranchised people could lead to trouble.

Population distribution is lopsided, since more than half the people in Qatar live in Doha. The remainder live mainly in small towns and villages on or near the coast. The interior is largely uninhabited except for a few nomadic Bedouins who still roam about with their flocks of sheep, goats and camels. The government is seeking to induce these nomads to adopt a settled existence and their way of life may soon come to an end.

The native Qataris are Sunni Moslems of the strict Wahabi sect. The foreign-born residents are chiefly Moslems of other denominations. The native Qataris are descended mostly from three famous Bedouin tribes, some of whose members entered the little peninsula over the centuries and settled there. These tribes are the Awamir, Manasir and Bani Hajir. The Qataris, like other peoples of the Arabian Peninsula, include a Negro strain.

HEALTH, EDUCATION AND HOUSING

Qatar provides free education and medical service for its citizens. The modern hospitals and clinics maintained by the Ministry of Public Health are equipped to deal with all but a few medical cases. If it is not possible to treat

The Qatar National Museum, housed in an old palace in Doha, contains examples of traditional Qatari crafts, jewels, manuscripts and rare books, as well as historical exhibits.

Ceremonies take place at the opening of the Fourth Arab Gulf Football Tournament, held in Doha in March, 1976.

The Vocational Training Institute at Doha trains Qatari workers for skilled jobs now held by foreign technicians.

a patient properly in Qatar, he is sent abroad for treatment, accompanied by his family, at government expense.

Government-built housing is available to Qatari citizens on generous terms. The land on which the house is built is provided free of charge and two interest-free loans are made, one for the house itself and a second to pay for the furniture. Repayment of the second loan begins when the first loan has been repaid. The time allowed for repayment varies according to income but it is usually 20 to 25 years. Free housing is provided for the disabled and for citizens over 60 years of age.

Free education is provided at all levels from primary school through university, and free adult education is available to foreigners as well as citizens. Books, school meals, transport, clothing, holidays and boarding accommodations are all free. In addition, monthly cash allowances are made to needy students and their parents. Overseas scholarships to universities are numerous and free study abroad is included in the curriculum of Qatar's Teachers Colleges.

CULTURE AND RECREATION

The official language of Qatar is Arabic, but English is widely taught and in common use, especially among the foreign communities.

The Qatar Cultural Centre was established in 1975 to further the arts. Projects in the arts are presently organized by the cultural sections of the Ministry of Information, and emphasize folk art, the graphic arts, and theatre—Qatar theatre troupes have performed in international festivals.

Qatar Broadcasting offers a variety of educational, cultural and news presentations on both radio and television in Arabic and English.

Sports are strongly emphasized by the government. Football (soccer) is the national game, and volleyball, basketball, table tennis and swimming are popular. A vast sports complex—Khalifa Sports City—has been built near Doha. The complex includes a stadium with a seating capacity of 40,000, an Olympic-size swimming pool, and facilities for numerous other sports and activities.

Fresh water for Doha and its environs is provided by the Ras Abu Abbud Desalination Plant, where sea water is freed of its salt and other impurities.

5. ECONOMY

QATAR HAS BEEN transformed since 1949 from a land whose only wealth lay in its pearl fisheries, into a modern state. The first step in this change came in 1935, when the first oil prospecting began. Oil was struck in 1940, but production was discontinued during World War II. However, after 1949, oil became the mainstay of the economy and oil revenues the basis of all social improvement.

Ports have been deepened and modernized, highways built and factories erected, including steel mills, desalination plants, and fertilizer and petrochemical factories. Irrigation has made Qatar an exporter of fruits and vegetables—where formerly nothing grew.

The pearl fishing industry had started to decline about the time that oil was discovered.

The reason for the decline was growing domination of the world pearl market by Japan, where the technique of producing cultured pearls had been perfected. By the mid-1970's the Qatari pearl industry had become virtually extinct—in the 1930's the Qatari pearl fishing fleet had numbered 400!

PETROLEUM

The oil fields of Qatar fall into two groups—an onshore belt along the west coast and an offshore zone along the east coast. The total daily output of Qatar's wells was 600,000 barrels in 1976. Qatar's petroleum reserves are extensive compared to Bahrain's, but modest compared

Only a few pearling vessels like this survive today—and six of them can be seen in an artificial lake on the grounds of the Qatar National Museum.

AGRICULTURE AND FISHERIES

In little more than a generation, Qatar has progressed from the point where agriculture (other than herding) hardly existed, to the point where it can now export fruits and vegetables. Vast water supply projects, involving the digging of deep artesian wells, are transforming barren wastes into woodland, fields and orchards.

to those of the United Arab Emirates, Kuwait or Saudi Arabia.

NATURAL GAS

Qatar's abundant natural gas is now being liquefied in local installations, and separated into propane, butane, and benzine. These fuels are then pumped aboard giant tankers for export.

OTHER INDUSTRIES

Residual gases from the liquid gas factories are diverted to the petrochemical plants to be made first into ethylene and then into plastics. Another government sponsored industry is cement manufacture—both Portland and sulphur-resistant types are produced.

The Qatar Fertilizer Company operates on natural gas and uses natural gas with a high methane content as raw material. The finished products are ammonia, which is exported, and urea, a nitrogen-rich fertilizer, for domestic use.

Gulf pearls are among the finest in the world. A man examines a string of Qatari pearls at a pearling industry exhibit.

This modern factory prepares the famous Gulf prawns for export.

The Qatar Earth Station, west of Doha, has a huge dish antenna beamed on the internationally owned Indian Ocean Satellite. It carries 30 international telephone circuits able to handle 5,000 calls at once, and two color television channels.

Qatar has modern communications, with a fully automatic telephone system with direct dialling to other Gulf countries.

Once barren soil now yields crops of luscious melons. Through the investment of oil profits, Qatar has expanded the production of fruits and vegetables to the point where it now exports them.

Among the 16 airlines served by Doha International Airport is Gulf Aviation, which is owned jointly by British Airways, Bahrain, Qatar, Oman and Abu Dhabi (largest of the United Arab Emirates).

Scientific animal husbandry is given priority among Qatari agricultural projects. Sheep such as these were long the chief livestock, but cattle raising is now expanding.

The principal farm products are cereal grains, dates, vegetables, fodder, hay, sheep, goats, cattle, poultry and eggs. Extensive forestry projects now grow trees to serve as windbreaks and to beautify the edges of highways, parks and public gardens.

The National Fishing Company, formed in 1966, has a fleet of six refrigerated trawlers. The principal catch is shrimp, which is frozen and packed for export.

OUTLOOK

Although Qatar is not faced with as rapid depletion of its oil reserves as is Bahrain, the government nonetheless is proceeding rapidly to convert oil revenues into foreign investment, into the development of agriculture, industry and water and electricity resources at home, and the education of its citizens for life in an advanced industrial society.

Mecca and the Great Mosque with the kaaba
as they appeared in the 19th century.

Saudi
Arabia

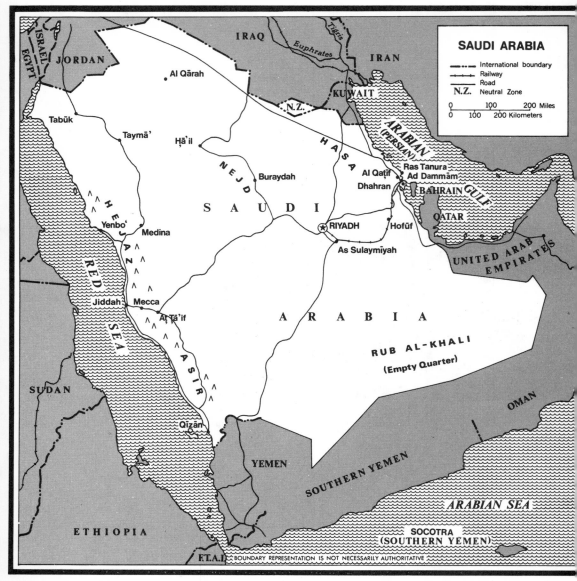

Note: the body of water between Iran and the Arabian Peninsula is called the Arabian Gulf in Arab countries, and the Persian Gulf in other countries.

An aerial view of the desert near the Hofuf Oasis reveals a sculptured effect created by strong winds. The black spots are date groves partially covered by the wind-blown sand.

INTRODUCTION

THE KINGDOM of Saudi Arabia occupies most of the Arabian Peninsula, but the history of this region is more than just the history of a country or a people. It was here that the Semites began to emerge on the stage of recorded history, and here was the birthplace of Mohammed, the prophet who established Islam, one of the world's major religions. It is a huge country, but much of it is an inhospitable sandy desert with little or no rainfall. There is not one river, and in the interior, daytime temperatures of 130° F (54° C) are common, suddenly giving way to the chill of night. It was from here that the first adherents of Islam charged out on their swift horses with the Koran in one hand and the sword in the other to conquer many lands.

Until about 1940 Saudi Arabia had changed little since Biblical times. Then, in the late 1930's, oil was discovered and suddenly the winds of change began to blow in the desert. Much has been altered and much has remained

Pilgrims' tents cluster at the foot of the fabled Mount Arafat, one of the main stops during the Mecca pilgrimage ceremony.

In the bazaars one can see camel saddles, ancient muskets, aromatic woods and holy water alongside souvenirs of Mecca made in Japan, and Persian prayer rugs made in Italy. A few donkeys along with cars of every type fight the traffic, the car drivers blow musical horns, while the donkey drivers shout to encourage their beasts to move faster. In the background radios blasting with the latest hit song from Cairo blend with the call of the *muezzin*, summoning the faithful to prayer.

The Saudi mechanic who operates an oil well today was most likely a camel driver a few years ago. His cousins probably still live in the desert in goathair tents, with a way of life that has changed very little since the time of Abraham.

the same. In settled areas the car has replaced the camel, but the nomadic Bedouin still clings to his ancient ways, forever moving with his goats and camels in search of new grazing land and water.

In the holy city of Mecca, a hotel was built by European architects, who were nonetheless forbidden to enter the city!

It is these contrasting elements that make up Saudi Arabia.

In Saudi Arabia, a man confronts fried chicken served by a United States fast-food company. A life-size cut-out of the firm's founder appears behind him.

The landscape of the Rub Al-Khali, or Empty Quarter, consists of an almost lifeless desert, 250,000 square miles in area. The characteristic elements of this desert landscape are withered shrubs, dunes and drifting sand.

I. THE LAND

SAUDI ARABIA occupies an area of nearly 900,000 square miles—about the size of the United States east of the Mississippi, and somewhat larger than all nine European Common Market countries, plus Spain and Portugal. On its western coast, running parallel with the Red Sea, is the narrow coastal plain of Tihama. Farther inland, the Hejaz mountains rise to 9,000 feet, then slope gently towards the east, forming a desert plateau with an average elevation of 2,000 to 3,000 feet.

The southern part of the country contains the Rub Al-Khali or Empty Quarter, one of the world's most isolated and forbidding terrains. Almost completely waterless and nearly devoid of life, this desert covers an area as large as the state of Texas.

Saudi Arabia is bordered on the west by the Red Sea, on the north by Jordan, Iraq, Kuwait and two Neutral Zones between Iraq and Kuwait. On the east, it is bounded by the Arabian Gulf, the Sheikhdom of Qatar, and the

Abha, the capital of Asir and one of the most scenic spots in the country, is 7,000 feet (2,100 m) above sea level.

United Arab Emirates (formerly called the Seven Trucial Sheikhdoms), and on the south by Yemen, Southern Yemen (formerly called the Aden Protectorate), and Oman. Many of these boundaries are ill-defined and border incidents have occurred, particularly along the frontier with Yemen.

REGIONS

Saudi Arabia is divided into four main geographical areas—Hejaz, Nejd, Hasa and Asir. Hejaz, in the western part of the country, contains the important cities of Mecca, Medina, Jiddah and Taif. Nejd is the central part of the country and contains the capital city of Riyadh. Hasa is frequently referred to as the Eastern Province, and it is here that most of the oil wells are located. Asir, in the southwest part of the country, has the best agricultural land due to heavier rainfall.

THE OASES

This vast country does not have any rivers or lakes except for *wadis* or river beds that contain water only during the seasonal rains. The only other running waters are small streams

A young Jiddah boy is delighted with the dates presented to him during a visit to a date grove on the Mecca road. Date production is still an important source of revenue in the kingdom.

For hundreds of years the Hofuf Oasis has had a sand dune area 20 miles long and 5 miles wide encroaching on it at the rate of 40 feet a year. ARAMCO *has completed a detailed study outlining a series of control measures which will halt the movement of the dunes.*

fed by wells. To a large extent, the country depends for its water on underground sources.

An oasis is an island of greenery in an otherwise barren desert. This fertility is due to the presence of underground water in the form of springs or wells. The amount of water that is available usually determines the size of the oasis. Some consist merely of a few palm trees edging a muddy water-hole, and support no permanent inhabitants, but provide life-giving water for the thirsty traveller. Other oases cover large areas and contain small towns supporting a permanent population of several thousand people, who make a living raising camels, sheep and goats and grow a variety of vegetables and fruits.

Wherever there is enough water to last for the whole year, large scale agriculture is possible. Through irrigation, the government is creating many artificial oases to encourage the people in the area to settle down and grow their own food.

Natural jigsaw puzzles are created when the fine desert sand, packed tightly by spring rains, cracks because of fast evaporation under high temperatures. In summertime, temperatures reach 130 degrees F (54° C).

CLIMATE

The Arabian Peninsula is a part of the great desert belt that stretches across Africa from Morocco in the west to Pakistan's Indus Valley in central Asia in the east. Along with the other countries of this belt, Saudi Arabia has a very dry, hot climate with frequent dust- and sandstorms. During the day the summer temperatures can rise to 130°F (54°C) dropping to about 40 to 50°F (4 to 10°C) at night. It is not so hot

along the coasts of the Red Sea and Arabian Gulf, but the humidity is much higher, particularly on the Arabian Gulf, known for its frequent heavy fogs.

In the central and northern parts of the country, temperatures drop below freezing in the winter, but snowfall occurs only at the highest altitudes. Riyadh is quite cool in the winter, with daytime temperatures dropping as low as 50°F (10°C).

The average rainfall is 3 to 5 inches annually, with the Asir region in the southwest getting the greatest amount, about 10 to 20 inches a year.

FLORA

The vegetation is generally very sparse due to lack of rain and the high salt content of the soil. True trees are rare—in most areas non-existent, while small shrubs and annual herbs are common. Most plants have had to adapt to the conditions of desert existence, some by reducing the leaf surface area—spiny or needle-like

Treeless hills form a back-drop for the oasis city of Medina.

In a small town in the southern province of Asir, the dome-shaped houses are thatched with reeds.

leaves lose less water from evaporation. Others have acquired the ability to store water, and some have developed a tolerance for salty water.

Among small trees and shrubs adapted to the desert climate are the aloe and tamarisk, found all over the country. In the higher altitudes are figs, carobs, and junipers, as well as cactus-like euphorbias.

Wild flowers are abundant in the higher elevations, particularly during the rainy season. Reeds grow in isolated areas where the water supply permits it, and are used by the people to build huts and to thatch roofs.

The most important cultivated plant is the date palm. The date fruit is a popular food, while the tree supplies valuable wood and other by-products. The palm leaves are used for thatching roofs.

FAUNA

Wild animals include two antelopes—the small, fleet-footed gazelle and the large, stately oryx (now close to extinction). The carnivores are represented by the fox, lynx, wolf, hyena, wildcat, cheetah, jackal and an occasional leopard. Smaller mammals include the hedgehog, hare and hyrax.

Locusts used to be so numerous as to constitute a plague. Curiously, they were also esteemed as food by some of the Bedouins. There are many other species of insects, snakes, lizards, and scorpions, and the coastal waters contain many varieties of fish.

Ostriches are found in some areas and on the coast, flamingoes and pelicans are common, along with many other shore birds. The most common bird in the oases is the bulbul, and this songbird figures often in the popular poetry of the country.

No mention of the animal life of Saudi Arabia would be complete without a word on the camel and the horse, although both of these are domestic, not wild, animals.

THE CAMEL

The most important animal in the history of Saudi Arabia is the camel, which has made travel possible in the barren and frequently waterless desert. The camel of Arabia is the single-humped variety, or dromedary, as opposed to the two-humped camel of Central Asia, the Bactrian. The dromedary has flat, broad, thick-soled, cloven hoofs that do not sink in sand. Because camels have the ability to go for days without water, and longer, if provided with

Bedouins and their camels camp near an oil drilling rig in eastern Saudi Arabia.

juicy plants, they are especially adapted to desert life.

Camels have been observed to drink as much as 30 gallons (114 litres) of water at one time. Capable of carrying loads of from 250 to 600 pounds (1,125 to 2,700 kilos) depending on the season and availability of water, they can travel 20 to 30 miles (32 to 48 km) a day. The milk of the camel forms an important part in the diet of the desert Arab, often being the only liquid that the nomadic Bedouin has access to.

A lightweight camel used only for riding is also raised.

Traditionally the camel has been a popular subject in the literature and folklore of Arabia, which have endowed the animal with mythical

The Arabian Horse is famous the world over for its speed and graceful lines.

Offshore drilling platforms, operated by ARAMCO, *obtain oil from the sea bottom. Much of the oil in Saudi Arabia comes from offshore wells.*

qualities of beauty, wisdom, endurance, and other highly desirable traits. Travellers to the desert who are not so romantically inclined have found the camel to be an ill-tempered beast that often bites, kicks and spits.

THE ARABIAN HORSE

The horse was introduced from the north ages ago and in the isolation of Arabia, a distinctive breed developed. The small, handsome Arabian horse has great stamina and speed, and is an ancestor of the Thoroughbred horse of the West.

The horse, like the camel, has played a very important part in the history of Arabia, for it was this animal that provided speedy transportation in the 7th century, when the Arabs set out on their famous conquests. For the Bedouin it was the perfect steed for making raids upon other tribes or desert travellers. Unable to compete with the camel, the horse was never used for long journeys through the desert, however. Today the horse is a status symbol in Arabia—only the wealthy can afford the price and upkeep of a good one.

NATURAL RESOURCES

Saudi Arabia has one great natural resource—petroleum. In the remote past, hundreds of millions of years ago, the Arabian Gulf extended over a larger area than it does today. The seas at one time covered much of the land mass east, west, and north of the Persian Gulf, including eastern and northern Saudi Arabia, Kuwait,

Oil prospectors set up camp in the Rub Al-Khali.

Efforts are being made for development of water resources. Here a newly constructed well provides badly needed water.

and parts of Iran. In time the land gradually rose, the Gulf shrank, and large areas of what had been sea bottom became dry land.

During the time that this land was under the sea, vast quantities of dead plant and animal life were deposited on the sea bottom. This organic material was slowly changed by geological processes into a mineral oil—petroleum.

The Gulf area contains perhaps the world's largest single deposits of oil.

Diving for pearls is still carried on in the Arabian Gulf, whose waters were formerly one of the main sources of pearls. However, in the last few decades, pearl fishing has decreased considerably, due to competition from the cultured pearl industry in Japan.

The Holy Kaaba in Mecca is covered with a richly embroidered dark curtain. Mecca is the place toward which all Muslims face when praying. In the background some of the buildings of the old part of the city itself can be seen.

OTHER RESOURCES

As a result of the development of oil, several other important resources have been created—petrochemicals, fertilizers, and liquid propane gas. Studies are in progress to determine if other minerals known to exist—such as phosphates, magnesium, silver, gypsum, and iron—can be profitably exploited. In 1939, a mining company was formed to work the ancient gold and silver mine at Mahad Al-Dahab, not far from Medina. This mine was in use in the days of King Solomon. After 1954, operations ceased because it was no longer profitable to run the mine.

After 1970, concessions were granted to several United States and European firms to explore the country for minerals.

Pearl fishing is carried on in the Arabian Gulf area, but only on a small scale.

CITIES

MECCA

The religious capital of the country and the most sacred city for all Muslims, Mecca is the birthplace of the prophet Mohammed and the site of the Great Mosque, towards which all Muslims face five times each day when praying. It is the spiritual hub of Islam, the religion of the Muslims (or Moslems).

Mecca has a population of 367,000 people and is located in the province of Hejaz in a dry rocky valley surrounded by hills. Due to the hot, dry climate of the area, there are few agricultural settlements near the city and, except for the manufacturing of religious articles, there is little local industry.

From early antiquity Mecca was crisscrossed by important caravan routes, thus making it an important market town. Even before Islam, the

A group of pilgrims wearing the traditional pilgrim's garb face the Holy Kaaba in the courtyard of the Great Mosque.

city was the sacred place of a cult of idol worshippers. Today Mecca owes its prosperity entirely to the pilgrim trade. Several hundreds of thousands of pilgrims come annually, and the housing, feeding and servicing of these people is a gigantic enterprise in which the Government lends a helping hand by organizing transportation and the distribution of supplies.

The Great Mosque which dominates much of the city, dates from the 8th century, but has been constantly enlarged. Presently it can accommodate 300,000 pilgrims; on the outside

A familiar sight to the pilgrim is the main entrance of the Great Mosque in Mecca. Behind this ornate façade is a vast courtyard where the Holy Kaaba is housed.

372 ◇ SAUDI ARABIA

Medina is the second sacred city after Mecca. Seen here at night is the section of the "suk" (market) where the food vendors are concentrated. Large quantities of meats, vegetables, and other spicy and fragrant foods permeate the air with their pungent aromas.

there is parking space for 4,000 vehicles. Mecca also houses a College of Education and the Sharia or Islamic Studies College.

Mecca the Blessed, as it is called by Muslims, has been ruled by many tribes and sects, but the most prominent among them was the Koreish tribe. It was from this tribe that Mohammed was descended. After the death of Mohammed, the members of the Koreish were afforded many privileges and were granted the honorary title of Sherif. The highest personage was the Grand Sherif, the ruler of Mecca. Most of the Grand Sherifs came from one of the most distinguished families, the Beni Hashem or Hashemites. The Hashemites ruled Mecca, with some interruptions, until 1924, when Ibn Saud overthrew them and proclaimed himself king.

MEDINA

Second sacred city, after Mecca, Medina has 200,000 people and is located in a flourishing oasis, growing great quantities of dates, fruits, and grains.

The main building is the Great Mosque, also known as the Prophet's Mosque, which contains the tombs of Mohammed, his daughter Fatimah, and the Caliph Omar, who is revered by Muslims for having laid down the legal and administrative principles of Islam. Medina also houses the Islamic University, an important school for Islamic studies, and nearby is the famous Medina Library, a treasure house of Arabic texts on religion, geography, and medicine. The most valued and cherished book in this library is a Koran, handwritten on parchment, dating from the 7th century.

An old house in Jiddah is decorated with classic arabesque designs executed in plaster. Geometric designs are the only decorations permitted by the Koran.

Before the flight (Hegira) of Mohammed to Medina in A.D. 622, the city was called Yathrib. After the arrival of Mohammed, the city began to grow in importance and eventually became the seat of the caliphate, or Muslim leadership. It began to lose its importance in 662, when the caliphate was transferred to the more centrally located Damascus. Constant fighting among the local tribes resulted in frequent changes of rule. Eventually Medina was occupied by the Mamelukes from Egypt, then by the Ottoman (Turkish) Empire in 1517. The Saudis took it from the Turks in 1804 only to lose it to them again in 1812. It remained part of the Ottoman Empire until the end of World War I, when Ibn Saud consolidated his rule over all Hejaz.

JIDDAH

Situated on the Red Sea with a population of 600,000, Jiddah is the country's most important seaport. The inhabitants are of varied ethnic backgrounds—Arabs, Persians, Negroes, Indians, and people of other races, too, for most of the foreign embassies are located in this city.

Rugs and religious articles are manufactured locally, but the biggest industry is the handling of pilgrims. About 90 per cent of all the pilgrims from foreign lands enter Saudi Arabia through Jiddah. They used to come by boat, but, in increasingly larger numbers, they now come by air.

Jiddah has the country's largest bazaar (market place), filled with the exotic products and spices of the Orient alongside the assembly-line goods of Japan, Germany, and the United States. Outside the city, near the Medina Gate, is the site of the reputed grave of Eve. Once about 200 feet (60 m) long and 10 feet (3 m) high, it was demolished in 1927 by the Wahhabi sect.

RIYADH

Riyadh is the largest city, the political and administrative capital of the country and the heart of the Wahhabi reform movement. With a population of about 660,000, it is situated in the Nejd region, in a well watered fertile valley lush with date groves, orchards, and fields of grain. Riyadh, connected with the Dhahran on the Arabian Gulf by a railway, has a modern airport, and is important for the manufacture of cement, plastics, and prefabricated houses. The Riyadh University has faculties in the arts, sciences, religion, commerce, agriculture, pharmacy, engineering and medicine. Also

Along Riyadh's Avenue of the Ministries, modern buildings house various government offices.

located in Riyadh are the Royal Vocational Institute, the Military College, the Air Force College and the Interior Security Forces College.

The city is surrounded by a number of villages and towns rich in palm groves. These communities provide most of Riyadh's requirements in fruits and vegetables.

DHAHRAN

This oil camp in the Eastern Province, with about 45,000 people, is a very important link in the country's oil exploration and development. The headquarters of the Arabian American Oil Company (called ARAMCO) is here. Dhahran has a busy international airport and is connected to Hofuf and Riyadh by a railway and linked by pipe lines with Ras Tanura and other important oil hubs. The area has grown up since 1938, an island of modernity in the middle of the desert, full of air-conditioned prefabricated houses and supermarkets. A College of Petroleum and Mineral Resources has been set up in Dhahran.

Dhahran, as it looked in 1936, had about a dozen buildings housing the early oil drilling crews. Today it is a modern place with supermarkets, jet airport and railway station.

Dammam, the most important port city on the Arabian Gulf and the capital of the Eastern Province, has a population of about 55,000.

DAMMAM

Dammam is a commercial city and the most important port on the Arabian Gulf. The local industries are based on fishing, agriculture, stock raising and oil operations.

TAIF

Located in central Hejaz at an altitude of 5,000 feet, Taif is blessed with a mild climate and serves as the country's chief summer resort. Here, many of Saudi Arabia's notables have luxurious villas surrounded by lush gardens. Taif is in the middle of an important orchard region producing much of the fruit of Hejaz. Taif is also famous for its superior attar of roses, an important item, for the pilgrims use it to scent the ritual water with which they wash themselves.

HOFUF

Hofuf lies in the largest oasis in Hasa province and is an important agricultural and commercial town, linked with Riyadh to the west and Dhahran to the east by railway. Hofuf raises large quantities of dates, vegetables, fruits and barley and has many small cottage industries producing textiles and copper and brass handicrafts.

AL-KHOBAR

Nothing but a few mud huts in 1958, Al-Khobar is today a thriving city with running water, sewers, and traffic jams. The population is a mixture of Arabs, Indians, Europeans, and Americans.

VILLAGES

Small villages ordinarily consist of densely packed groups of houses surrounded by orchards and fields and frequently by a mud wall. Each house often has a small garden or orchard of its own. Beyond the fields and orchards on the outskirts of the village are the grazing lands. The larger and older villages are generally built around a *suk* or bazaar where the periodic markets are held. The bazaar also serves as a gathering place for special occasions, and is usually located close to the village mosque.

The former monarch, King Saud, brother of the present King, is seen here shaking hands with United Nations Secretary-General Dag Hammarskjold on January 29, 1957. The King addressed the U.N. General Assembly on that occasion. He died in 1964.

2. HISTORY

FOR THOUSANDS of years the Arabian Peninsula had been the home of nomadic Semitic tribes, some of whom established settlements in the oases and along the more important caravan routes.

Southern Arabia (Yemen and Southern Yemen) was for a long time the prime source of frankincense and myrrh which were used in large quantities by the Romans and the Egyptians for religious purposes, embalming and cosmetics. Other important commodities traded and carried north by the nomadic merchants of

Arabia included silk and spices from India, ivory, animal skins and slaves from Africa, and semi-precious stones, gold, and possibly copper, from Arabia itself. Starting from southern and western Arabia a network of important caravan routes crisscrossed the peninsula eventually ending in Egypt, Palestine, Syria and Babylonia.

The early inhabitants of what is now Saudi Arabia performed the important rôle of middlemen between southern Arabia with its precious commodities and the densely settled areas

In Medina, the First Mosque, or as it is sometimes called "The Prophet's Mosque," contains the tombs of Mohammed, his daughter Fatimah, and the Caliph Omar.

Arabia in 24 B.C., but their troops were given wrong directions by their guides and were swallowed up by the desert. Thereafter the desert tribes were left to themselves until, following the founding of Islam in the 6th century A.D., the Arabs swarmed over much of the known world.

THE BIRTH OF ISLAM

Islam, which in Arabic means "submission to, or having peace with, God," is the religion of which Mohammed is the prophet. A follower of Islam is called a Muslim or Moslem (Arabic for "one who submits"). It is better not to call a Muslim a Mohammedan, as that implies the worship of Mohammed, and a Muslim must worship only God (Allah), not His messenger Mohammed.

The prophet Mohammed was born in A.D. 570 in Mecca. Both his parents belonged to the Koreish, the ruling clan of Mecca, and at the age of 24 he married Khadija, a widow much older than himself.

Until he reached the age of 40, Mohammed led the normal life of a well-to-do merchant. Then at about 40 he began to have revelations that God had chosen him to be the prophet of the true religion. These revelations continued all his life—and were collected and eventually recorded in the Koran, the holy book of Islam.

During this time Mecca, the home of the black stone (Kaaba) and assorted pagan gods, attracted great numbers of idol worshippers. The prosperity of the city depended on this "commerce in gods." The merchants of Mecca viewed the activities of Mohammed with great suspicion, as he openly preached the destruction of the many gods and advocated instead the invisible "only" God, Allah. By 622, Mohammed had made many enemies, who forced him to flee to the city of Yathrib, as Medina was then called, in order to save his life. His flight to Medina is called the "Hegira," and it is from this year of 622 that the Muslim calendar starts.

In the next few years Mohammed began to consolidate his power and spread his influence and teachings over much of Arabia. In 630 he

north and west of Arabia—Egypt, Syria, and Mesopotamia. These countries, due to a more adequate water supply, developed civilizations far more advanced than Arabia. These civilizations to the north badly needed the commodities that southern Arabia had to offer, as well as the goods that came from East Africa and India by caravans and by the traditional Arab sailing ship, the *dhow*.

Most of the cities of later centuries began as settlements established alongside the important trade routes in order to supply the caravans with pack animals, foodstuffs and lodging. Many of these routes still exist and are in use today.

Most of the Arabian peninsula was bypassed by the many conquerors of the Middle East. The Romans sent an expeditionary force to

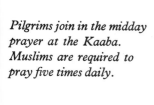
Pilgrims join in the midday prayer at the Kaaba. Muslims are required to pray five times daily.

invaded and occupied Mecca without a fight. His first act was to destroy the pagan gods, but he kept the sacred nature of the black stone (Kaaba), turning it into a relic of Islam.

THE GREAT ARAB CONQUESTS

A century after Mohammed's death in 632, Arab horsemen stormed out of Arabia with the Koran in one hand, and the sword in the other and conquered Egypt, North Africa and Spain in the west and Syria, Persia, Mesopotamia (modern Iraq), Afghanistan, and parts of India and Central Asia to the east and north. The so-called "great flowering of Arab civilization" came about through contact with the other civilizations which they conquered, notably those of Egypt, Persia, Syria, Turkestan and Spain.

During these great conquests Arabia itself was declining in importance. The greatly enlarged borders called for the moving of the caliphate, or leadership of Islam, to the more centrally located Damascus in Syria, thus weakening the ties between Arabia and the conquered lands and cultures. This caused the Arabs in Arabia once again to fall into political chaos and become disunited. Through the cen-

turies there were many unsuccessful attempts to unite the various tribes, but the Arabian Peninsula remained politically fragmented until the early part of the 16th century when the Ottoman Empire occupied much of Arabia. They stayed, with some interruptions, until 1913.

TRAVELLERS TO ARABIA

Arabia was always a difficult country to visit, and for non-Muslims it was almost impossible. Most European explorers travelled in disguise and at great risk to their lives. They had to master the language, religion, and customs of the country in order to avoid detection. The traveller whose disguise was discovered never returned home.

BURCKHARDT

Among the first European travellers to Arabia and the first Christian to visit Medina was Johann Ludwig Burckhardt. A Swiss explorer, born in 1784, he set out to explore Africa and the Near East. Disguised as a Muslim scholar, he wandered through Arabia and left behind vivid descriptions of the country and of Mecca in particular. He was the first to give an accurate description of the Kaaba.

Mount Arafat and the pilgrim camp appeared this way to Sir Richard Burton during his visit in 1853.

BURTON

Another famous explorer to visit Mecca and Medina was the Englishman, Sir Richard Burton. In 1853, disguised as a pilgrim under the name of Al-Hajj-Abdullah, he arrived at Jiddah, then proceeded to Mecca and Medina to complete the pilgrimage, all the while making detailed notes of everything he saw. His diary was later published and to this day it is one of the best descriptions of life and customs in Arabia.

DOUGHTY

Charles M. Doughty spent two years travelling with the Bedouins of Arabia from 1875 until 1877. His book "Travels in Arabia Deserta" is ranked among the best travel books ever written. Due to its ponderous style, it is not easy reading, but those willing to give it the attention it deserves will be rewarded with a rich panorama of desert life.

PHILBY

H. St. John Philby, British explorer and diplomat, was born in Ceylon and came to Arabia in 1915. He eventually became a close friend and adviser to King Ibn Saud. Philby became a Muslim and spent close to 40 years in Arabia

Sir Richard Burton, the English adventurer and traveller, visited Mecca and Medina in 1853 disguised as a Muslim pilgrim.

during which time he explored and studied the country in greater depth than anyone else, writing about a dozen books on the subject.

THESIGER

Wilfred Thesiger, British explorer, was born in Ethiopia in 1910, grew up in Africa and came

The city of Medina appeared like this in the early 19th century, as seen by an Arab artist of the period.

to Arabia in 1945 to head a team of specialists investigating the plague-like periodic movements of the locusts, which were suspected of originating in the Empty Quarter of Arabia.

Eventually he crossed the Empty Quarter disguised as a Bedouin. Barefoot and with a few Arab companions, he travelled through much of that area. His descriptions of life in the desert are unique, due to his almost mystical affinity for the primitive way of life of the Bedouin.

THE WAHHABIS AND THE SAUDI DYNASTY

Saudi Arabia became for the first time a distinct political unit in the late 18th century when the religious reformer, Abdul-Wahhab, under the patronage of the Saudi dynasty of Nejd, embarked upon unifying the country and reforming and purifying Islam.

The Saudis encountered the hostility of the Turks and Egyptians, and in 1818 the Turkish and Egyptian forces invaded and occupied Nejd. The Egyptians were unable to maintain control and the Saudis returned to power in 1824.

A period of strife between Arab factions forced the Saudi dynasty into exile, when another family, the Rashids, won control of Riyadh.

The modern history of Saudi Arabia starts in 1902, when Abd Al-Aziz Al Saud, known in the outside world as Ibn Saud, left Kuwait,

A public square in Jiddah appeared like this about 125 years ago. Since then Jiddah has become the main commercial city of the country, but many of these ancient buildings still remain in the old quarter of the city.

where the Saud family was living in exile. With a handful of followers, he recaptured the family's traditional capital, Riyadh, from the Rashids. By 1914, Ibn Saud had reconquered most of the provinces of Nejd and Hasa and was recognized as Emir of Nejd by the British during World War I. During this war the walls of the Ottoman Empire were crumbling and the Turks were losing their grip over the Middle East, setting the stage for the independence of Arabia.

The British were sympathetic to Ibn Saud because of his harassment of the Turks, but they gave most of their support to his rival, the Emir Hussein, ruler of Hejaz. With the aid of the famous English adventurer, Lawrence of Arabia, the Emir Hussein was induced to revolt against the Turks by the British. Hussein then declared himself King of Hejaz, but was subsequently defeated by Ibn Saud, who by 1925 consolidated his rule over Hejaz.

SAUDI ARABIA ESTABLISHED

In 1926, Ibn Saud was proclaimed King of Hejaz and Sultan of Nejd. In 1932, the two areas were united into the Kingdom of Saudi Arabia. The imposing figure of Ibn Saud began to dominate as he ended the tribal divisions of the country. He established a firm, autocratic rule and by strictly enforcing the laws, he ensured the safety of the pilgrims travelling to Mecca and Medina, thus gradually forging a unified country.

OIL TRANSFORMS THE DESERT

In 1933, King Ibn Saud granted an oil concession to the California-Arabian Oil Company, later to become the Arabian American Oil Company (ARAMCO). The first important well was discovered in 1938 and major production started shortly after World War II.

This early 19th-century engraving depicts the camel-borne litter of Arabia called the "taktarawan." This strange conveyance formerly served to transport people of high class only, but it is no longer in use.

Barely 25 years later, the huge incomes from oil royalties had brought about incredible changes. A country that existed in almost complete isolation from the outside world was transformed within two decades into a country with jet airports, television stations, and diesel trucks in place of camels.

This rapid transformation took its toll. King Ibn Saud himself lived an austere life, but the plentiful easy money pouring into the country was often mismanaged. In 1953, he died at the age of 73, and was followed on the throne by his eldest son, King Saud Ibn Abd Al-Aziz, who exercised direct rule until 1958 and then again from 1960 to 1962.

The traditional, simple garb of the pilgrim contrasts with that of the veiled woman. This engraving was made almost 150 years ago.

The late Ibn Saud founded the Kingdom of Saudi Arabia in 1932 by uniting Hejaz and Nejd. Here the ruler of Bahrain, Sheikh Hamab Al-Khalifah is on his left.

In early 1958, King Saud's rule was interrupted by chaotic financial conditions at home due to reckless spending, and strained relations with President Nasser of Egypt. The Royal Family convinced King Saud to delegate the direct running of the government to his younger but more efficient brother, Feisal. In 1960, Saud took back full control, but in 1962 poor health coupled with internal pressures for reform and external pressures generated by Egyptian propaganda, and Saud's involvement on the royalist side in the Yemen war, forced the King to delegate powers again to Feisal.

In 1964, Crown Prince Feisal assumed complete authority and on November 2 of the same year he was proclaimed king by the senior members of the royal family and religious leaders. Saud subsequently died in exile in 1969. King Feisal, who had been born in 1906, from an early age showed administrative ability. In 1925, he was appointed Viceroy of Hejaz and in 1930, he was given the post of Foreign Minister. King Feisal travelled widely and through the years visited the United States, Iran, Kuwait, Jordan, Pakistan, Spain, Turkey, Morocco, Mali, Tunisia and many other countries.

THE EMBARGO

King Feisal assumed a new rôle in world politics in 1973 after the outbreak of war between Israel and the Arab nations of Egypt and Syria in October of that year. The king until then had refrained from serious involvement in the Middle East situation, although he was under pressure from the leaders of other Arab states to use Saudi oil as a political weapon. These leaders called for an embargo on Arab oil shipment to nations giving support to Israel. Feisal gave in after the 1973 war began and agreed to cut down oil shipments to the West. Then, when President Nixon indicated his intention of stepping up the flow of arms to Israel, Feisal cut off all Saudi oil to the United States. He was joined in this move by the other Arab oil-producing nations, causing an energy crisis among the industrial nations, some of whom, like Japan and the Western European countries were heavily dependent on Arab oil. Most of these countries were forced to change their stand on the Arab-Israeli conflict. The United States, much less dependent on Arab oil, held out, along with the Netherlands.

Then, following the negotiation of a cease-fire between Israel and its opponents by U.S. Secretary of State Henry Kissinger, the embargo came to an end in March, 1974, pending further working out of details. Whatever the outcome, Saudi Arabia had taken the decisive measure of using its vast oil resources as a political weapon.

RECENT EVENTS

In March, 1975, King Feisal was assassinated by a young prince of the Saudi royal family who had a record of instability. The King's brother, Crown Prince Khalid, succeeded to the throne. The assassin was later beheaded in public according to Saudi custom. No important policy changes were expected to be made by the new King.

The market in the city of Buraidah, northwest of Riyadh, is a busy place. Buraidah started out as an oasis but grew to become an important commercial city.

3. THE PEOPLE

THE POPULATION of Saudi Arabia was about 7,000,000, according to a census that was conducted in 1974. Unofficial estimates placed it as high as 9,000,000 in 1979. About 90 per cent of the population is pure Arab, descendants of the native Arab tribes with some admixture of Negro blood from slaves imported from Africa over the centuries.

Along the Arabian Gulf there are some inhabitants of Iranian and Pakistani descent, but otherwise the population is homogeneous, both in language and religion. The main division is between the settled people and those who are nomadic, the Bedouins. These two groups have traditionally been antagonistic to each other.

Until recently a large proportion of the

Until recently a large proportion of the people were nomads or semi-nomads, but under the impact of general economic growth, the settled population is steadily increasing.

The rapid development of the oil industry has attracted a large number of skilled and semi-skilled workers from Arab countries, mostly Egyptians, Lebanese and Palestinian Arabs, and a large number of migrants from other areas. Nomadic and semi-nomadic people have also flocked in large numbers to the cities, drawn by the promise of good wages, electricity and ample water.

THE BEDOUINS

About 15 per cent of the population are still Bedouins, who are constantly on the move in search of water and grazing lands. The Bedouins living in the relative isolation of the desert have changed very little through the centuries. The desert surrounding them acts as the ocean does with an island—it limits contact with other peoples and cultures. As a matter of fact, Arabia is sometimes referred to as "The Island of the Arabs."

Until very recently the typical Bedouin still lived as he always had, in tents of goat or camel hair called "houses of hair." He was highly individualistic and would not readily give allegiance to anyone. Even in the practice of religion, he had an independent approach. His social organization followed a set pattern—each tent represented a family; a group of families made up a clan; and a number of clans constituted a tribe.

Reputation and dignity were greatly valued, and any insult, bodily or otherwise, upon any member, was revenged. Sometimes the clan or the entire tribe acted in revenge, but generally an offense was dealt with by the immediate family of the injured person. Blood feuds could last for years, sometimes for generations, and "an eye for an eye" was the rule of the desert.

One of the main features of Bedouin life used to be the "razzia," or raid. It was the only way a Bedouin could prove his manhood—and, when successful, it also increased his worldly possessions. Razzias were carried out most often against the settled people, travellers in the desert, or Bedouins belonging to a different tribe. Raids are now outlawed in Saudi Arabia.

In sharp contrast with the custom of raids is the Bedouins' renowned hospitality. In principle, even a stranger must be given food, water and shelter, for to deprive a traveller of these essentials in the inhospitable desert would mean certain death for him. For the first few days the "guest" is treated like a member of the family. However, custom decrees that he does not overstay his welcome, which is usually a maximum of three days. After this time, his special status expires and his hosts may become rather unpleasant if he lingers longer.

The largest and most important Bedouin tribes are the Ataiba, Harb, Shammar, Mutair and Dawasir.

The Bedouin's main diet consists of a flat bread made of flour, dates, and milk from his goats and camels. Occasionally he will have a feast of rice pilaf and roast mutton. Roasted locusts are considered a delicacy.

A legendary well (believed to be in use for 4,000 years) is located in the courtyard of the Prophet's Mosque in Medina. Here a group of pilgrims drink water from faucets installed by King Ibn Saud.

RELIGION

Virtually all the population are Sunni Muslims, adherents of the puritan Wahhabi sect.

Religion has been the single most important element in the history of Arabia. It was the birth of the new religion, Islam, that first gave an identity to the inhabitants of the Arabian Peninsula, who, until the coming of the prophet Mohammed, had no common identity.

Islam rests upon five tenets or pillars, faith and the declaration of faith, prayer, giving alms, periods of abstinence and fasting, and finally, the pilgrimage to Mecca. It is the latest of the three major monotheistic religions, the other two being Judaism and Christianity, both of which greatly influenced Islam.

Islamic teaching holds that God keeps sending prophets through whom He reveals himself to man, but man does not see the light and keeps falling away from God. Abraham, Moses, and Jesus are among the many early prophets recognized by Islam. But Islamic teachings claim that Islam is mankind's last chance to redeem itself through the revelations of God, sent through his messenger, the prophet Mohammed.

In principle, Jews and Christians, as opposed to idol worshippers, have a special status in Islam. In the Koran they are referred to as "People of the Scriptures." In practice, this preferred position is all but non-existent. When Mohammed fled to Medina, the city had a large Jewish and a small Christian settlement and his ideas about Judaism and Christianity were formulated through his personal contact with these two faiths. Since these religions were opposed to Mohammed and to Islam, Mohammed and his early followers developed little tolerance towards the Jews and Christians.

Religious freedom exists in varying degrees in other Muslim countries, but in Saudi Arabia, only Islam is permitted and the practice of any other religion is strictly forbidden.

THE KORAN

The Koran, sacred book of all Islam, is considered to be the sum of a series of revelations by God to Mohammed. A number of versions appeared after Mohammed's death, but the only accepted one was that written by his secretary. The Koran consists of 114 *suras* (chapters), written in classical Arabic, and it is the main link among the 600,000,000 Muslims of different races and languages.

THE PILGRIMAGE

The burning desire and ambition of every Muslim is to make the pilgrimage to Mecca. Muslims from the four corners of the earth gather each year to make this sacred journey. During the pilgrimage, all social and political differences are temporarily laid aside. Every pilgrim, whether beggar, prince, wealthy landlord, or poor camel-driver, wears the same simple white garment and participates in the same rituals. However, some arrive in Mecca in air-conditioned Cadillacs, others are crowded into huge trucks or buses, and still others arrive on foot after walking for days.

The first goal of the pilgrims is the Kaaba, a large structure in the shape of a cube. In one corner of the wall, set in a silver frame, is the sacred black stone. Legend has it that the original structure was built by Abraham, but was subsequently destroyed and rebuilt several times. The building is covered with heavy dark curtains, embroidered with verses from the Koran. It is towards the Kaaba that all Muslims turn five times each day when praying.

During the pilgrimage each pilgrim has to circle the Kaaba seven times. The sick and crippled are carried on litters. The following day the pilgrims' next goal is the plain of Arafat, about 12 miles outside of Mecca. Here they

Pilgrims arrive at the airport in Jiddah.

The streets of Medina are crowded during the pilgrimage season. The minaret of the Holy Mosque rises on the left.

Pilgrimage City—hundreds of thousands of Muslim pilgrims encamp annually on the plains adjacent to Mount Arafat and the city of Mina, near Mecca. Each year Saudi Arabia is host to approximately 250,000 Muslims who make the Hajj (pilgrimage) to Mecca. The Hajj is one of the five pillars of the Islamic faith, but only those Muslims who are financially and physically able are required to make the journey.

congregate in vast numbers, waiting for the roar of the cannon at sunset, signalling them to proceed to the town of Mina, about five miles away. At Mina are the three white pillars believed to mark the place where Abraham was tempted by the devil as he was about to sacrifice his son to God. Each pilgrim then hurls seven stones at the white pillars, enacting the ceremony called "stoning the devil."

When Abraham was about to sacrifice his son, God replaced the son with a ram, according to scripture. This symbolic sacrifice survives to this day, when tens of thousands of sheep and a smaller number of cattle and camels are slaughtered yearly. Half are butchered in special slaughterhouses set up for this purpose, while the others are killed where they stand in the valley, often right next to the pilgrim's tent. The owner reserves a choice cut of meat for himself, and distributes the rest among the poor.

The valley is a scene of feverish activity—animals being offered for sale by their owners, and butchers and knife sharpeners loudly offering their services amid the cries of the animals. Whatever meat is not consumed is preserved by drying it in the fierce heat of the sun, by a special group of workers from Mecca. Some of the dry meat is carried home by foreign pilgrims as a sacred keepsake.

One of the most common health hazards dur-

A pilgrim to Mecca suffering from heat prostration (one of many) is treated by being dipped in a tub of ice water.

ing the pilgrimage is heat prostration. The government has mobile ambulance units where the affected pilgrim is plunged into a bathtub of cold water, and then transferred to a temporary hospital for additional treatment. All along the pilgrim's route free ice-water is available, and he is encouraged to consume large quantities, to prevent dehydration. A sign of the changing times—the thirsty pilgrim can now purchase ice cream and soft drinks.

The shrine of Al-Safa is one of the required stops for the pilgrims. Here they recite certain prayers in a soft voice, after which they praise God three times, then start to trot (not walk) to the next shrine.

Muslims pray under the graceful arches of the Great Mosque in Mecca. Built in the 8th century, the mosque is constantly being enlarged.

Arabic letters have different forms. The row on the top is for everyday use, the row in the middle is a highly stylized and ornamental version, and the row on the bottom is a highly decorated style used for headlines and titles.

THE WAHHABIS

The Wahhabis were a reform movement founded by Muhammed Ibn Abdul Wahhab who lived in the middle of the 18th century in Ayaina, near Riyadh. By all accounts it seems that he displayed strong religious tendencies even as a youth. It is said that by the time he was 10 he knew the whole Koran by heart, at the ripe age of 12 he was married, and at 14 completed his pilgrimage to Mecca.

At that time most of the Bedouins took religion rather lightly and Ibn Abdul Wahhab made it his mission to return the people of Arabia to strict observance of the Koran and to bring back the strong penalties introduced by Mohammed against those who did not observe the religious rules. The present ruling family still adheres to the strict Wahhabi creed, but the strong fanatical tendencies have diminished.

LANGUAGE

Throughout the country, Arabic is spoken. There are local dialects, but these are minor and do not prevent people from different parts of the country from understanding each other. Arabic is a Semitic language related to Hebrew and Aramaic. The written language is cursive, that is, written in flowing, rounded and connected characters and is read from right to left.

EDUCATION

The literacy rate is about 15 per cent. In the past, many of the people, particularly the Bedouins and those who lived in small villages, never saw any book other than the Koran, and sometimes not even that. To provide education to many is one of the government's main challenges.

Schooling is free and is provided on three levels—elementary, intermediate and secondary—and there are also commercial, agricultural

Typesetters are at work at the Al Mutawa Press in Dammam, where both Arabic and English publications are printed.

A fountain graces the campus of the College of Petroleum and Mineral Resources in Dhahran.

—and there are also commercial, agricultural and vocational schools. Co-education does not exist—boys and girls attend separate schools. Adults without previous education can enroll in night school for a four-year course to qualify them for an elementary educational certificate. The first two years are devoted entirely to teaching them to read and write.

In 1978, Saudi Arabia had 3,597 schools with a total enrolment of 805,000 students. There are 34 teacher training schools and four commercial schools. The country is divided into 23 administrative educational districts.

The Agricultural Department of Riyadh University, with advice from the Food and Agriculture Organization and the help of private consultants, has established a model agriculture project. The Royal Vocational Institute in Riyadh can accommodate 8,000 students in two shifts and has provisions for boarding students.

The University of Riyadh, founded in 1957, has faculties in the arts, sciences, commerce, pharmacy, agriculture, engineering, education, and medicine. There is also a University in Jiddah, which has two faculties in Mecca, and the Islamic University in Medina. In 1963, a College of Petroleum and Mineral Resources was established in Dhahram to develop trained personnel for the country's most important industry, oil.

Students and teachers leave one of the college buildings in Riyadh as classes end.

LITERATURE

In pre-Islamic Arabia, poetry and literature reached its highest form of expression. After Mohammed and the coming of Islam, poetic expression changed, as Mohammed did not approve of the easy-going and romantic poetry common during that time.

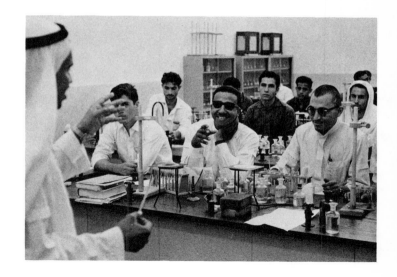

An instructor of chemistry conducts a class of first-year students at the College of Engineering, Riyadh.

The literature of Arabia is full of stories and poems extolling the virtues of romantic love, heroes, war, and the beauty and intelligence of Arabian horses and camels. Poetry and story-telling are ways to hand down a country's history and traditions in a land where most of the population is illiterate.

The best stories and poems were translated into English by 19th-century travellers and scholars, but they do not take well to translation and seem overly ornate, flowery, and without much content. Like everything else in Arabia, literature is dominated by the Koran. In it, poetic expression reached an unsurpassed majestic quality.

It should be noted that part of the literature in the Arabic language did not originate in Arabia itself, but in the highly advanced countries conquered by the Arabs.

LIBRARIES

Mecca, Medina, Riyadh, and Jiddah have a number of libraries. As the holy places of Islam, Mecca and Medina have accumulated through the centuries a priceless collection of manuscripts and printed books—many of them the only ones in existence. Medina has the largest and most important collection, while the best private collection is in Jiddah.

MUSIC AND ART

According to a strict interpretation of the Koran, music is not allowed in religious services and its use is even limited in private life. The Bedouins have evolved a rather monotonous chant accompanied by a one-string guitar and

A 14th-century enamelled oil lamp from a mosque is embellished with decorations of the type permitted by the Koran.

A worker at a marble factory in Jiddah inspects designs in arabesque and geometric patterns.

drums. Currently, there is a trend to play more music, primarily through the influence of radio and television. The newer music is a mixture of the traditional and the more modern, borrowed from other Arabic countries.

Visual arts used to be virtually unknown in Saudi Arabia. The Koran has strict injunctions against the making of graven images and this injunction has been taken literally by puritan Muslims, resulting in the complete absence of painting and sculpture in the country. Artistic expression has found an outlet in the making of hand-lettered and illuminated Korans with the illustrations based on geometric or floral designs. There are no art museums in the country.

ARCHEOLOGY

The Arabian Peninsula possibly has one of the oldest and richest histories in the world. The Old Testament and the Koran are full of accounts of nations, peoples and cultures that

Inscriptions and pictographs (rock paintings), found on a large rock near Sakakah in the northern part of the country, date from ancient times.

This ancient stone tablet, about 2,000 years old, was found at Qatif near the shores of the Persian Gulf. The writing is in the ancient South Arabian script.

flourished at one time or another in Arabia. Throughout the country, many ancient relics, inscriptions, cave paintings, mounds, and cities carved out of stone are still waiting for a systematic exploration. Although recently there have been a few minor archeological expeditions, the surface has been barely scratched. The absence of museums and the very difficult access to the country by foreigners are also responsible for the lack of archeological research.

Until recently there was no attempt in Saudi Arabia to study and explore its early (pre-Islamic) history, since anything that preceded Islam was not considered a worth-while subject. Frequently the remains of earlier civilizations were diligently searched out and destroyed by the Muslim zealots.

A great deal of amateur archeological exploration has been done by American employees of ARAMCO, and they have also been instrumental in inviting archeologists like Geoffrey Bibby and his Danish team.

MARRIAGE, SOCIAL LIFE AND CUSTOMS

The Koran permits a man to have four wives, but it stipulates that all have to be treated equally. That is why most of the Saudi Arabians have only one wife. Marriages are usually between distant relatives and are arranged by the parents. Often the young couple

Nabatean rock tombs in the northern part of Saudi Arabia are similar to the more famous Nabatean tombs found in Petra, Jordan.

SAUDI ARABIA ◈ 397

After the fast of Ramadan, friends and family gather for coffee and sweets. The fast lasts for one month, during which no food or drink is allowed during the daylight hours.

see each other for the first time during the marriage ceremony. Before the marriage is agreed upon, a dowry must be paid to the bride's family by either the prospective groom or his family. Some of the more modern, educated young people are breaking with these traditions and are choosing their own mates.

A man can divorce any of his four wives relatively easily, but not without certain obligations, such as providing for the children. It is much more difficult for a woman to secure a divorce. Although the Koran has many references to the rights and fair treatment of women, their position in all the traditional Arab societies is inferior.

Men and women rarely socialize together, and when families gather the women keep to themselves. Saudi women are generally required to wear veils in public and in the presence of strangers. They have been insulated from the social, business and political life of the country.

Only in recent years have women begun to emerge slowly to participate in some social and charitable activities—but they are still not allowed to drive cars! Social and cultural activities in which both sexes participate are virtually non-existent and while men often gather in coffee shops to smoke, gossip and drink innumerable cups of coffee, women's place is in the home or in women's clubs.

In fact, Saudi Arabian society is just beginning to organize for social, economic and

A veiled and timid mother arrives with her children at the Wadi Fatimah Community Centre, where the clinic is the most popular service and attracts many families. (UNICEF)

Boys in a class at the Wadi Fatimah Community Development Centre, wear a long white robe with a headcloth, or "ghutra." When a boy reaches manhood he adds a black, crown-like cord, or "agal," to the ghutra. (UNICEF)

political purposes. The government permits associations or clubs for cultural and athletic purposes, and large gatherings are to be seen on religious occasions or at soccer games.

FOOD

The customary meal of the country consists of mutton roasted whole, served on a large platter with great heaps of rice, side dishes of eggplant roasted or fried, mixed green salad, eggs and cheese, and for dessert, fruit or a custard-like sweet with raisins or almonds. The bread is flat and round and is often large enough to be folded over several times. Originally one ate only with the right hand as the left hand was traditionally used for performing so-called "unclean functions."

Knives, spoons and forks are now coming into use. When they are not available, the diner dips his plate in the heap of rice and withdraws it with the desired amount of food. Meat has to be broken by hand into pieces and vegetables scooped up with pieces of bread. Rice is squeezed with the fingers into small balls and dropped into the mouth. In the traditional manner, a host frequently selected choice bits of food and gave it to his guests. Both before and after meals, people wash their hands, after the meal usually with scented water. Once coffee is served, conversation stops—the meal is considered over, and the guests take their leave.

Alcoholic beverages are strictly forbidden and unavailable in Saudi Arabia and even visitors or foreigners working in the country are not allowed alcohol.

COFFEE

In Arabia, coffee is more than just a beverage, it is a social institution. Between meals, whenever two Arabs get together, coffee is served. It is very much a part of the Arabian scene— in fact it is believed that coffee originated in

Coffee beans are roasted over an open fire and then ground to a fine powder by mortar and pestle. Sometimes cardamom seeds or other spices are added to the coffee.

The coffee beans are roasted in a brass pot and stirred constantly, so that they will brown evenly. An open fire in the sand suffices in this tent home.

Arabia, near Mocha in Yemen. To this day some of the best coffee is grown in Yemen.

The green coffee beans are roasted in small quantities, pounded very fine, mixed with sugar and water and then cooked in coffee pots that come in all sizes to fit the need of the moment.

Arabian coffee is not syrupy, but a thin watery liquid tasting of cardamom. It is poured into small cups, which are only half-filled, then re-filled twice more—three cups being the usual amount. To have more is considered poor taste.

At the Riyadh orphanage, teen-age boys play volley-ball. Boys' clubs are a vital part of community development. (UNICEF)

At Riyadh a unique "wall" newspaper is produced weekly by children at the Community Development Centre.

SPORTS

Until recently, sports, in the strict sense of the word, were almost unknown in Arabia, with the exception of falconry and hunting. The nearest thing to "sport" with the Bedouin was the "razzia" or raid, but as it is now outlawed, it is being replaced with more conventional pastimes.

Falconry is the traditional sport of Arabia particularly among the wealthy. Most of the falcons are brought from Iraq and Persia and are very expensive. These birds of prey are trained to hunt other birds and small animals. Carried on the wrist of their keeper, they are kept hooded, but once the keeper sights the quarry, the hood is taken off and the falcon released for the attack. Falcons usually have only one keeper, who is completely responsible for their care.

MODERN SPORTS

Since 1950, there has been a trend in the country toward the more modern sports. Particularly in the cities and at the oil installations, basketball and soccer are popular. Calisthenics and gymnastics are now part of the schools' physical education courses.

HOLIDAYS

The most important religious observance, lasting one month, is Ramadan. The aim of Ramadan is to lead the faithful to a deeper perception of God and to remind man of the deep obligation he owes to God. According to the Koran, Muslims must abstain from eating, drinking and sex during the daylight hours for the entire month. The start of each fast day is determined when there is enough light for a white thread to be distinguished from a black one, and the day lasts until sunset. The last 10 days of Ramadan are especially sacred.

Since both eating and drinking are forbidden during daylight hours, this is a very difficult period for Muslims. When Ramadan falls during the hot summer months, the whole tempo of life noticeably slows down.

There are two other religious holidays, and National Day is celebrated as a patriotic holiday. It commemorates the unification of the country under the new name of Saudi Arabia. This is the only official holiday that is not observed according to the Islamic calendar, but is based on the Gregorian calendar—presumably for the convenience of foreign diplomats who take part in the festivities on September 23.

SAUDI ARABIA ◈ 401

A page from an Arabic calendar shows, side by side, the Gregorian and Islamic dates.

TELLING TIME

The task of telling time is not so simple in Saudi Arabia. The day officially begins at sunset. This means that night precedes daylight in the span of one full day. Thus Islamic noon (12 hours after the start of the new day) comes at approximately 6 o'clock in the morning, depending on the time of year, and on the time at which sunset takes place. The oil companies use daylight saving time and the domestic airlines use Greenwich time plus three hours as a form of compromise. One can purchase watches in Saudi Arabia which have two faces—one showing Greenwich, and the other, local (Islamic) time.

Saudi Arabia uses the Islamic calendar, which is dated from A.D. 622 when the prophet Mohammed fled from Mecca to Medina. Thus the first year of the Islamic calendar corresponds to A.D. 622 of the Gregorian calendar, and 1973, according to the Islamic calendar, is 1393.

The Islamic year is based on the lunar calendar, which has only $29\frac{1}{2}$ days in a month, therefore making the year 11 days shorter than the Gregorian year. Thus, an event or holy day based on the Islamic calendar takes place about 11 days earlier each successive year on the Gregorian calendar, causing events to revolve around the year—completing a cycle every 33 years. If the first day of Ramadan in 1972 was October 22, in 1973 it would be October 11, and in 1974, October 1, and so on until the full cycle of 33 years, at which time it would once again start on October 22. Therefore, according to the Islamic calendar the months have no permanent relation to the seasons.

The Saudi Arabian Government railway, which went into operation in 1951, spans the 375 miles from Dammam to Riyadh.

4. GOVERNMENT

SAUDI ARABIA is a monarchy with the Koran as the constitution. Executive and legislative authority is exercised by the King, who is chief of state and head of government. The council of ministers are appointed by and responsible to the King, who is also the supreme religious leader of the country.

The country functions on a framework of Arab tradition and Koranic (or Islamic) law called Sharia. The courts, whose magistrates are appointed by the Islamic leadership, are guided by the Sharia law, which is based entirely on the Koran. The Sharia is, in effect, the commentary and explanations added through the centuries by Islamic scholars to clarify and explain at greater length the basic points and rules set down in the Koran. Since the penal code is also based on the Koranic tenet of "an eye for an eye," the punishments meted out to offenders are at times quite cruel by Western standards.

Slavery was practiced on a wide scale until 1963, when it was officially made illegal by King Feisal.

Political parties or electors, in the Western sense, are unknown. Despite the rapid economic progress, the society remains conservative and religious. Although there is a total absence of representative government, there is a strong element of equality, which gives the individual certain rights, particularly the right to present grievances.

The country is divided into 18 administrative districts. Tribal and village leaders report and are responsible to the district governors, assuring a certain amount of central control in the remote areas. From 30 to 40 per cent of the population is organized on a tribal system. Each local tribe is headed by a sheikh and several tribes are grouped to form a main tribe headed by the paramount sheikh.

The war dragged on until 1967, with heavy Egyptian army and air involvement. After Egypt was defeated by Israel in 1967, it could no longer afford to support the republicans in Yemen and thus was forced to withdraw, ending the tension with Saudi Arabia. In 1967, Saudi Arabia along with Kuwait and Libya agreed to pay annual subsidies to Egypt and Jordan to offset losses suffered by those nations during the 1967 war with Israel.

RELATIONS WITH THE WEST

Formal diplomatic relations with the United States have been in existence since 1940. United States oil interests in Saudi Arabia makes the security of that country a matter of great concern to Washington—ARAMCO represents the largest single American investment in any foreign country. The continued availability of Saudi oil is also very important to the security and prosperity of Western Europe and Japan, as the 1973-74 embargo dramatically demonstrated.

In 1945, the United States signed an agreement with the late king, Ibn Saud, for the construction of an airport at Dhahran, to be used as an air base. The agreement also called

FOREIGN RELATIONS

Saudi Arabia follows an independent foreign policy oriented toward the other Arab states and the defence of Arab interest. Its basic objectives are to maintain its leading position in the Arabian peninsula and its prestige in the Muslim world as protector of the holy places and tenets of Islam. It is a charter member of the United Nations and a member of several U.N. specialized agencies.

Saudi Arabia does not have diplomatic relations with any of the Communist nations, and no known Communist is allowed to reside in the country.

THE WAR IN YEMEN

In 1962, when the absolute ruler in adjacent Yemen was deposed in a coup by republican forces, a full-scale war developed between Yemeni royalists and republicans. The republican troops were financed and armed by Egypt, whose President Nasser wanted to use Yemen as a jumping ground for the "liberation" of the entire oil-rich peninsula. Nasser coupled his involvement in the Yemen with verbal attacks against the rulers of Saudi Arabia, who reacted by supplying aid to the royalist side.

The Royal Emblem of Saudi Arabia displays two crossed swords and a date palm.

King Feisal paid a visit to United Nations head-quarters in New York on June 24, 1966. Here he is with Secretary-General U Thant.

for a military mission in Saudi Arabia, as well as a grant of economic assistance to improve the port facilities at Dammam and to construct a civilian air terminal at Dhahran. In 1962, King Saud terminated the airfield agreement and nationalized the airfield, but the U.S. Military Training Mission continues to operate.

An important development has been the complete withdrawal of Britain from the Arabian Peninsula. For a long time, Saudi Arabia was bordered on the south and east by British colonies and protectorates. All of these areas—Southern Yemen, Oman, Qatar, Bahrain and the United Arab Emirates—had become independent states by 1973.

Whatever the long-range results of the 1973-74 embargo, the emergence of Saudi Arabia as a political power was a fact. Whether the Arab states could successfully use oil to force the United States to call for a "full withdrawal by Israel from occupied territories" remained to be seen.

A sidelight of the "new deal" in Saudi Arabia was the rise to world prominence of the Saudi Oil Minister, Sheik Ahmed Zaki al-Yamani, who became a principal figure in the international negotiations relating to the embargo.

In April, 1974, Saudi Arabia and the United States signed a pact calling for military and economic co-operation on both sides. The United States hoped that the pact would induce Saudi Arabia to increase its petroleum production and thus help to lower the world price of oil. However, Saudi Arabia later indicated that this was unlikely to happen soon, in spite of the pact. At the same time, Saudi Arabia began a large-scale scheme for investing its huge oil revenues in foreign countries, including Western ones.

Modern houses in the residential section of Medina still exhibit traditional Islamic motifs.

At the oasis town of Diriyah, a little girl stands outside the Community Centre. UNICEF is providing supplies and equipment for child-care facilities as part of community development.
(UNICEF)

Late in 1974, King Feisal forced the 4 United States oil companies owning part of ARAMCO to agree to sell their remaining shares in the company to the Saudi government.

HOUSING

The settled people living in the oases and cities dwell in houses built of adobe and palm fronds. Wood is seldom seen, but galvanized steel and cement are being used more and more frequently. Prefabricated homes are becoming popular, particularly around oil installations where the oil companies assist the workers with loans. Due to the rapid influx of people to the cities, urban housing is still one of the main problems in spite of the great strides the government has made in this field.

SOCIAL WELFARE

Traditionally the family or tribe took care of its old, handicapped, and orphaned. However,

due to the change from a tribal to an urban society, these traditional ways are disappearing. The government is trying to fill the void with improved health and welfare services. The oil companies have provided a good example—ARAMCO has an efficient plan for its employees that includes a pension fund, free medical care, and accident compensation.

The Saudi Government has established facilities for the housing and care of the old, disabled, and orphans. Presently these facilities can accommodate about 2,000 people. Other recent accomplishments include social service bureaus to advise people on social, cultural and agricultural problems. The first experimental bureau was established near Riyadh in 1960, with the help of United Nations specialists.

HEALTH

Saudi Arabia's chief health problems are typical of most other underdeveloped countries. Malnutrition was once widespread, resulting in anemia, scurvy and tuberculosis. Dysentery, trachoma, bilharzia (a worm infection) and typhoid are common. Since 1950, however, impressive improvements have taken place. It is one of the main goals of the government to provide the people with better health care.

A long-standing health problem has been the yearly influx of pilgrims, who frequently bring with them a variety of communicable diseases. New health care facilities are planned to serve both the Saudi citizens and the pilgrims. There are 47 hospitals with a total of 6,926 beds, 531 clinics, and 325 health units, of which 23 are mobile units that regularly tour the remote parts of the country.

Strict laws have now been enacted to curb communicable diseases. Immunization is being offered throughout the country and special mobile teams are regularly inspecting water and sewer systems. Various U.N. agencies have assisted in the establishment of medical facilities with particular attention to preventive medicine.

The main entrance of the international departure section at the beautifully designed Dhahran Air Terminal appears deserted. Actually, the airport is one of the busiest in the country and handles large jets.

5. THE ECONOMY

IN RECENT years Saudi Arabia has had an average economic growth of 9 per cent annually. The greatest single factor of economic importance is oil. Production is constantly increasing, and in 1977 it reached 38,214,000 metric tons per month. Saudi Arabia is one of the largest producers in the world, and with proven reserves of 150,000,000,000 barrels, it has one of the largest reserves. In 1972, it replaced Venezuela as the world's largest exporter of oil. Oil royalties account for more than 85 per cent of the nation's total revenue. More than 90 per cent of the oil is produced by ARAMCO.

OIL DEVELOPMENT

The country is rapidly expanding and diversifying its industrial potential through the use of income derived from the petroleum industry. The government is also developing its own petroleum industry, including refining and marketing facilities. With the assistance of several international firms, exploration for oil is also being planned in the central part of the country—an area relatively unexplored so far.

Offshore oil developments are also being extended. To facilitate this, ARAMCO is putting

To facilitate and speed up the loading of oil aboard tankers, the oil companies are installing "Sea Islands," which enable many huge tankers to take on oil simultaneously. This picture shows a model of ARAMCO's *Sea Island IV, with a tower crane in the middle, an elevated control house behind it, loading arms at both ends, and multi-purpose towers at the corners.*

Sea Island IV was placed in position on June 27, 1972. In this view the legs have been lowered to the sea bottom and are being driven in by crane-hung pile drivers.

The control house of ARAMCO's *Sea Island IV was installed in an inlet of the independent Gulf island of Bahrain, and its eight legs inserted and lowered 24 feet into the water. The structure was then towed from this location to waters off the Ras Tanura Marine Terminal, where it became a part of the company's growing offshore oil-loading facilities.*

into operation a gigantic floating storage vessel. Anchored off shore, moored to a single buoy in water about 130 feet deep, the vessel has a storage capacity of 1,800,000 barrels and is capable of taking in and discharging crude oil simultaneously.

Much Saudi oil is shipped by tankers to Europe and Japan to be refined, although some of it is now being refined in Saudi Arabia—there is a huge refinery operated by ARAMCO at Ras Tanura. Some of the oil is shipped by tankers to the Red Sea port of Jiddah, where a new refinery has been constructed. Some is carried by pipelines to the island of Bahrain, and some through another pipeline to the Mediterranean.

Ras Tanura is the largest oil shipping port on the Persian Gulf. The huge tanks are used to store the oil until it is loaded aboard tankers for shipment to refineries.

Cargo ships lie at anchor off the Red Sea port of Jiddah.

ARAMCO

The Arabian American Oil Company began as a United States holding company, and was one of the largest single United States investments abroad. ARAMCO has played a very important rôle in the development of Saudi Arabia. In 1933, when the first concession was granted to ARAMCO the country was a primitive tribal society and it was the discovery of oil and its development by ARAMCO that created the need for new roads, jobs, airfields and housing.

Much of the country was explored and mapped for the first time by ARAMCO engineers.

The influence of ARAMCO has been also quite impressive in providing technical training and in the field of social services by providing its workers with benefits unheard of in Saudi Arabia—housing, health, insurance and recreation facilities.

WATER AND ELECTRICITY

One of the greatest problems is lack of water, and due to this scarcity only about 15 per cent of the land is arable. To combat this problem

An ARAMCO technician adjusts a multiple valve called a "Christmas Tree," atop an oil well in Dhahran. In the background is a mosque built for the Muslim employees of the company.

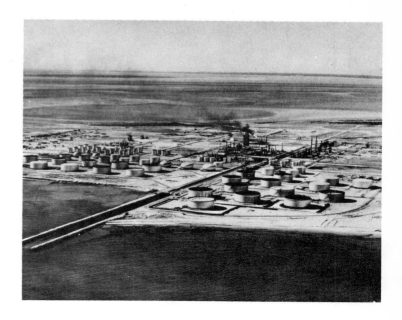

An oil refinery with its huge storage tanks is now a common sight in Saudi Arabia's eastern region.

the government has enlisted the help of the FAO (the U.N. Food and Agricultural Organization) to help in irrigation projects and water conservation. Several small dams have been constructed, and in 1971 the government signed a contract with an Italian firm to build a large dam at Abha, in the south.

A huge water desalinization plant has been set up at Jiddah with a daily capacity of 5,000,000 gallons, and another is being built in the eastern part of the country.

The largest industry after oil is the production of electricity. Presently there are six large plants supplying electricity to the major cities. There are also small generating plants throughout the country. All the generating plants use diesel engines, thus enabling them to utilize the plentiful local oil as fuel.

ARAMCO has several industrial training facilities to educate workers in the various skills needed. This is the training shop for basic and specialized manual skills.

Dates are packed in a modern plant at Hofuf, the largest oasis in the Hasa province and an important agricultural hub.

INDUSTRY AND COMMERCE

In addition to oil and electricity, other industries are being set up. Although there are manufacturing plants for cement, plastics, soap, shoes, clothing and other consumer items, the country still relies heavily on imported consumer goods, foodstuffs, and machinery of all sorts. The major trading partners are the United States, England, Japan, West Germany, and France.

TRADE UNIONS

Since 1965, it has been illegal to use collective bargaining as a method to settle disputes. Trade unions are banned, and all agreements between workers and owners have to be settled on an individual basis with the government acting as a third party to safeguard the interests of the workers.

AGRICULTURE

Agriculture is limited to the few areas with adequate rainfall, sufficient well water, or rain-catching basins. In some places water is brought to the surface by primitive methods, but mechanical pumps are increasingly coming into use.

One of the most important food crops is the date, which until recently was the staple diet for a large segment of the population. This dependency on dates is changing as the people are beginning to grow a wider variety of vegetables and fruits. Wheat, millet and barley are the grains most commonly cultivated. Much of the country will never be suitable for agriculture, and is used by the nomadic Bedouins moving with their herds of camels, goats and sheep to take advantage of the meagre pastures. Thus the Bedouin forms an important link in the country's economy by raising animals for meat and other food products. It is an indication of the fast-changing times and customs that nowadays large herds of animals are supplied with water by diesel tanker trucks.

An American agriculturist inspects a crop of dates in Qatif. Dates used to be the country's most important food crop, but are decreasing in importance as farmers change to more varied food crops.

The Japanese tanker "Tokyo Maru" is moored at the Arabian American Oil Company's marine terminal at Ras Tanura.

SHIPPING

The main ports are Jiddah, Dammam, Yenbo, and Ras Tanura, with Jiddah being the most important. Port facilities are being expanded to accommodate the increasing flow of exports and imports. Ras Tanura is the most important oil loading port, handling thousands of tankers yearly. Among the most picturesque sights are the large numbers of traditional Arab sailing ships, or dhows, anchored alongside the large ocean-going vessels. Built by hand of the finest hardwoods, soaked and impregnated with shark oil, they still travel the Red Sea, the Arabian Sea, and the Persian Gulf with their varied cargoes.

TRANSPORTATION

The diesel truck has gradually replaced the camel as the main source of transportation, although donkeys are still used in the settled areas. There are 8,000 miles of roads capable of carrying motor traffic. In 1967, the most ambitious road project to date was completed, a 950-mile asphalt road connecting Dammam on the Arabian Gulf with Riyadh and the Red Sea port of Jiddah. By 1980 the country expects to have about 7,000 miles of paved roadways.

There is only one railway line, connecting Dammam with Riyadh. It is about 360 miles long, with some spurs added to provide a link-up with other towns and industries in the

Fishing boats in the Red Sea port of Yenbo are framed by the hulls of dhows, the traditional sailing ships of the Arabs.

The modern airport terminal in Jiddah receives pilgrims from as far away as Morocco and Indonesia.

general area. Work is being done to reactivate the famous Hejaz railway, in order to provide rail communication with Jordan and Syria. This railway has been out of service since World War I. Maintained by the Turks as their main supply line for their occupation of Hejaz, it became a primary target of the raiders organized by Lawrence of Arabia and the forces of Hussein, Emir of Mecca.

AVIATION

Saudi Arabia has a large fleet of commercial aircraft, ranging from DC-3's to modern jets. The main airports at Jiddah, Dhahran and Riyadh are capable of handling the huge modern jets, while the other smaller airports form an important link in the country's growing transportation network. Saudi Arabian Airlines, a government-owned company, flies to North Africa, Beirut, London, Geneva, and Frankfurt.

Travelling by air in Saudi Arabia gives one an excellent opportunity to see the traditional and the modern side by side—for instance, a desert sheikh accompanied by an attendant sitting next to an American engineer. Planes now land on airfields where until a few years ago roads did not even exist.

CURRENCY

For many years the country did not have paper currency, in fact the law specifically forbade the printing and use of paper money. All transactions were carried out with silver, gold or with foreign currency.

To facilitate matters, in 1953, the Saudi government issued a paper currency called

Saudi Arabian banknotes—official paper currency—were issued for the first time in 1961. Until then paper money was officially called "pilgrim's receipts." The banknote on the top is worth 100 riyals and the one on the bottom, 50 riyals.

A recording session is in progress at a Saudi Arabian television station operated by ARAMCO.

"pilgrim's receipts." Officially the purpose was to relieve the pilgrims of the necessity of carrying large quantities of silver and gold. However, it proved to be so successful that it was gradually adopted for all transactions. In 1961, the government formally issued a new official paper currency and in 1963 the pilgrim's money went out of circulation.

COMMUNICATIONS

TELEVISION AND RADIO

Television and radio are the primary sources

of entertainment, and there are five television and several radio stations. The offerings are varied, consisting of educational broadcasts, readings from the Koran, and Egyptian "soap operas." The voice of a Saudi woman was heard for the first time on the radio in 1963, and since then women are playing a more prominent rôle in radio and television.

PRESS

There are five daily newspapers and 15 newspapers and magazines that appear weekly or monthly. The magazines range from popular pictorials to literary and scientific reviews.

Most of the newspapers are privately owned, but are subsidized through government advertising and special tax privileges. The government keeps an eye on the press and, although there is no direct censorship, newspapers are expected to refrain from publishing anything offensive to the state. Attacks or criticisms on the institution of the monarchy are not permitted.

The Food & Agriculture Organization (FAO) of the United Nations sent a fishing trawler to the Red Sea to demonstrate modern fishing methods. As a consequence, a company was formed to exploit the country's Red Sea resources.

This photograph shows the construction in Mecca of a hotel, mosque, and conference hall complex, supervised by European architects. As non-Muslims are forbidden in Mecca, the European architects and supervisors followed the progress of the construction from a distance of 10 miles via closed-circuit television cameras.

TOURISM

Tourism is undeveloped. Visitors are allowed to enter the country by applying for special permission from the Ministry of Foreign Affairs. Journalists are admitted by special invitation of the government. Employees of oil companies and other firms conducting business in Saudi Arabia can secure permission more easily. The holy cities of Mecca and Medina are forbidden to non-Muslims.

A trend towards improved tourist facilities was launched in June, 1974, when a modern Inter-Continental Hotel opened in Riyadh. Similar hotels were planned for Jiddah and Dhahran.

The Saudi Arabian flag is green with white lettering bearing the inscription, "There is no god but God, and Mohammed is His messenger."

Dammam fishermen lay their fish traps in the shallow waters of the Arabian Gulf. Fishing along the coast is an important source of protein.

The highway from Mecca to Taif winds its way over the mountains.

At Mount Arafat, about 12 miles from Mecca, a pilgrim shaded by a parasol climbs a rock to view the vast tent city.

The ruins of Palmyra tower above the Syrian steppe.

Syria

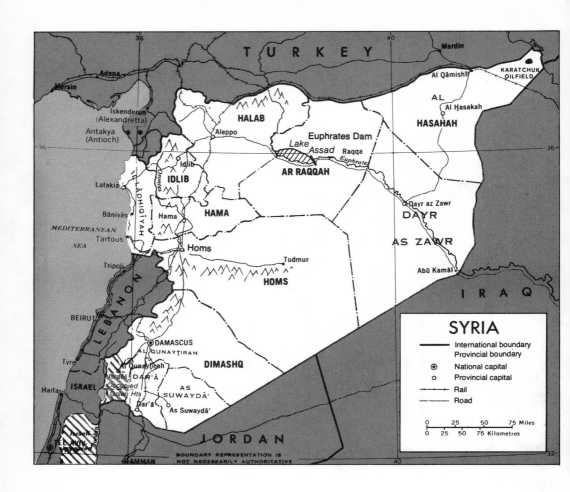

SYRIA

International boundary
Provincial boundary
⊛   National capital
o   Provincial capital
⊢—⊣   Rail
– – –   Road

0   25   50   75 Miles
0 25 50 75 Kilometres

Latakia, on the Mediterranean, is a famous resort as well as Syria's leading seaport and the hub of the tobacco industry.

I. THE LAND

SYRIA LIES AT the eastern end of the Mediterranean Sea, bounded by Turkey on the north, by Iraq on the east, by Jordan on the south, and by Israel, Lebanon and the sea on the west. Officially called the Syrian Arab Republic, the country has an area of 71,000 square miles (185,000 sq km). It is thus slightly larger than Oklahoma and just about the size of Ireland, Scotland and Wales combined.

The land includes several distinct natural regions. A narrow coastal plain is separated by a north-south chain of mountain ridges from an interior comprising fertile plains and river valleys, scattered highlands and extensive steppes and deserts.

COASTAL PLAIN

The plain of Latakia is a discontinuous strip extending for a distance of over 70 miles (112 km) along the Mediterranean coast. North of the port city of Latakia, the coast tends to be rugged, with rocky cliffs and promontories, while to the south of the city, the coastline is less severe.

The plain of Latakia is well-watered, intensely cultivated and densely populated—with few wilderness areas remaining.

In the Katanah district, a fisheries expert of the U.N. Food and Agriculture Organization shows how to catch trout with an electric net. With United Nations aid, rainbow trout have been introduced into the cool streams of Syria's mountain regions.

In the southeast are the Jebel Druse Mountains, and along the northern border are the foothills of Turkey's Taurus range. West of the Jebel Druse lies the Plain of Hauran, a treeless region studded with volcanic cones.

THE INTERIOR

Eastern Syria is composed chiefly of a plateau with an average elevation of 2,000 feet (600 metres). The northern part of the plateau is steppe or grassland, while the southern end forms part of the Syrian Desert. The Syrian Desert extends far into Iraq and Jordan, merging on the south into the desert of Saudi Arabia.

MOUNTAINS AND VALLEYS

The Jebel Ansariya parallels the coastal strip and reaches its highest point at the peak of Nabi Yunis, 5,123 feet (1,537 metres) at the northern end of the range. The mountains of the Jebel Ansariya are rounded and are interspersed with deep transverse valleys.

East of the Jebel Ansariya lies the Great Rift Valley through which the Orontes River flows northward. This is the same Rift Valley that contains the Dead Sea and extends southward far into Africa.

Forming the eastern rim of the Rift Valley, the Anti-Lebanon range also marks the boundary between Lebanon and Syria. The highest peak in this range, and in Syria, is Mt. Hermon (of Biblical renown) which attains an elevation of 9,232 feet (2,769 metres). East of the Anti-Lebanon, the Kalamein ridges stretch northeastward almost to Tudmur (Palmyra).

RIVERS

Two famous rivers water Syrian soil—the Euphrates and the Tigris. The Euphrates flows from its source in Turkey through a broad stretch of Syria before entering Iraq. The Tigris forms a small part of Syria's extreme northeastern boundary. These two rivers flow roughly parallel to one another until their junction in Iraq near the Persian (Arabian) Gulf. The ancient name of Iraq and northeastern Syria was Mesopotamia, a Greek word meaning "between rivers."

The Orontes River rises in Lebanon, flowing north through Syria towards its mouth in Turkey. There are no other rivers of any importance.

CLIMATE

The climate of Syria varies greatly from east to west. The eastern plateau region has a continental climate, meaning that it has hot

Trout made considerable weight gains in the year following their introduction. Here, United Nations experts weigh a specimen, as snow begins to fall.

summers and cold winters. The western rim has a Mediterranean climate, with mild winters and summers tempered by the sea wind. In the valleys of the interior, the climate is sub-tropical.

Rainfall is heaviest along the coast and in the mountain ranges flanking the coastal strip. Here the annual rainfall varies from 20 to 40 inches (50 to 100 cm), and may exceed 50 inches (125 cm) in some mountainous districts. Inland the rainfall may be as low as 0.5 inch (12.5 mm) annually in the desert. The rainy season lasts from November to March, with additional rains sometimes coming in the middle of spring. Snow occurs regularly in the mountains.

FLORA AND FAUNA

The coastal plain has been so heavily cleared for farming and housing that not much of the original vegetation survives. Scrubby plants of the Mediterranean type, such as tamarisk and buckthorn, grow in waste areas, while bright wildflowers grow as weeds in cultivated fields, notably species of poppy and anemone.

Forests of oak and pine grow in the northern part of the Jebel Ansariya, while scrubby hardwood trees are found in the southern part of the same range. Stands of oak, pine, cedar

and cypress cloak the upper slopes of the Anti-Lebanon range.

In the steppes a common small tree is the terebinth, or turpentine tree. A member of the sumac family, this tree is the earliest known source of turpentine (the English word, turpentine, is derived from terebinthine).

Wild mammals include deer, gazelles, and rodents such as dormice, porcupines, squirrels and rats. A distinctive animal often mistaken for a rodent is the hyrax, which is actually a hoofed mammal that can climb. Other small mammals include hares, hedgehogs and such lesser carnivores as otters, wildcats, weasels and foxes. Lions and leopards were encountered in the past, but the only large carnivores reported in recent times are bears.

Birds include hawks and kites, cormorants, pelicans and flamingoes, cuckoos and wood-peckers and, in the desert, ostriches.

NATURAL RESOURCES

The chief minerals exploited commercially in Syria are phosphates, salt, lignite (brown coal), gypsum and asphalt. First discovered in 1957 in the Karatchuk area in the extreme northeast, petroleum is now a leading export, although Syrian oil resources are small compared to some other Arab countries.

The oasis surrounding Damascus, known as the Ghouta, has the look of a giant garden, with rows of fruit trees rising above cover crops.

The Barada River cuts through Damascus, dividing the old city from the new.

The Omayyad Mosque in Damascus, dating from the 8th century, is one of the most renowned shrines of the Islamic world.

CITIES

DAMASCUS

With over 1,000,000 people, Damascus, the capital, is Syria's largest city and the hub of finance and communications. Situated between the Anti-Lebanon range and the Syrian Desert, the city lies in the oasis of Ghouta, a delta-shaped network of irrigation canals fed by the Barada River.

Damascus has been a focal point of trade since the most ancient times. The city is mentioned in the Book of Genesis, and there are some authorities who claim that it is the oldest continuously inhabited city in the world. Long renowned for its textiles and ironwork, the city has given its name to a type of cloth, damask, and to a method of inlaying steel with precious metals, damascene. The damson plum,

Details of the Omayyad Mosque in Damascus show pre-Islamic influences, such as the capitals of the columns in the foreground.

The interior of the Omayyad Mosque in Damascus clearly shows pre-Islamic Hellenistic and Byzantine features.

The head of John the Baptist is supposedly contained within this domed structure inside the Omayyad Mosque in Damascus.

Parliament Boulevard cuts through the new quarters of Damascus to the edge of the Oasis of Ghouta.

first grown in the extensive orchards of the Ghouta, also derives its name from that of the city.

The modern city of Damascus extends north of the Barada, while the ancient city lies south of the river. Among the landmarks of the latter is the Great or Omayyad Mosque, one of the most renowned houses of worship in the Islamic world, erected in A.D. 705 by the Caliph al-Walid on the site of a former Christian church. Also in the old town is the "Street called Straight," a covered thoroughfare lined with bazaars, which looks today much as it no doubt did when it was mentioned in the New Testament Book of Acts in the 1st century A.D.

The modern part of the city boasts wide avenues, modern office buildings and numerous cultural institutions.

ALEPPO

The second largest city of Syria, Aleppo has over 700,000 inhabitants, and like Damascus, is a place of great antiquity. There is evidence that it may date from before 5000 B.C.

Aleppo is a commercial and industrial city and a market for the surrounding agricultural regions of northeastern Syria. Its chief industries are textile manufacturing and food processing, mainly of dried fruits and nuts.

The city has numerous historic remains, one of the most famous being the Zakariyeh Mosque, which is supposed to house the tomb of Zachary, father of John the Baptist. Another

The Hamadiyeh Souq (bazaar) in Damascus is covered by a vaulted roof.

A panoramic view of Aleppo shows the Citadel at the left and just below it, the dome and minaret of the Zakariyeh Mosque. The Citadel's walls are 1,230 feet (369 metres) in circumference, making it the largest castle in the world.

mosque, the Kikanah, incorporates a stone block bearing Hittite inscriptions. On a bluff dominating the older part of the city is an extensive citadel dating from the 12th century A.D.

HOMS

Homs (also called Hims), with 216,000 people, lies in west-central Syria on the Orontes River. In ancient times the city was known as Emesa and was a focal point in the worship of

Enormous storage tanks at the Homs refinery rival in size the great monuments of Syria's past.

A panoramic view of Aleppo can be seen from the ramparts of the mighty Citadel that rises on a bluff above the city.

Baal, the sun god. The ill-reputed Roman Emperor Heliogabalus was born there about A.D. 205 and served as high priest of the Temple of Baal before succeeding his cousin Caracalla on the imperial throne.

Set amid one of the most fertile countrysides of Syria, Homs is famous for the manufacture of silk and for the mosque and mausoleum erected in 1908 to venerate the 7th-century Moslem general, Khalid ibn el-Welid.

HAMA

Also a city of ancient renown, Hama was a Hittite stronghold long before 1000 B.C. Built on the banks of the Orontes River, the city lies about 30 miles (48 km) due north of Homs, in a district where grain and cotton are raised on a large scale. Hama is the site of the Great

Ancient Homs, one of Syria's most historic cities, is the site of this modern oil refinery.

Giant water wheels built in the 14th century lift water from the Orontes to irrigate the farmland surrounding the city of Hama.

Mosque of Djama al-Nuri, which was a Christian basilica before the Moslem conquest of Syria.

Other curiosities are a Roman aqueduct that is still used and nine enormous water wheels that pump water from the Orontes for irrigation. Dating from the 14th century (when there were 30 such wheels), some of these devices are 90 feet (27 metres) in diameter.

Hama's chief industries are food processing and the manufacture of textiles, clothing and carpets, activities employing a large part of its 137,000 people.

LATAKIA

Latakia, with 125,000 people, is the chief seaport of Syria. Founded by the Phoenicians, it was known as Ramitha until 290 B.C., when

Seleucus Nicator, a general of Alexander the Great, rebuilt and renamed it Laodicea (of which Latakia is a corruption).

The city is the hub of the Syrian tobacco industry, which was begun in the 17th century, and exports raw cotton, asphalt and foodstuffs, as well as tobacco. Latakia is also known as a leading resort city and for its sponge fisheries.

OTHER TOWNS

Tartous, another ancient town, lies close to the Lebanese border. It is Syria's second largest port and the chief exporting point for Syrian crude oil and phosphates. The seaport of Baniyas, halfway between Tartous and Latakia, is the terminus of a pipeline from northern Iraq. Dayr az Zawr, on the Euphrates in eastern Syria, is a market town for farm produce and for salt mined in the vicinity.

El Azm Palace in Damascus, built in 1749, now houses the National Folk Museum. This folk group is demonstrating a traditional dance called el-samaha.

2. HISTORY

THE LAND KNOWN in former times as Syria once covered a greater area than does the modern Syrian Arab Republic. At different times, areas of what are now Turkey and Iraq as well as all of Lebanon, Jordan and Israel, were considered part of Syria.

EARLY HISTORY

Throughout the long history of the region, the population has largely consisted of Semitic peoples, despite numerous invasions and conquests by non-Semites. Excavations made at Ebla in northern Syria during the 1970's, have established the existence of a great Semitic culture that flourished there about 2500 B.C.

This previously unknown civilization rivalled those of Mesopotamia and Egypt. Its discovery has changed our view of the history of the ancient Middle East.

About 2100 B.C., a Semitic tribe called the Amorites entered the area from the Arabian Peninsula. A branch of this people, the Canaanites, occupied the Mediterranean coast, and from them sprang the Phoenicians. The ancient Egyptians and the Hittites, an Indo-European people of Anatolia, extended control over parts of Syria at various times during the second millenium B.C. Two other Semitic peoples, the Hebrews and the Aramaeans, became important toward the end of the 11th century B.C.

Near the modern village of Tudmur, the magnificent ruins of ancient Palmyra are being rebuilt. Palmyra was the capital of Septimius Odenathus, who ruled an extensive autonomous state within the Roman Empire in the 3rd century A.D. *His ambitious widow Zenobia, however, provoked the Romans and in* A.D. *272, the splendid city was sacked by the forces of the Roman emperor Aurelian.*

A well-preserved Roman theatre still stands at Busra, a few miles from the Jordanian border.

One of Syria's chief Christian monuments is the ruined Monastery of St. Simeon Stylites, completed in
A.D. *490, on the spot where the famous hermit sat on a pillar for seven years.*

From the 11th to the 6th centuries B.C., Syria was held intermittently by the Assyrians and Babylonians, with occasional forays by the Egyptians. From the 6th to the 4th centuries, the land was part of the Persian Empire, until that vast realm was conquered by the Greek (Macedonian), Alexander the Great. When Alexander's empire fell apart at his death in 323 B.C., Syria fell to one of his generals, Seleucus Nicator.

THE SELEUCIDS

Seleucus Nicator assumed the throne of Syria as Seleucus I, founding a dynasty called the Seleucids. The Seleucids established Antioch (now in Turkey) as their capital and introduced Greek civilization and European settlers. During this period the country pros-

pered, although the Seleucid kingdom was constantly threatened by the rival Macedonian dynasty of the Ptolemies, who ruled Egypt.

THE ROMANS

In the 1st century B.C., the Armenians and Parthians, Indo-European peoples from the north and east, began a series of invasions. In 64 B.C., the Romans under Pompey defeated the Armenians and added Syria to their growing empire, but they did not throw back the Parthians until 39 B.C. The Roman period in Syria was generally prosperous. Antioch became one of the chief cities of the Roman Empire, famous for the magnificence of its architecture and its schools of law and medicine.

The Krak of the Knights, Qualat al-Husson, is one of the great crusader citadels rising above the Mediterranean coast of Syria.

Another flourishing city was Palmyra, the capital of a powerful semi-independent kingdom that reached its height in the 3rd century. In A.D. 272, Palmyra was sacked by the Romans. Today its splendid ruins are a tourist attraction. When the Roman empire split into eastern and western parts in A.D. 395, Syria fell to the Eastern Empire and was ruled from Byzantium. During the Byzantine period, the country became completely Christianized.

ISLAM AND THE ARABS

The Byzantines maintained their hold on Syria, until weakened by invasions from Persia that lasted into the early 7th century, when a new force appeared—Islam and the Arabs.

The Arabs conquered Syria in A.D. 633, bringing the new religion of Islam, which largely replaced Christianity there. Damascus became the Arab capital and enjoyed a period of fame and wealth as the hub of the Arab Empire that stretched from Spain to Central Asia.

Then, in 715, the Omayyad dynasty that ruled from Damascus was overthrown by the Abbasids, a rival family, who made Baghdad in Iraq the Arab capital. Syria sank to the level of an outlying province.

SELJUKS AND CRUSADERS

Under the Abbasids the Arab Empire began to fall apart. Until the invasion of the Seljuk Turks in the 11th century, Syria was either divided into petty states or ruled by Egypt. The Seljuks, a Central Asian people who had adopted Islam, established two states in Syria, one with its capital at Aleppo, the other at Damascus.

Soon after the arrival of the Seljuks came invaders from western Europe, the Crusaders. These Christian knights conquered parts of the Seljuk domains and set up states with capitals at Antioch, Tripoli, Jerusalem and Edessa. Damascus, Homs and Hama remained in Moslem hands, however.

El Azm Palace in Damascus was built by Assad Pasha, an Ottoman governor of Damascus in the 18th century.

MONGOLS AND MAMELUKES

In 1187, the Seljuk ruler Saladin reconquered Jerusalem from the Crusaders and broke their hold on Syria. After Saladin's death, Syria broke up into several states and in 1260 was devastated by the Mongols. The Mameluke sultans of Egypt intervened, repulsed the Mongols and took the last remaining Crusader strongholds in 1291. Syria prospered under Mameluke rule until 1400, when a new Mongol horde under Tamerlane once more laid it waste.

THE OTTOMANS

The country never recovered from the damage inflicted by Tamerlane and, in 1516, it fell to the Ottoman Turks, who had earlier occupied Anatolia and absorbed the remains of the Byzantine Empire. Syria stagnated for most of the next three centuries as a province of the huge Ottoman Empire, which during this time spread over much of southeastern Europe, North Africa and the Middle East.

EUROPEAN INTERVENTION

In 1799, Napoleon Bonaparte invaded Egypt and briefly held a bit of the Syrian coast. This interlude dramatized the growing interest of the European powers in the Levant as the Ottoman Empire declined.

At this time, Russia was emerging as the champion of the Syrian Orthodox Christians. France backed the Maronites, Christians in communion with Rome. The British began to show an interest in the Druses, a religious group that had broken away from Islam. The outbreak of bloody hostilities between the Druses and Maronites led to French intervention in 1860, and the establishment of predominantly Christian Lebanon as an autonomous province.

THE FRENCH MANDATE

Syrian nationalists participated in the Allied campaigns against the Turks during World War I, in the expectation that an independent Syrian state would be established after the war. In 1920, a Syrian national congress elected Faisal ibn Hussein King of a Syria

Syrian refugees from the Israeli-occupied Golan Heights set up housekeeping in tents.

which included the lands of Palestine and Jordan (then called Transjordan). He was not to be installed, however, for the French, who had occupied Lebanon, wished to establish a mandate over Syria. In the face of strong opposition, the French mandate was declared later in the same year and Faisal left the country. A French mandate over Lebanon was also declared, as well as British mandates over Palestine and Iraq.

The French divided Syria into several states, under the administration of a French high commissioner residing in Beirut, the capital of Lebanon. A revolt broke out in 1925, which the French put down brutally. Syrian dissatisfaction mounted in 1939, when France ceded to Turkey the northwestern district of Alexandretta, including the historic city of Antioch. The mandate continued until after the outbreak of World War II. In 1941, the British and Free French occupied Syria and overthrew the Vichy-controlled French régime which ruled the country after the fall of France in 1940.

At the Yarmouk Refugee Camp south of Damascus, Palestinian women learn sewing and home economics.

INDEPENDENCE

In 1945, Syria and Lebanon, though still technically under the French mandate, were admitted to the United Nations. In 1946, the

French finally evacuated their troops from Syrian soil and Syria became a fully independent republic. The new government faced many problems left over from the French régime, as well as new situations, such as the establishment of the Jewish state of Israel in part of the former British mandate of Palestine.

In 1958, following a series of political crises climaxed by the Israeli action against the Suez Canal in 1956, Syria united with Egypt to form the United Arab Republic. This union lasted only until 1961, when Syrian army officers seized control of their country and seceded from the United Arab Republic.

In the Arab-Israeli War of 1967, Israeli troops occupied the Golan Heights district of southwestern Syria and retained the area after a cease-fire was effected. In 1973, following the Yom Kippur War with Israel, Syria and Israel accepted a United Nations Security Council cease-fire, agreeing to the establishment of a United Nations buffer zone along the Golan cease-fire line.

Palestinian refugees look to the day when the political difficulties in the Middle East are settled.

The restoration of the Hedjaz Railway, connecting Damascus with Medina in Saudi Arabia was a major transportation project of the 1960's, carried out with United Nations aid.

3. THE GOVERNMENT

THE SYRIAN ARAB Republic is governed by a constitution approved by the Syrian electorate in 1973. The constitution was drafted by a 173-member People's Council appointed in 1971. In the same year, Hafiz-al-Assad was elected President by means of a popular referendum. Following the adoption of the 1973 constitution, parliamentary elections were held and President Assad was re-elected for a 7-year term, and a legislature called the People's Assembly was chosen at the same time.

The presidency is provided with considerable authority—the president, for example, is empowered to appoint cabinet ministers, to declare wars and states of emergency. He can also amend the constitution and appoint members of the People's Assembly.

The 1973 Constitution replaced a provisional constitution of 1964, which it basically resembles. One difference is that the 1973 Constitution does not declare Islam to be the state religion. However, the president must be a Moslem and Islamic law must be the main basis for legislation. The judicial system of Syria includes features of Turkish and French origin, however, in addition to traditional Islamic influences.

On the local level, Syria is divided into 14

A United Nations expert (left) and a Syrian agricultural engineer inspect solar-energy transmitting instruments on a rooftop in Damascus.

units consisting of 13 provinces and the City of Damascus. The provinces are headed by governors proposed by the Ministry of the Interior and announced by presidential decree. Each province has a Provincial Council, three fourths of whose members are elected and one fourth appointed by the Minister of the Interior and the governor.

POLITICAL PARTIES

Since the late 1950's, the dominant political group in Syria has been the Ba'ath, or Arab Socialist Resurrection Party, whose slogan is "Unity, Freedom and Socialism." The party advocates state control of the means of production and the redistribution of farm land, and is committed to "spreading Socialist revolution" to other Arab countries. Other parties, including the Syrian Communist Party, have been rendered ineffective.

FOREIGN RELATIONS

Syria is a member of the Arab League and of the United Nations. In 1971, it established, with Egypt and Libya, the Confederation of Arab Republics, a loose political grouping that has so far been inactive owing mainly to disputes between Egypt and Libya. Syria is an avowed supporter of the Palestine Liberation Organization, which it recognizes as the only legitimate spokesman for the Palestinian Arabs.

Relations with Jordan were improved in 1975 when that country and Syria formed a Joint High Commission to co-ordinate policies of the two governments on economic and political affairs.

Syria intervened in the civil war in Lebanon in 1976, sending a force of 20,000 troops into that country to help maintain order.

Men of a military unit carry their insignia as they march in a parade opening an athletic event.

4. THE PEOPLE

THE SYRIAN PEOPLE number 7,580,000, most of whom are Arabs. About 10 per cent of the people belong to non-Arab ethnic groups—mainly Kurds, Armenians, and Circassians, with some Turks and a small community of Jews. The people show traces of the many races that have entered Syria during its long history, but most are of the Mediterranean type, dark-haired, dark-eyed and olive-skinned. A blond strain is widely discernible, however, and here and there a Negroid trait appears.

RELIGION

Syria's population is 85 per cent Moslem, mostly of the Sunni sect, which is the chief branch of Islam. Of other Islamic denominations, the Alawites are the most numerous, especially in Latakia. There are small numbers of Ismailis and Shiites.

The Druses number about 120,000, and are found mostly in the southwestern district of Jebel Druse. Christians, who account for nearly

All over the Islamic world, Moslems are called to prayer from minarets such as these at Al Lekiyyeh al-Suleimaniyeh.

Schoolgirls learn about the climatic zones of Africa, the vast continent that begins almost at their doorstep.

14 per cent of the Syrian population, belong to many sects. The largest Christian denominations are the Greek Orthodox, Armenian Orthodox, Syrian Orthodox and Greek Catholic.

Other Christians are Maronites, Nestorians, Chaldeans, Roman Catholics and Protestants. The once sizeable Jewish community has dwindled to about 4,000 members.

A Christian church in the new part of Damascus is a reminder of Syria's sizeable Christian minority.

These schoolboys doing calisthenics may wish they were playing basketball with the boys behind them.

Teachers lead children in play in a Damascus kindergarten.

Basketball is a popular sport in Syria, where physical fitness is being given strong emphasis.

EDUCATION

The government provides free, compulsory education for children of 6 to 11 years of age. In 1977, there were over 1,500,000 students enrolled in 6,446 primary and secondary schools.

The University of Damascus was founded in 1923, and that of Aleppo in 1960. The total enrollment at these and other institutions of higher education is over 60,000.

In spite of recent advances in education, the literacy rate is only about 40 per cent.

WAY OF LIFE

Syria's people range from the sophisticated citizens of Damascus and Aleppo to the strongly independent Bedouins of the desert. Most of them, however, are rural villagers—farmers and shepherds of the mountains and steppes—called *fellahin*.

Most of the Bedouins are nomads, driving their camels over the vast stretches of the Syrian Desert. The traditional loose robes of the desert Arab are still worn by them. People in the cities and larger towns often wear Western dress, while the villagers wear the peasant clothes of their region which often show a Turkish influence.

Traditional Arab hospitality includes coffee served in graceful vessels of hammered copper or silver and music played on ancient instruments.

The fez, a headdress dating from the days of Turkish rule, is now largely restricted to theatrical presentations.

Girls of Dayr az Zawr in eastern Syria model the traditional dress of their region.

Rich embroidery adorns the traditional costume of women of the Jezirah region of northeastern Syria.

This man combines the traditional Arab headdress and robe with a Western-style jacket and pullover.

A girl carries water from a makeshift well in a graceful metal vessel. Syria's extensive water supply projects are expected to make scenes such as this a thing of the past.

The *fellahin* subsist mainly on lentils, bread, olives, yogurt and cracked wheat, or *bulghur*, supplemented by meat, fresh vegetables, dates and other fruits on occasion. The city-dwellers have a more varied diet, with greater amounts of protein and fresh produce. Syrian cuisine resembles that of other countries of the Middle East, with many dishes based on lamb, eggplant

At a coffee stall in the market place, one man grinds while another brews and pours.

The man on the right is puffing on a hookah, or water pipe.

(aubergine), rice, chick peas and yogurt. The large numbers of Syrians who have emigrated to North and South America brought their cuisine with them, and Syrian restaurants can be found in New York, Buenos Aires and other New World cities.

NON-ARAB GROUPS

The Kurds inhabit the northeast corner of Syria, adjoining Persia and Turkey. An ancient people whose language is related to Persian, the Kurds are mountaineers with a distinct culture of their own, although they are Moslems. The 150,000 Syrian Kurds are only a small part of the Kurdish people, several millions of whom inhabit the region where Iraq, Iran, Turkey and Syria come together.

Another Moslem people, the Circassians, came originally from the Caucasus. When Circassia was occupied by Russia in the 19th century, many of its people took refuge in Syria and Turkey. Today about 25,000 Circassians live in villages of their own in southwestern Syria.

Another displaced group are the Armenians, Christian fugitives from Turkish oppression in the early 20th century. Numbering about 120,000 they live mainly in and around Aleppo.

LANGUAGE

Arabic, the official language of Syria, is spoken by all but a few of the people. Kurdish is the language of daily life in the extreme north-

With United Nations help, the Syrian government is working to improve sanitation, sewerage, and water supply in villages such as Arbine, near Damascus, where these children are playing.

The "debke" is a cheerful traditional Syrian dance.

east corner of the country, and Armenian is used in the home by the Armenian community. French is spoken by many people in the large cities.

Syria is the land of origin of two historic Semitic tongues—Aramaic and Syriac. Aramaic, brought into the country by the Aramaeans, became a *lingua franca* of the ancient Middle East and even replaced Hebrew as the language of the Jews of Palestine in the centuries preceding the birth of Jesus. Aramaic later developed into several dialects, of which Syriac was the most important. Today Syriac survives as the language of scattered communities in Iran and Iraq, and as the liturgical language of Syrian Christians.

These toddlers will grow up in a different Syria from the one their parents and grandparents knew.

In the Mezze quarter of Damascus new housing for middle-income families has been constructed on a large scale.

5. THE ECONOMY

After centuries of foreign domination and after decades of recent instability, Syria emerged in the 1970's as a country with an expanding economy. This came about through economic planning, through an increase in the value of exports and through sizeable loans and grants from Arab oil states and Iran.

AGRICULTURE

Syria, unlike most Arab states of the Middle East, is basically able to feed itself. The large amount of productive land has made this possible, even though, until recently, old-fashioned agricultural methods were in general use.

Today new agricultural projects are increasing both the amount of arable land and the yield of existing acreage. Foremost among these projects is the Euphrates Dam west of Raqqa, completed in 1973. The damming of the river created a vast reservoir, Lake Assad, which will eventually double the amount of Syrian land under irrigation. In addition, the hydro-electric power from the dam will, when current projects are completed, furnish 80 per cent of the power required by new industries and provide lighting for the entire country, as well.

In the Food-Processing Laboratory in Damascus, a chemist trained at the University of Damascus examines newly arrived equipment.

CROPS AND LIVESTOCK

Cereals, cotton, sugar beets, tobacco, fruits and vegetables are the principal agricultural crops. The chief cereals are wheat, barley, sorghum, millet and maize. Among orchard crops, olives are of first importance, and in the Aleppo area, pistachios. Other leading fibre crops than cotton are hemp and silk, although the latter is declining.

Sheep, poultry and cattle are the leading livestock, with production of both beef and dairy cattle being greatly expanded. Together, these three animal groups represented about 35 per cent of Syria's total agricultural production in 1977. Other farm animals raised are goats for meat, milk and hides, and water buffaloes as draught animals.

INDUSTRY AND TRADE

Until the 1960's, Syrian industry consisted chiefly of processing the country's agricultural products. Syrian factory workers were employed

mainly in making cigarettes, ginning cotton, weaving, extracting olive oil, packing dried fruit and similar activities.

While these industries are still important, the Syrian economy is no longer so dependent on them. New factories are now turning out glass, paper, fertilizers, cement, iron and steel,

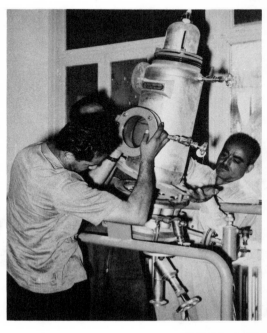

Food-processing is an important and expanding industry in Syria. Here workmen are installing a machine for producing concentrated fruit juice.

This extensive textile factory boasts the latest equipment and also provides housing for its employees, schools for their children, and subsidized meals and medical care for all.

television sets, household appliances—many of these with the aid of foreign investors.

Syria under President Assad has adopted an open-door trade policy—that is, restrictions on foreign trade have been removed and foreign investment has been encouraged.

Syria's principal exports are cotton, crude petroleum, textiles, wool, phosphates and fruits

The National Bank typifies the buildings of the new part of Damascus. The old man in the foreground sports the now rarely seen fez.

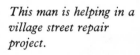

This man is helping in a village street repair project.

and vegetables. The European Economic Community (Common Market) buys 48 per cent of Syria's exports, the Communist bloc buys 22 per cent, and other Arab states 9 per cent.

Imports consist mainly of fuels, machinery and equipment, foodstuffs and various other manufactured goods. The Common Market is the source of 33 per cent of these products, the Communist states, 17 per cent, and the Arab states, 9 per cent.

Syria is famous for the craftsmanship of its metal work, especially copper, brass, silver and steel. This artisan is finishing an engraved brass tray.

A modern well and storage tank rising above the stony desert typify Syria's drive to increase its water resources.

The Syrian government owns and operates nearly 1,000 miles (1,600 km) of railway track. Nearly half this total was completed in the 1970's with Russian aid, when a new stretch was built connecting Latakia with Al-Qamishli in the far northeast.

Trade with the United States has grown rapidly—in 1973, Syria imported U.S. $20,000,000 worth of United States goods, while by 1976, the amount had increased tenfold to U.S. $200,000,000.

PETROLEUM

The petroleum industry in Syria began production in 1968, with an output in that year of 1,000,000 metric tons. Production rose to 9,500,000 metric tons by 1975. On the basis of known reserves, it is estimated that production will level off at 10,000,000 metric tons a year until the early 1980's, after which a decline will set in unless new fields are discovered.

TRANSPORTATION AND COMMUNICATION

Most of Syria's surfaced roads are in the western part of the country and total about 5,000 miles (8,000 km) altogether. The government owns and operates the railway system as well as the national airline, which flies to many points in Asia, Europe and Africa. Damascus boasts an ultra-modern international airport.

Communications, including press, television and radio are under government ownership or control.

TOURISM

The uncertain political situation in Syria before the time of President Assad inhibited the growth of tourism, as did the general tension in the whole Middle East. Under the Assad régime, tourism is being developed. Chains of new hotels have been built to make Syria's archeological treasures more accessible to foreigners—there is now a modern hotel at Palmyra, for example, and there are new hotels in most of the major cities. These efforts resulted in an influx of 1,390,000 tourists in 1976—up from 870,000 in 1970.

The Al-Ain Hilton at Abu Dhabi
is one of the new hotels
springing up in the larger towns.

United
Arab
Emirates

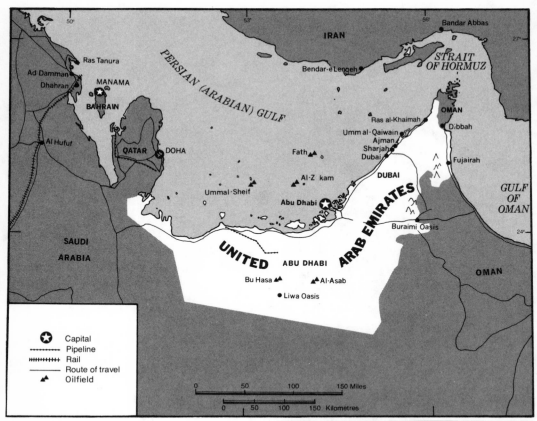

Legend

⭐ Capital
········ Pipeline
⫟⫟⫟⫟⫟⫟ Rail
——— Route of travel
▲▲ Oilfield

0   50   100   150 Miles
0 50 100 150 Kilometres

454 ◇ UNITED ARAB EMIRATES

Shallow, meandering inlets or creeks are a common feature of the Persian Gulf coast of the Emirates. Seen here is the creek at Dubai before it was bridged. A tunnel beneath it is also planned.

I. THE LAND

THE UNITED ARAB EMIRATES is a federation of 7 sheikhdoms on the Persian (Arabian) Gulf. The federation is bounded by Qatar on the west, Saudi Arabia on the west and south, and Oman and the Gulf of Oman on the east. With an area of 32,000 square miles (83,200 sq km), the Emirates are about equal in size to Maine or to all of Ireland.

Over the centuries this cluster of small monarchies has been known by such names as the Pirate Coast, the Trucial Coast, the Trucial States, the Trucial Sheikhdoms and Trucial Oman. The states composing the federation are Abu Dhabi, Dubai, Sharjah, Ajman, Umm al-Qaiwain, Ras al-Khaimah and Fujairah. Of these, Abu Dhabi and Dubai are the largest and most important—in fact, Abu Dhabi dwarfs all the others in area, with its 27,900 square miles (72,540 sq km).

The boundaries of the Emirates are somewhat confusing since all but Abu Dhabi are composed of several separate fragments of territory separated by parts of other Emirates. In this respect, they rather resemble the small German states of Europe before the unification of Germany.

Dubai is second in size with 1,500 square miles (3,900 sq km), and Sharjah is third, with 1,000 square miles (2,600 sq km). The others in descending order of size are Ras al-Khaimah (650 square miles or 1,690 sq km), Fujairah (450 square miles or 1,170 sq km), Umm al-Qaimain (300 square miles or 780 sq km), and Ajman (100 square miles or 260 sq km). Fujairah is the only Emirate without a coastline on the Persian Gulf—it lies entirely on the Gulf of Oman.

TOPOGRAPHY

Most of the land is flat and barren coast that merges inland with empty, sandy desert. The coastline stretches for about 400 miles (640 km) from Qatar in the west to Oman in the east, and

Trees and flowers adorn the grounds at Abu Dhabi Airport.

is broken by extensive salt marshes and fringed with numerous barren islets. In the east, where the mountains of Oman extend into the territory of the Emirates, broad gravel plains separate the highlands from the enormous shifting sand dunes of the Rub al-Khali or Empty Quarter of Saudi Arabia.

There are oases in the interior of Abu Dhabi, of which Liwa and Buraimi are the most extensive, and in the eastern Emirates of Sharjah and Fujairah fertile, well-watered mountain valleys and coastal plains provide a certain amount of greenery. The Emirate of Ras al-Khaimah, however, is the most productive, since it is endowed with abundant underground water coming down from the mountains of Oman.

OTHER FACTORS

The climate of the Emirates is similar to that of the other Gulf countries—hot and dry. The long, dry summer lasts from May to October, while the remainder of the year is more temperate. January is the wettest month—if the term wet can be used for a country whose average annual rainfall is almost 5 inches (125 mm). In the eastern mountains, however, annual rainfall averages 15 inches (375 mm).

Too much wind is as much a problem as too little water. The growth of vegetation is checked by the fact that the prevailing northwest winds often expose the roots of young plants. Sometimes the winds reverse direction and heap up sand upon the younger plants, burying them completely.

The flora and fauna of the Emirates are virtually the same as those of adjacent Qatar and Saudi Arabia. Palms grow in the oases, and acacias, tamarisks and other thorny and scrubby plants, in the arid regions. Hares, gazelles, falcons, quail, foxes, jackals, and jerboas are common, and fish abound in the offshore waters.

The natural resources of the Emirates were virtually non-existent until the discovery of petroleum in 1958. Today, oil and natural gas constitute the principal sources of wealth. Gypsum and limestone are found and some copper deposits exist but are not developed.

CITIES

Each of the Emirates bears the name of its capital, but some of these capitals are little larger than villages. The city of Dubai was for long the only important town in the region, owing to its excellent port. Both Dubai and Abu Dhabi today have populations of 60,000, while

The port at Sharjah, capital of the third largest Emirate, is a busy place since the expansion of docking facilities. Here, cement is being unloaded from a ship.

Fountains spray in Jamel Abdul Nasser Square, in Dubai, a city where water was once scarce.

Sharjah is next with 25,000, followed by Ras al-Khaimah with 10,000. Abu Dhabi is the provisional capital of the country until a new federal capital is built.

The cities of the United Arab Emirates are among the most modern in the world and are growing daily, as new port facilities, highways, housing, banks, factories, offices, hospitals, schools and mosques are added.

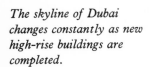

The skyline of Dubai changes constantly as new high-rise buildings are completed.

The representative of the United Arab Emirates (middle) to the United Nations signs a technical assistance agreement.

2. HISTORY

RECENT DIGGINGS by Danish archeologists and others have revealed evidence of a civilization existing 5,000 years ago and having possible connections with both ancient Mesopotamia and the Indus Valley of India and Pakistan. Otherwise the early history of the Emirates left little trace until recently. Present excavations, however, may add much to our knowledge of the area.

After the arrival of Islam in the 7th century A.D., the history of the region was bound up with that of the great Arab Empire and its subsequent break-up into smaller states. By the 17th century, the Persian Gulf had become infested with pirates, both European and Arab, and many of them had operated from the area that is now the United Arab Emirates. It was at this time that the name "Pirate Coast" came into use.

THE TRUCIAL COAST

By the 19th century, piracy in the region had become such a problem that the British intervened. In 1820, following several British expeditions against Ras al-Khaimah, the principal pirate headquarters, a "General Treaty of Peace" was signed by the sheikhs of the area. Renewed outbreaks of piracy occurred until 1853, when a "Perpetual Maritime Truce" was signed with the British. This treaty put the "Trucial Sheikhdoms" or "Trucial States," under British influence, giving Britain the right to enforce the treaty terms and the power to settle disputes among the sheikhs. In 1892, the Trucial States formally became British protectorates, with Britain assuming full control over their foreign relations.

MODERN TIMES

The Trucial States continued under the British protectorate until 1971, when the British withdrew from the Persian Gulf. Plans for the seven states to federate with nearby Bahrain and Qatar fell through, and on December 1, 1971, they all became independent. On December 2, six of them formed the United Arab Emirates—the holdout being Ras al-Khaimah, which did not join until early in 1972. The United Arab Emirates joined both the United Nations and the Arab League in 1972.

The National Council Building is located in the city of Abu Dhabi, the temporary capital of the United Arab Emirates. Eventually, a new capital city will be built at a site on the boundary line between Dubai and Abu Dhabi Emirates.

3. GOVERNMENT

THE UNITED ARAB EMIRATES has a government that seems to be a contradiction in terms—a federation of monarchies that in effect form a republic. Each emirate has control over mineral rights within its own boundaries, taxation, police and other matters, and some of the larger ones maintain their own armed forces.

THE CONSTITUTION

The Constitution, which became effective on December 2, 1971, was officially named the Provisional Constitution of the United Arab Emirates. The term "provisional" was chosen

to allow room for change as the federation developed in its first five years—in fact, the document was a full constitutional instrument with 152 articles. In 1976, the Constitution was amended slightly to increase federal control, and was extended until 1981.

EXECUTIVE POWER

Responsibility for policy decisions and for the ratification of federal laws lies in a Supreme Council, a body composed of the seven rulers of the individual emirates. The council also elects the country's President and Vice-President,

(Left) In 1958, the only primary school at Dubai was housed in the Emir's Palace. (Right) By the mid-1970's, new schools were rising everywhere, including this new secondary school at Abu Dhabi.

who serve five-year terms. The first President and Vice-President were respectively the Rulers of Abu Dhabi and Dubai, who were re-elected in 1976. The President appoints the Prime Minister, and, in consultation with him, also appoints the other cabinet members.

PARLIAMENT AND LEGAL SYSTEM

The legislative function is carried out by the National Council, a 40-member body that also debates a wide range of matters of public interest. Of the National Council members, Abu Dhabi and Dubai return eight each, Sharjah and Ras al-Khaimah, six each, and the remaining emirates four each. The members are appointed by the Rulers of their respective states.

The constitution provides for the establishment of an independent judiciary, composed of a Higher Federal Court and several lesser courts. Within each emirate, traditional law is observed, but the aim of the government is to standardize the legal system throughout the entire land. Sharia, the traditional Islamic legal code is the basic law of the land.

Low-cost modern housing is under construction all over the Emirates, replacing the simple reed and mud cottages that formerly housed the people.

4. THE PEOPLE

THE POPULATION of the United Arab Emirates is about 750,000, with the greatest concentrations in Abu Dhabi, Dubai and Sharjah. About 72 per cent of the people are Arabs and the rest are Iranians, Pakistanis and Indians. Only about one fourth of the population is native-born—since the 1960's large numbers of Arabs from other countries have come in to work in the oil fields and the booming construction industries.

Like the people of other oil-producing Gulf countries, the residents of the Emirates are people in transition. Before the development of

In 1973, when this picture was taken, there were 37,000 children in schools in the Emirate. In 1977, the number was approaching 100,000.

The sprawling Rashid Hospital at Dubai was erected in 1972.

oil resources, fishermen, herdsmen and villagers made up the small and scattered populace. Now industrial urban workers and modern farmers predominate.

The Sunni form of Islam is the official religion and Arabic is the national language. English is in wide use, however, and Hindi and Urdu are spoken by many foreign immigrants. Education is regarded as a major field for development and a modern school system has been established in a few short years. In 1953, there were only 700 students in school, over half of them in one emirate—Sharjah. In 1977, 90,000 were enrolled in all levels of education, a phenomenal growth. In 1977, the University of the United Arab Emirates was opened and four junior university colleges were scheduled.

Health and housing, like education, are generously financed by state grants and loans.

Traditional fishing methods of the kind seen here are yielding to modern techniques.

Workmen lay incoming pipe in one of Abu Dhabi's new plants.

5. THE ECONOMY

NOT ALL of the Emirates are rich in oil as are Abu Dhabi, Dubai and Sharjah—but a balance exists, since Ras al-Khaimah and Fujairah are the breadbaskets of the country. For the present and for some time to come, the oil resources of the Emirates are the basis of all modernization and development.

OIL

Before 1958, the rulers of the Emirates received a certain amount of income from oil exploration rights and British Government grants. Then heavy oil strikes were made in Abu Dhabi between 1958 and 1960. The economy had until then been based on subsistence farming, raising sheep and goats, fishing, and in Dubai a certain amount of trade.

Abu Dhabi began pouring its oil revenues into modernization, health, education and irrigation projects not only for itself, but for the other Emirates. In 1971, large offshore oil strikes were made in the territorial waters of Dubai, and again in 1974 off the coast of Sharjah. In 1976, exploration began off the coasts of Ras al-Khaimah and Umm al-Qaiwain. The total oil income for the Emirates rose to U.S. $5,556,000,000 in 1976.

A production platform tops an underwater oil storage tank off Dubai.

OTHER INDUSTRY

Financed by oil money, new factories are being built to produce cement, tile, pipe, petro-chemicals, fertilizers, paint, plastics, asbestos, aluminium, flour and air-conditioning units. When in full operation these new installations will greatly reduce the need to import manufactured goods, which at present is considerable.

Highways, international airports, hotels and commercial buildings have been completed, along with modern electric power and telecommunications systems. Once sleepy Gulf fishing ports have almost overnight been turned into modern cities with broad, tree-lined boulevards and bustling port facilities.

The power and desalination installations at Abu Dhabi are seen shortly after completion.

Technicians in traditional garb man the Emirates' new television stations.

AGRICULTURE

A good example of the new techniques being developed to expand agriculture can be observed at Salmayat in Abu Dhabi, where a 1-inch (2.5 mm) layer of asphalt is being laid down under a tract of sand at a depth of about 3 feet (0.9 metre). The "carpet" will prevent irrigation water from sinking into the sand and will also prevent salt, which is injurious to plants, from seeping up from the sub-soil. If successful, this technique could be widely used in many areas.

In the historically productive Emirate of Ras al-Khaimah, the chief crops are fruits, vegetables and fodder. New roads have made it easy to transport produce from this area. Among the items grown and shipped are such vegetables as eggplants, tomatoes, cucumbers, turnips, radishes and cabbages, and a wide variety of luscious fruits—bananas, oranges, lemons,

The satellite aerial at Dubai links the United Arab Emirates with cities all over the world.

At Al-Ain, near Abu Dhabi, an irrigation channel brings fresh water to a flourishing farming area.

strawberries, mangoes, pomegranates, mulberries and figs. Tobacco is also grown for local consumption.

Ras al-Khaimah also produces cattle, goats, milk, eggs and poultry—and the quality of all these is constantly being improved. Fujairah has extensive date plantations along with market gardens.

Fisheries are earmarked for extensive development and sizeable areas have been set aside for afforestation projects.

The new airport at Sharjah is now an important link with other parts of the Middle East.

Yemeni architecture has its own distinctive style,
although recognizably Arabic.

Yemen

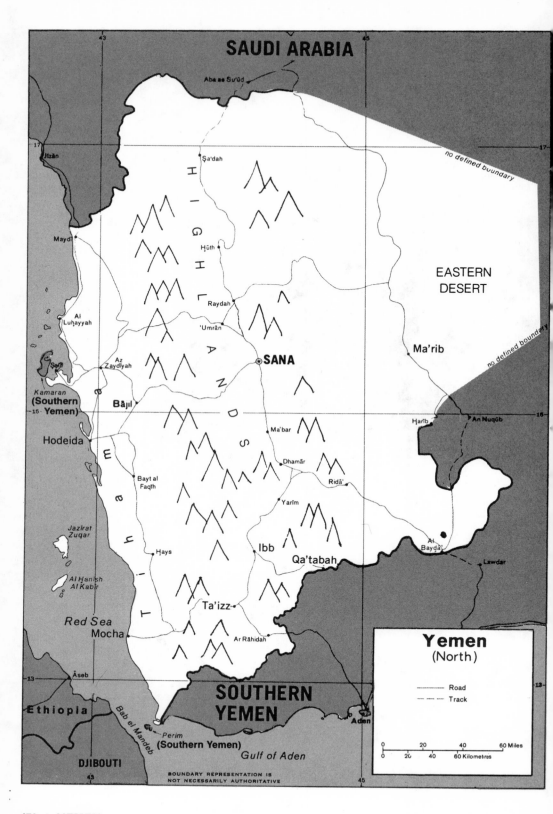

SAUDI ARABIA

Aba as Su'ūd

no defined boundary

Jīzān

Ṣa'dah

H
I
G
H
L
A
N
D
S

Maydi

Hūth

EASTERN
DESERT

Al
Luḥayyah

Raydah

'Umrān

Ma'rib

Soffi

Az
Zaydīyah

SANA

Kamaran
(Southern
Yemen)

Bājil

Harib

An Nuqūb

no defined boundary

Hodeida

Ma'bar

Bayt al
Faqīh

Dhamār

Ridā'

T
i
h
a
m
a

Jazīrat
Zuqar

Yarīm

Hays

Ibb

Al
Bayḍā'

Al Hanish
Al Kabīr

Qa'tabah

Lawdar

Red Sea
Mocha

Ta'izz

Ar Rāhidah

Āseb

SOUTHERN
YEMEN

| Yemen |
| (North) |

Ethiopia

Bab el Mandeb

Perim
(Southern Yemen)

Gulf of Aden

Aden

	Road
	Track

DJIBOUTI

BOUNDARY REPRESENTATION IS
NOT NECESSARILY AUTHORITATIVE

0   20   40   60 Miles
0   20   40   60 Kilometres

Tier upon tier of terraced fields cling to the hillsides in the mountain zone.

I. THE LAND

THE YEMEN ARAB REPUBLIC lies at the southwest tip of the Arabian Peninsula. Sometimes referred to as North Yemen to distinguish it from the People's Democratic Republic of Yemen, which adjoins it on the south and east, it is bounded on the north by Saudi Arabia and on the west by the Red Sea. With an area of 75,000 square miles (195,000 sq km), it is almost the same size as Nebraska, or half again as big as England.

TOPOGRAPHY

Yemen is unique among the states of the Arabian Peninsula, since a large part of it is green and well-watered, although an unin-

formed visitor landing on the Red Sea coast would never guess this. The Tihama, or zone along the Red Sea, is a torrid, parched strip 40 miles (64 km) wide, quite unlike the mountainous interior.

The Tihama merges into a range of foothills and lesser mountains known as the lower mountain region, with elevations up to 6,000 feet (2,700 metres). Eastward of this zone the high mountains begin, reaching elevations over 12,000 feet (3,600 metres). The highest peak in Yemen, and the highest on the Arabian Peninsula, is Jebel al-Nuabi Shuaib, 14,000 feet (4,200 metres) above sea level.

The north and west are desert regions merging into the deserts of Saudi Arabia.

Near Sana, water is carried from a well in little tank carts complete with rubber tires.

CLIMATE AND WATER SUPPLY

Very little rain falls along the barren Tihama coast, where summer temperatures average well over 100°F (37.8°C). This region cools off somewhat from November to March, when the temperature usually falls between 75° and 95°F (23.9° and 35°C).

In the central highlands the climate is temperate—summer temperatures vary between 63°F and 81°F (17.2°C and 27.2°C), while winter temperatures may drop to 23°F (−5°C) in the higher elevations.

Rain falls heaviest in the southwest province of Taizz, less heavily but still sufficient in the northern mountains. The rainy season begins in March and ends in August.

The streams (there are no real rivers) of Yemen are fed by springs in the mountains and swollen by rain during the rainy season. Those flowing west drain intermittently into the Red Sea, while those descending the eastern slopes of the highlands disappear into the desert.

FLORA AND FAUNA

The semi-desert coastal strip contains soil too salty to support much vegetation, although scattered oases of palm trees are found. The eastern half of the Tihama has fertile soil but insufficient water and here scrub grows, especially along the water courses, whose beds are dry, however, for much of the year.

The slopes of the mountains are heavily terraced for agriculture. Forests of junipers occur along with such broadleafed trees as figs, tamarinds and carobs.

Among mammals, a species of ibex occurs in the mountainous regions, and wildcats, wolves, hyenas, foxes, jackals, hares and hyraxes

Two farm women near Hodeida take a break in the course of their work in a parched Tihama field.

are common, and several species of monkey are found. Birds include ostriches and bustards in the desert areas, while elsewhere partridges, quail and doves are fairly common. Insects and other arthropods are numerous, especially locusts, centipedes, scorpions and ants.

NATURAL RESOURCES

The mineral resources of Yemen have not been prospected or developed except for salt, which is mined for export as well as domestic use. There are indications of the presence of petroleum in Tihama, and of copper, sulphur and iron ore deposits in other regions.

Near Sana, a farmer uses two camels to draw water from a well to irrigate his fields. Mechanized farm equipment is in use on only a few Yemeni farms.

Modern motor cars flow by the ancient walls of Sana. Motor vehicles are on the increase in Yemen as more and more modern highways are built.

CITIES

SANA

Capital and largest city of Yemen, Sana (also spelled San'a) is a place of considerable antiquity—it was important before the rise of Islam. The city, which is surrounded by an ancient wall, has a population of 125,000 and is a cultural and commercial hub. At an elevation of 7,250 feet (2,175 metres), Sana has a healthful climate and is renowned for the luscious grapes grown in the surrounding countryside and abundant in the city's markets.

HODEIDA

Connected by road to Sana, Hodeida on the Red Sea coast is Yemen's chief port and most modern city—much of it was destroyed by fire in 1961 and completely rebuilt, with Russian

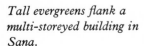

Tall evergreens flank a multi-storeyed building in Sana.

Citizens of Sana move briskly through a typical street of the city, propelled no doubt by the bracing mountain air.

aid. The city's importance as a port dates only from the 19th century, when Yemen was under Turkish rule. Hodeida has 90,000 people.

TAIZZ AND MOCHA

Taizz, with 80,000 people, the leading town of the southern part of the country, is chiefly a market town for farm produce. From Taizz a road leads to Mocha on the coast. Formerly Yemen's leading port (until surpassed by Hodeida), Mocha gave its name to the fragrant coffee shipped from its once busy wharves.

Al Mudhafar Mosque in Taizz has a minaret typical of the Taizz region—a series of recessed round-headed alcoves one above the other.

YEMEN ◇ **475**

Present day Marib rises above ruins of the ancient Marib, capital of the Sabaeans, who are supposed to be the people of the biblical Queen of Sheba. In the vicinity are the remains of a huge dam built about 800 B.C., which once provided water to this semi-arid area.

2. HISTORY

YEMEN is an ancient land, the home of several pre-Islamic civilizations, of which the most renowned is the Saba or Sheba mentioned in the Bible. The beginnings of civilization in Yemen are obscure. The earliest culture about which much is known is that of the Minaeans, whose capital was Ma'in and who flourished from 1200 to 650 B.C., although these dates are disputed.

THE SABAEANS

It is not certain whether the Minaean kingdom predated or co-existed with the Sabaean kingdom. In any case, the earliest records of the Sabaean state date from the 10th century B.C. Until the 7th century B.C., Saba was under priest kings, the Mukarribs, who ruled from Serivah (modern Khariba). The

The Talha quarter in Sana provides a good example of Yemeni multiple housing. Since ancient times tall apartment houses have been built in South Arabia—sometimes 20 storeys high!

Mukarribs were succeeded about 650 B.C. by a line known as the "Kings of Saba," whose capital was Marib. The Queen of Sheba mentioned in *I Kings* is supposed to have visited Solomon about 950 B.C. Some scholars doubt that her story is factual.

Two other kingdoms existed during the Sabaean period—those of Qataban and Hadhramaut, with which the Sabaeans warred continually, but little else is known about these states.

The Sabaean kingdom prospered for 500 years. One source of wealth came from the fact that Sabaean ports were the principal points of transfer for goods travelling by sea between Egypt and India. When an overland trade was established with India by Egypt's Ptolemies, the wealth of Saba declined.

THE HIMYARITES

Another South Arabian people, the Himyarites, succeeded the Sabaeans about the end of the second century B.C. as the dominant South Arabian group. These people possessed an ancient alphabet and have left many inscriptions on bronze tablets among the ruins of their buildings. Sana was their principal city.

During the Himyaritic period, a Roman invasion was repelled in 24 B.C. and later Yemen was invaded by the Ethiopians, who occupied

Mumtaza el Rawdah Mosque in Sana is important for its schools of Islamic law and theology.

it from A.D. 340 to 378. Following this, both Christianity and Judaism were introduced into Yemen, and for a time a Jewish kingdom was established among some of the Himyarites. The Ethiopians, who were Christians, again invaded the country in 525. The Himyarites invoked the aid of Persia, which succeeded in gaining control over Yemen in 575, and ruled it until 628.

ISLAM

The coming of Mohammed and the spread of the Islamic religion in the 7th century engulfed Yemen. Many Yemenis rose to leadership in the Arab armies that carried the new religion into the ancient countries of the Mediterranean and the Middle East. Yemen

itself became a province of the great Arab empire that was ruled first from Damascus and then from Baghdad.

After the breakup of the caliphate, as the Arab empire was called, Yemen was largely ruled by local Moslem dynasties, with a period of domination by the Fatimite rulers of Egypt from about 1000 to 1175. The most important native dynasty was that of the Rassites, religious rulers called *imams* of the Zaidi sect of Islam, founded in 898. The imamate survived as an institution until 1962, sometimes under nominal foreign domination, at other times, independent.

During the 16th century the Ottoman Turks invaded Yemen and added it to their dominions. The Ottomans, however, were unable to maintain more than nominal control over

A Yemeni official signs an agreement to promote locust control in 19 Asian and African countries, with United Nations officials looking on.

Yemen during most of the period of their rule, which ended with the breakup of their empire in 1918.

THE 20TH CENTURY

In 1911, the Turks recognized as imam a descendant of the 10th century founder of the imamate. The new imam, Yahya, however, held sway only over the central and northern highlands. In 1915, the imamate extended its control to include the Tihama. When the Turks pulled out after their defeat in World War I, Imam Yahya sought to extend his control further, laying claim to the British-controlled areas south and east of Yemen, now included in Southern Yemen. It was not until 1934, however, that Yemen's boundaries were fixed by treaties with Britain and Saudi Arabia. Following World War II, Yemen abandoned a policy of isolationism and joined both the Arab League and the United Nations.

In 1948, Imam Yahya was assassinated by insurrectionists, but his successor, Imam Ahmad put down the insurgents. Following Ahmad's death in 1962, his successor Imam Badr was deposed and a republic proclaimed. Civil war between the republican and royalist forces continued until 1970. Egypt intervened to aid the republicans, while Saudi Arabia aided the royalists. Stability did not come about until 1970, when Saudi Arabia recognized the republican régime.

In 1972, border clashes took place between Yemen and Southern Yemen. Southern Yemen is the name popularly given to the former British-controlled areas of Aden and the Aden Protectorate, south and east of Yemen, which became independent in 1967. Later, in 1972, the two governments signed an agreement to end the border clashes, and to work towards a merger of their countries into a single Yemeni state. Occasional border clashes occurred after the agreement, but both governments continued to support the concept of unification.

In 1979, Southern Yemen invaded Yemen. The League of Arab States arranged a cease-fire and sent a special force to patrol the border between the two Yemens.

United Nations technical assistance to Yemen began in 1953, when Prince Saif al Islam Abdullah (left) signed for his country, then a kingdom.

3. GOVERNMENT

THE YEMEN ARAB REPUBLIC is governed by a 4-member Command Council. The Council appoints a prime minister, who then appoints a cabinet of his own choosing. All high-level decisions, however, are made by the Command Council, and the prime minister and his cabinet ministers are responsible to that body.

The head of state is the chairman of the Command Council, who is also president of the republic. A parliamentary body called the Consultative Council, or Assembly, was dissolved in 1975.

On October 12, 1977, the incumbent president, Ibrahim al-Hamdi was assassinated just before he was to leave on a state visit to Southern Yemen. The surviving members of the Command Council assumed control under Ahmad Hussein al-Ghashmi and pledged to continue the policies of President al-Hamdi, including eventual union with Southern Yemen. They also imposed martial law on the entire country. President Al-Ghashmi was assassin-ated in 1978 and was succeeded by Ali Abdulla‌ Saleh.

LOCAL GOVERNMENT

Yemen is divided into 10 provinces c emirates, each under the administration of a emir appointed by the central governmen However, since Yemen is largely a trib‌ society, local government within each distri‌ is handled by traditional headmen or loc‌ leaders with the approval of the emir. Th emirates in turn are divided into districts.

Yemen's legal system is a mixture of trib‌ and Islamic law. The *sharias,* or Mosle‌ courts, are headed by Islamic judges, but th execution of their decisions is referred to th central government. There are also civil, th‌ is, non-religious courts administered by th prime minister through the Minister of Justic‌

Political parties in the Western sense do n‌ exist—differing points of view are usuall‌ tribal or regional in orientation.

At Amran, the Monday morning market gets underway within sight of hillsides terraced for farming.

4. THE PEOPLE

MOST YEMENIS are of Arab stock, although there is a strong Negro strain in the population of the Tihama, which faces Africa across the Red Sea. Certain Arab traditions claim that the mountains of the south of Arabia, and particularly Yemen, were the ancestral home of the desert Arab stock. Whatever the facts are, the history and archeology of Yemen show that it has had a sedentary population since ancient times.

This condition holds true today—there are virtually no nomadic Yemenis. About 10 per cent of the people live in cities and the rest in small villages throughout the highlands and the coastal strip.

RELIGION

Although monotheism was introduced in the forms of Judaism and Christianity in the 4th century A.D., most of the people of Yemen remained under the influence of pagan beliefs until the arrival of Islam. The ancient South Arabian creeds were polytheistic, with many gods, whom their adherents worshipped in magnificent temples.

Islam replaced both the pagan cults and Christianity, but a sizeable Jewish community survived until the middle of the 20th century, when its members emigrated to Israel.

The 7,000,000 modern Yemenis belong to

A two-storeyed vocational school in Sana is in marked contrast with the tall buildings in the background.

A World Health Organization expert from Sudan (left) gives practical training in handling a young patient to two Yemeni nurses.

two main Islamic groups—the Zaidis, who adhere to the Shiite sect, and the Shafa'i's, who are Sunni Moslems. The Zaidis occupy the central and northern regions of the country, while the Shafa'i community occupies the south, with Taizz as its stronghold. The two groups are roughly equal in number, but the Zaidis dominate, since Sana is their traditional capital, as well as the capital of the country.

EDUCATION

Although an anciently civilized country, Yemen has a severe education problem—75 per cent of its people are illiterate. Since the establishment of the republic, however, considerable progress has been made in opening new schools. Primary and secondary schools in 1977 numbered 3,000, with an enrolment of 250,000. There is one university, at Sana, and several technical colleges.

Yemeni dwellings are often multi-storey buildings—but not all are perched on top of a column of rock as is this one (middle of photo) near Sana.

WAY OF LIFE

Yemen is still a highly traditional country, reflecting little of the change taking place in other Islamic states. City women, other than servants, still go veiled, while country women usually do not wear their veils. The latter, however, do wear scarves and head covers that partially conceal their faces. A few young women in the chief cities, who work as nurses, teachers and in broadcasting, wear Western dress on the job, but cover up with cloaks and scarves when they go out.

The clothing of men is much more varied. Many wear Western dress and many more wear the *lungi*, a sarong-like garment, while others wear combinations of traditional and Western dress.

A United Nations expert from Nepal (right) aids a Yemeni laboratory technician in an experiment at the FAO Research Centre in Taizz.

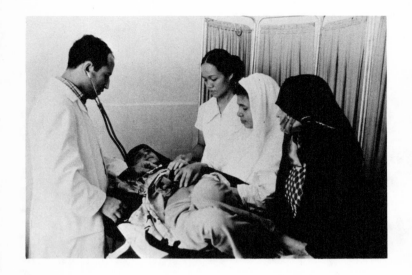

A United Nations volunteer from the Philippines (middle) assists a Yemeni doctor at the Republican Hospital in Taizz.

Food is similar to that of other Arab countries, but because of the abundance of crops in the well-watered highlands, offers a greater variety. Barley and maize are the staple cereal foods. As one might expect in a land where Mocha coffee originated, coffee is widely available.

A custom prevalent in Yemen—a national pastime, in fact—is the chewing of *qat*. Qat is the leaf of a small tree or shrub of the spindle-tree family. When chewed in wads over a period of several hours it produces a feeling of euphoria, although, like coffee, it can produce insomnia. People of both sexes and all ages often start chewing qat immediately after breakfast. The leaves are chewed until they form a soft paste and are then swallowed.

The well-to-do have qat parties in whitewashed rooms provided with cotton mattresses. Hookahs, or water pipes, are available for those

Male nurse trainees attend a lecture on nutrition at the Institute of Health in Sana.

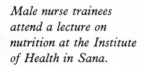

Yemeni houses are usually built of brick and stone, with whitewashed decorative details. Windows are tinted glass set in plaster frames, and balconies, grillwork and walled gardens add to the Arabian Nights quality of these structures.

who wish to smoke tobacco while chewing qat. Also on hand are vacuum bottles of spiced ice water, bottles of soft drinks and a brew made from coffee husks.

The habitual qat chewer eats a heavy lunch before attending a qat party, usually held in the afternoon. Such a lunch consists of fatty soup, mutton, bread, fenugreek, and a profusion of salad greens and fruits. Chewing qat on an empty stomach can bring on a severe headache.

Although there is opposition to the use of qat, it seems unlikely to disappear soon from the social scene, since it is part of the Yemeni way of life. It is also an inexpensive way of entertaining, since everyone brings his own qat, tobacco, and other comforts—and a democratic one, since anyone may attend a qat party without invitation.

In spite of this, the Yemeni government launched a campaign in 1972 to discourage the use of qat. All government-grown qat plantations—a substantial source of revenue—were ordered to be uprooted in that year.

At a research farm near Hodeida, operated with the help of the Food and Agriculture Organization, a United Nations expert (left) supervises work in a maize field.

5. ECONOMY

THE YEMEN ARAB REPUBLIC has a basically agrarian economy, with relatively little modern industry. Until recently, Yemen was self-sufficient in food, but the civil war of the 1960's badly upset the country's agriculture system.

AGRICULTURE

The principal cereal crop of Yemen is durra, a kind of millet, which can be grown at altitudes up to 9,000 feet (2,700 metres). Other cereals of importance are maize, barley, wheat, oats, rice and sorghum.

Fruit production is important and varied. Dates and bananas grow in the lowlands, along with citrus fruits. Apricots, grapes, almonds, and other fruits flourish at higher elevations.

Other important crops are cotton, tobacco and sesame, all grown in the Tihama. The principal export crops had long been coffee and qat, both grown in the lower highlands, but cotton now accounts for 43 per cent of the volume of exports. The coffee of Yemen is world-famous, but production has declined in recent years, owing to a prolonged drought that occurred about the same time as Yemen's disruptive civil war, also a cause of the decline.

The most numerous domestic animals are sheep, grown for meat, milk, hides and wool. Next in importance are goats and cattle, and a

Fishermen, clad in lungis, both plain and plaid, examine their catch on the beach near Hodeida on the Red Sea.

small number of stockraisers are engaged in breeding horses and camels.

FISHERIES

The fishing industry is undergoing considerable expansion. A modern cannery has been built at Hodeida to process fish from the Red Sea. Among the chief species caught off the Yemen coast are grey mullet, sea bream, snapper, kingfish, queenfish, parrotfish and prawns.

INDUSTRY

Since the 1950's the number of light industries has increased, although most manufacturing is still on the handicraft level. In 1956, a textile mill was built at Bajil, near Hodeida, and another was erected later at Sana. Hodeida is the site of a cement plant and a cotton-seed oil factory. Other factories turn out cigarettes and soft drinks.

The artisans and craftsmen of Yemen turn out beautiful objects in silver, copper, brass, and leather, as well as handwoven rugs and textiles.

TRANSPORTATION AND COMMUNICATIONS

With United States and Russian aid, Yemen's highways have been improved and extended. Railways, however, are non-existent. There are major airports at Sana, Hodeida and Taizz, served by the Yemen Airlines, which also provides international service to nearby countries.

Telephone, telegraph and broadcasting facilities are government-controlled. There are four radio stations and one television station.

Using a reaping hook in the way his forebears did a thousand years ago, a farmer near Sana harvests his grain.

TRADE AND FOREIGN AID

Yemen's chief imports are consumer goods, refined petroleum, machinery and equipment and foodstuffs. Yemen spends far more on what it buys from abroad than the amount earned from exports.

The difference in the trade balance is made up by revenues sent home by 1,000,000 Yemeni workers in Saudi Arabia, Kuwait, the United Arab Emirates and other petroleum boom states.

In addition, Yemen has received extensive aid from both the West and the Communist bloc, and even more from Saudi Arabia and Kuwait.

A precarious building site—perhaps that is why this structure was allowed to deteriorate!

Yemen, People's Democratic Republic

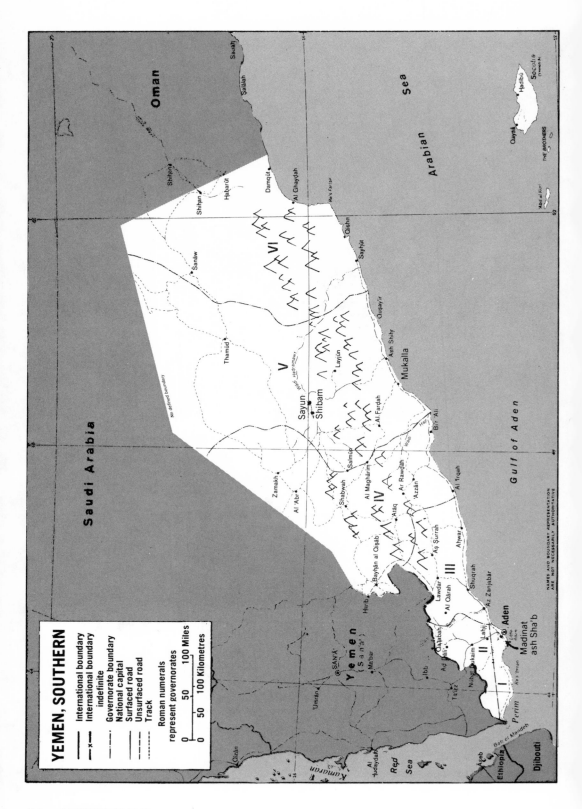

YEMEN, SOUTHERN

International boundary
International boundary
  indefinite
Governorate boundary
National capital
Surfaced road
Unsurfaced road
Track

Roman numerals
represent governorates

0   50   100 Miles

0   50   100 Kilometres

Oman

Saudi Arabia

Yemen
(Sanʻa')

SANʻA

Arabian Sea

Gulf of Aden

Red Sea

Ethiopia

Djibouti

Socotra
(Yemen S.)

Ḥadbū

Qayṣ

THE BROTHERS

ʻAbd al Kūri

Ṣawlah

Salālah

Shiḥain

Shiḥan

Ḥabarūt

Damqūt

Al Ghaydah

Raʼs Fartak

Qishn

Sayḥūt

Saʼnāw

Thamūd

Wādī Ḥaḍramawt

Sayun

Shibam

Layjūn

Quṣayʻir

Ash Shiḥr

Mukalla

Bīʼr Alī

Al Fardah

Zamakh

Al ʻAbr

Shabwah

Salmīn

Al Maghārim

IV

Ataq

Ar Rawḍah

ʻAzzān

Al ʻIrqah

Bayḥān al Qiṣāb

Ḥarīb

Lawdar

Aṣ Ṣurrah

Aḥwar

Shuqrah

Az Zanjibar

Madīnat
ash Shaʼb

Aden

III

Al Qārah

Laḥij

Nūba

Bukaim

II

ʻUmrān

Al Baydaʼ

Maʼbar

Ibb

Ad Dāliʻ

Qaṭabah

Taʼizz

Perim

Bāb el Mandeb

Raʼs Imrān

I

Kamaran

Al
Ḥudaydah

Qizān

NAMES AND BOUNDARY REPRESENTATION
ARE NOT NECESSARILY AUTHORITATIVE

V

VI

490 ◇ YEMEN, P.D.R.

Scrubby vegetation grows sparsely on the mountain slopes above a wadi in the highlands.

I. THE LAND

THE PEOPLE'S DEMOCRATIC Republic of Yemen, formerly and still popularly called Southern Yemen, stretches for 700 miles (1,120 km) along the southern edge of the Arabian Peninsula, from the Strait of Bab el Mandeb in the west to the borders of the Sultanate of Oman in the east. Saudi Arabia borders it on the north, the Yemen Arab Republic on the north and west, and the Gulf of Aden and the Arabian Sea on the south. With an area of about 112,000 square miles (291,200 sq km), the republic is somewhat smaller than Italy or Arizona.

TOPOGRAPHY

The land consists of a narrow coastal plain, rising abruptly to interior mountain ranges, which in turn fall off into the sandy desert of the Rub al Khali, or Empty Quarter of the Arabian Plateau. The interior highlands, which are cut by deep valleys, rise to elevations of 10,000 feet (3,000 metres). There are no permanent rivers—the dry riverbeds or *wadis* of the valleys come to life only during the rainy season.

Kamaran, an island in the Red Sea, close to the coast of the Yemen Arab Republic, is the locale of this tranquil scene.

ISLANDS

The territory of Southern Yemen includes a number of outlying islands, some of them close to the shores of other countries. The largest of these is Socotra, at the wide mouth of the Gulf of Aden and nearer to the Horn of Africa than to Arabia. Socotra, with an area of 1,383 square miles (3,596 sq km), is mountainous, with elevations up to 5,000 feet (1,500 metres).

The small, barren island of Perim guards the entrance to the Red Sea, from the middle of the narrow Strait of Bab el Mandeb. With an area of 8 square miles (20.8 sq km), Perim's importance is chiefly strategic. Formerly part of Southern Yemen, the Kuria Muria Islands off the coast of Oman were ceded to Oman by Britain in 1967. The island of Kamaran, 80 square miles (208 sq km) in area, hugs the coast of the Yemen Arab Republic, 200 miles (320 km) north of Perim in the Red Sea.

CLIMATE

Most of the country is hot and dry, except for the western highlands, adjoining the Yemen Arab Republic, where rainfall may reach 30 inches (75 cm). Elsewhere, rainfall averages 3 inches (7.5 cm) annually. Temperatures can exceed 130°F (54°C) on the coast and in much of the interior, but June temperatures average about 90°F (32°C), while in January the average is 76°F (24°C).

CITIES

ADEN

Aden, the chief port and the largest city with a population of 264,000, is situated on a small rocky peninsula 100 miles (160 km) east of the Strait of Bab el Mandeb. The peninsula, or promontory, reaches heights up to 1,776 feet (533 metres) and is connected to the mainland by a low-lying sandy neck. The old part of the city is built in the curving remains of a volcanic cone, providing it with a natural wall of rock. The port of Aden is flanked by this peninsula and a lesser one to the west, called Little Aden.

Aden is an ancient site, known to the Greeks and Romans of old, and its importance through the ages is due to the fact that it has the best port on the Arabian coast. It is also the capital of the republic and the hub of commerce and industry. The administrative offices of the government, however, are at Madinat Asha'ab (the People's City) a few miles to the west, formerly called Madinat al Ittahid.

OTHER CITIES

Mukalla, with 45,000 people, is the second largest city and a major fishing port. Sayun,

The bay at Aden is flanked by two promontories, each connected by low ground with the mainland, and each with a volcanic crater. The lesser of the two is Little Aden, seen here with its extensive oil refinery in the foreground.

These culverts form part of the water supply system of Aden.

The old city of Aden, seen from the rim of the crater that walls it off, borders on the old port, now in disuse. The rocky islet of Sirah is in the left background.

Mukalla is the second largest city of the Republic and an important fishing port.

Clouds blanket the rim of the crater that surrounds the old city of Aden. The new city and port are located on the bay of Aden, north and west of the crater.

with 20,000 people, is the chief city of the interior highlands. Near Sayun, is Shibam, which is famous for its concentration of South Arabian "skyscrapers," multi-storeyed dwellings built hundreds of years ago and still inhabited. Sayun and Shabam both lie in the Valley of Hadhramaut, largest, most productive and most historic of the wadis.

Wide streets, motor traffic and new buildings typify the new districts of Aden.

South Arabian "skyscrapers" rise above date palms, against the barren ridges of the highlands in the Wadi Hadhramaut.

2. HISTORY

THE HISTORY of the People's Democratic Republic of Yemen is closely linked with that of the Yemen Arab Republic. The region embracing both countries was called in Roman times *Arabia Felix,* or fortunate Arabia, possibly because of the fertility and greenness of the western part of it.

EARLY HISTORY

The early history of Southern Yemen relates to the same ancient South Arabian cultures that flourished in Yemen proper—the Minaean,

Sabaean and Himyarite. The rise of Islam led to the absorption of the country into the great Arab empire, or caliphate, in the 7th century A.D., of which it remained a part until the caliphate broke up. After this, the region split up into a number of small states.

The island of Socotra, which was called the Isle of Dioscorides in classical antiquity, was in early contact with Egypt, Greece and Rome. Socotra was later Christianized by the Nestorian sect and did not accept Islam until the 16th century.

Early in the 16th century both Aden and

Dhala, in the Second Governorate, was the seat of a former sheikhdom of the West Aden Protectorate.

Socotra were occupied briefly by the Portuguese. However, the Europeans were driven out with the aid of the Ottoman Turks, who later occupied Aden and other points on the coast and claimed suzerainty over the interior.

RECENT HISTORY

In 1799, British troops occupied Perim, but the lack of water on the island forced them to withdraw. In 1839, the British occupied Aden; in 1854, they took over the Kuria Muria Islands; and in 1857, they retook Perim. In 1876, Socotra was made a protectorate.

Through a series of treaties made between 1886 and 1914, the British next established protectorates over the numerous small states—sultanates and sheikhdoms—of the mainland. Certain areas were also purchased outright from the local rulers. Aden and its protectorates were governed as a part of British India from 1839 until 1937.

In 1937, the British declared Aden a crown colony under the direct control of the Colonial Office in London. At the same time, the 24 protected states were grouped into a single entity called the Aden Protectorate. This in turn was divided administratively into the West Aden and the East Aden Protectorates.

INDEPENDENCE

Following World War II, Britain began taking steps towards granting Southern Yemen independence. In 1959, six states of the Aden Protectorate were joined in the Federation of Arab Emirates of the South. After other states joined, the name was changed to the Federation of South Arabia, in 1962.

In 1966, the British transferred responsibility for South Arabia from the Colonial Office to the Foreign Office. In the meantime, two rival nationalist groups emerged—the Front for the Liberation of South Yemen and the National

A ceremony is in progress at Mukalla on October 14, the national holiday of the People's Democratic Republic of Yemen.

Liberation Front (NLF). The British had intended to grant independence to the territory in 1968, but rising violence induced them to withdraw their troops in 1967.

The British withdrawal led to a collapse of the Federation and the leaders of the NLF took control. Later in 1967, the People's Republic of Southern Yemen was proclaimed, with British concurrence. In 1976, the name of the new state was changed to the People's Democratic Republic of Yemen.

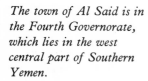

The town of Al Said is in the Fourth Governorate, which lies in the west central part of Southern Yemen.

Demonstrators parade in motor vehicles during the stormy days leading to independence.

3. GOVERNMENT

THE PEOPLE'S DEMOCRATIC Republic of Yemen is governed by a three-man Presidential Council and a Council of Ministers, which jointly serve as the executive arm of the government. The Chairman of the Presidential Council is the Chief of State, and the Prime Minister is the Head of Government.

Under the Constitution of 1970, legislative power is vested in a 101-member body called the People's Supreme Council. The People's Council and the government is dominated by the National Front Party. This party's 10-member Executive Committee is answerable to a 40-member body called the General Command, whose members are elected by regional party representatives meeting in an assembly called the Congress of the National Front. The General Command appoints the members of the Presidential Council.

The legal system in the area that was formerly the Crown Colony of Aden is based on British concepts. In the areas formerly making up the Aden Protectorate, Islamic law (*sharia*) and tribal tradition are the rule.

For purposes of local government the country is divided into six governorates, each with a governor appointed by the National Front. The former sultanates and sheikhdoms have all been abolished.

In foreign policy, the government has proclaimed a policy of non-alignment in world affairs. Southern Yemen's relations with adjacent Arab states have been touchy. There have been border clashes with both the Yemen Arab Republic and with Oman. In spite of the clashes with Yemen, Southern Yemen still officially supports a 1972 agreement to merge with that country.

Southern Yemen, which had actively supported a rebellion in Oman's Dhofar Province, negotiated a cease-fire with Oman in 1976. In the same year, diplomatic relations were established with Saudi Arabia, the only country that had not recognized the People's Democratic Republic.

Southern Yemen, which is socialist-oriented, has close relations with both Russia and China and has received economic aid from both of the Communist giants. Military aid, however, is provided exclusively by Russia.

Traditional Islamic architectural motifs prevail in the older parts of Aden.

4. THE PEOPLE

THE POPULATION of the People's Democratic Republic numbers about 1,800,000, most of whom are of the same South Arabian stock as the people of the Yemen Arab Republic. Along the coast are minorities of Indians, Pakistanis and Somalis, who are especially numerous in the city of Aden and the territory of the former Aden colony at the western end of the country. As in the Yemen Arab Republic, there is a Negroid strain in the Arabs of the Coast. The people of Socotra are a mixture of the various groups—Somali, South Arabian, Indian and others—who have reached the island at different times. The small population of the island of Kamaran is also mixed—a blend of Arab, Ethiopian, Indian and Somali.

LANGUAGE

While Arabic replaced the South Arabian languages in the Yemen Arab Republic, this was not wholly the case in Southern Yemen. The Himyaritic tongue survives in the Mahri district in the eastern part of the country and on Socotra. Himyaritic and the extinct South Arabian tongues such as Minaean and Sabaean, are closer to the Semitic languages of Ethiopia than to Arabic.

Arabic is the official language as well as the speech of most of the people, and English is widely used.

RELIGION AND EDUCATION

Unlike the people of the Yemen Arab Republic, who are divided between the Shiite and Sunni branches of Islam, the Southern Yemenis are nearly all members of the Shafai'i rite of the Sunni denomination. They are thus part of the mainstream of Islam, since 80 per cent or more of all Moslems belong to the Sunni (orthodox) branch.

Members of the Women's Union march in formation. Southern Yemen's Constitution guarantees equal rights for men and women.

Illiteracy is a serious problem—only 20 per cent of the population can read and write. Education is therefore a major concern of the government. Enrolment in primary and secondary schools now stands at about 240,000. There are four teachers' training schools and a College of Higher Education, founded in 1970.

The village of Al-Thumair in the Second Governorate is clearly not a South Arabian "skyscraper" community.

Ships lie at anchor in the port of Aden.

5. ECONOMY

SOUTHERN YEMEN is a very poor country, heavily dependent on foreign aid. For years, under British rule, the economic life of the land was focused on the bustling city of Aden, a major naval base and a port of call for world shipping. Except for some fishing along the coast, the remainder of the Aden protectorate was an agrarian backwater, with few paved roads and no railways. There are still no railways, although there is a national airline.

Then in 1967 the British left and the income generated by their military installations was stopped. The closing of the Suez Canal in the same year was an added blow. Before then Aden was one of the world's greatest oil bunkering ports, handling an average of 6,000 ships a year. The closing of the Canal during the Arab-Israeli War of 1967 brought this figure down greatly, as shipping was diverted around South Africa and relatively few ships continued to use the facilities at Aden.

An additional cause of decline was the internal conflict in Southern Yemen following the British withdrawal, which inhibited any government action to bolster the sagging economy.

AGRICULTURE

The basis of the economy today is agriculture, even though only a small part of the total area is cultivable. Most farming is of the subsistence type, although some agricultural produce is marketed, and some exported.

Wheat, millet and sorghum are the chief cereal crops, grown mostly in the western part of the country. The coastal belt produces cotton, bananas, watermelons and winter vegetables. The Wadi Hadhramaut grows coffee and tobacco, while in the western highlands, plums, peaches and apricots are raised at higher altitudes, and citrus fruits and dates at lower elevations. Another crop is qat,

Irrigated banana plantations are a familiar sight in the coastal plain.

the mildly narcotic leaf chewed widely in southern Arabia and East Africa.

Livestock raising is a major farm activity, sheep and goats being the most numerous domestic animals. Others are cattle, poultry and camels, the latter a principal means of transport and one that will remain important until a surfaced highway system for motor vehicles is completed. Fishing is important locally along the coast, but the methods in use are antiquated.

Socotra is famous for the quality of its aloes and dates, as well as its livestock. The island exports ghee (clarified butter), hides, fruits, dried fish and dragon's blood, a red resin from a native tree.

INDUSTRY AND TRADE

The only large industry is the oil refinery at Little Aden, across the bay from the city of Aden. Built in 1954, this sizeable installation was forced to operate at less than half of capacity following the closing of the Suez Canal. The

Tractors now work the fields at Abyan in the cotton belt of the Third Governorate.

Jaar is situated somewhat to the east of Aden, not far from the coast, where the coastal plain meets the foothills of the highlands.

Coffee "cherries" are deep red berries growing in clusters among the smooth oval green leaves of the coffee tree.

re-opening of the Canal in 1975 was expected to restore Aden's importance as a refining and bunkering hub, but this recovery did not take place to any marked degree.

Light industries, situated for the most part near Aden, produce goods such as soap, tobacco, textiles, furniture, cooking utensils, bricks and tile on a limited scale for domestic consumption. Exports consist mainly of raw cotton, hides, incense, petroleum products and fish products. The principal imports are food, textiles and crude petroleum.

Most of the foreign aid received by the People's Democratic Republic comes from Communist and Socialist countries and not from the conservative, oil-rich Arab states, which are suspicious of the leftist Southern Yemen government.

A fisherman displays his catch with the fortress-crowned islet of Sirah looming behind him.

Masses of downy cotton bolls are being fed into the gins, where the seeds are removed.

Salt is obtained in coastal areas by flooding enclosed areas with sea water and allowing it to evaporate.

509

511

ACKNOWLEDGMENTS

The publishers wish to thank the following for the use of photographs in this book: Paul Almasy; Arab Information Center, New York; Aramco World Magazine; Habib Bedewi, Cairo; Philip Boucas; Consulate General of the State of Kuwait, New York; Directorate General of Antiquities, Baghdad; Directorate General of Information and Tourism, Sultanate of Oman, Muscat; Djambatan Publisher, Amsterdam; Economic Features, Ltd., London; Egyptian State Tourist Administration; Khalil Abou el-Nasr; Embassy of Lebanon; John Fistere and Associates, Beirut, Lebanon; Albert Flouty, Amman, Jordan; Food and Agriculture Organization; R. Grunbaum/ARA; George Holton; Inter-Continental Hotel Corporation, New York; Iraq Ministry of Culture and Information; Iraq National Petroleum Company; Jordan Ministry of Information, Amman; Jordan Ministry of Tourism and Antiquities, Amman; Jordan Tourism Authority, Amman; Jordan Tourist Information Center, Beirut; Kuwait Airways; Kuwait Hilton; Kuwait Oil Company, Ltd.; Kuwait Radio and Television, United Nations Bureau, New York; Kuwait Sheraton; Dominique Lujoux; F. Mattioli; Middle East Airlines Airliban; Ministry of Guidance and Information, Kuwait; Ministry of Information, Doha, Qatar; Ministry of Information, Manama, Bahrain; Ministry of Information, United Arab Emirates; Ministry of Tourism, Cairo; Mission of the Republic of Iraq to the United Nations; Patrick Morin; Al Morshid, Manama, Bahrain; Werner Muckenhirn; Kay Muldoon; NASA, Washington, D.C.; National Council of Tourism in Lebanon; The New York Public Library; H. Null; Oman News; People's Democratic Republic of Yemen Ministry of Information and Culture; Photo Manoug, Beirut; P.A. Pittet; Royal Embassy of Saudi Arabia, Washington, D.C.; Sheraton News Photo (Worldwide service of ITT); Camille Mirepoix Stegmuller; Southern Yemen Information Office, New York; Syrian Consular Affairs; Hagop Toranian, Amman; M. Tzovaras/ARA; UNESCO; UNICEF; United Nations; United Nations Relief and Works Agency for Palestine Refugees; United Press International; World Food Programme; World Health Organization; Yemen Arab Republic Tourism Department, Sana. The publishers wish to extend special thanks also to Mr. Haytham el-Abed of the Kuwait Mission to the United Nations and Dr. Tarik el-Erris, Press Officer, The Iraq Mission to the United Nations.